A Guide to
Library of Congress
Classification

LIBRARY SCIENCE TEXT SERIES

A Guide to Library of Congress Classification

JOHN PHILLIP IMMROTH

1968

LIBRARIES UNLIMITED, INC., ROCHESTER, N.Y.

LIBRARY SCIENCE TEXT SERIES

Science-Engineering Reference Sources.
Introduction to Bibliography and Reference Work, 4th ed.
Introduction to Cataloging and Classification, 3d ed.
Guide to Reference Materials in Political Science. 2 vols.

Library of Congress Card No. 68-19094

Libraries Unlimited, Inc.
P. O. Box 9842
Rochester, New York 14623

Printed in the United States of America

TABLE OF CONTENTS

4

Chapter 3.   Special Problems in the Use of
L. C. Classification

Chapter 4.   Examples of the Use of Tables

Chapter 5.   Individual Classes of Library of
Congress Classification

6

TABLE OF FIGURES*

*These pages and class outlines in Chapter 5 are reproduced from official L. C. schedules.

8

Chapter 5.

PREFACE

When the Library of Congress was developing its present classification system in 1900, it was assumed that this system of classification would be used only by the Library of Congress. Almost immediately, however, other libraries requested copies of the classification tables; since that time the number of libraries changing to Library of Congress Classification has increased annually. The curricula of graduate library schools in this country include courses in Library of Congress Classification and national and regional conferences are held to acquaint librarians with problems involved in the adoption and use of Library of Congress Classification. During this time three books were written about Library of Congress Classification; two of these represent theses or dissertations while the other was written by a member of the staff of the Library of Congress. In 1938 Catherine W. Grout wrote, as her master's essay at Columbia University, Explanation of the Tables Used in the Schedules of the Library of Congress Classification. In 1940 this work was published by the School of Library Service at Columbia University in mimeograph form. A second study from Columbia University is A. Annette Lewis Hoage's doctoral dissertation, "The Library of Congress Classification in the United States: A Survey of Opinions and Practices" (1961). Also published that year was Leo E. LaMontagne's American Library Classification with Special Reference to the Library of Congress. Although all three of these works represent significant contributions, none of them is designed to be a simple introduction to the use of Library of Congress Classification. The intent of this guide is to fill that gap.

This guide is organized into five chapters covering: a brief historical orientation to early systems of classification at the Library of Congress; a survey of general characteristics of the format of the schedules and tables and of the notation; special problems in the use of Library of Congress Classification including auxiliary tables and successive Cutter numbers; an examination of typical tables and their use; and, an introduction to each class schedule illustrating special problems, tables or unusual notation pertaining to each schedule. Every table or problem discussed is accompanied by one or a series of examples. The portion of the table required for the example is shown on the page and the actual page from the L. C. schedule is reproduced; these "Figures" are numbered and placed at the end of each chapter. A Table of Figures is provided at the beginning of the book. A bibliography of readings and schedules is included at the end of the text for each chapter, and there is an index to the guide. The detailed Table of Contents is intended to serve as a subject index to the guide.

This guide is an introduction to the Library of Congress Classification and as such, does not include instructions for every subclass or table, but attempts to provide the reader with an understanding of the characteristics of the classification, the arrangement within the classes, the format of the schedules and tables and special problems of use and notation. The reader should trace the analysis of each example of classing through the Figures provided in the guide. It is important to remind the reader that a thorough study of each class schedule in addition to the recommended readings is essential. The author realizes that many imperfections may be present in this guide, and will appreciate suggestions for changes from readers.

The author wishes to acknowledge encouragement given him by colleagues both at the University of Denver and at the State University College at Geneseo, New York. To Paul Frame and Helen Rowe I am indebted for my introduction to Library of Congress Classification. Finally, I wish to thank my wife, Barbara, for her patience and assistance.

J. P. I.

January 25, 1968.

CHAPTER 1.

A BRIEF HISTORY OF

THE LIBRARY OF CONGRESS CLASSIFICATION SYSTEMS

EARLIEST SYSTEMS

The Library of Congress was established by the fifth section of the "Act to make provision for the removal and accommodation of the Government of the United States" which was approved on April 24, 1800. Prior to that time Congress used the Library Company of Philadelphia and the New York Society Library. Senator Samuel Dexter of Massachusetts was chiefly responsible for the selection of the initial collection of the Library of Congress. He ordered 740 books from the London booksellers Cadell & Davies. These books were sent from London on December 11, 1800 and reached Washington by May 2, 1801. On January 26, 1802 "An Act Concerning the Library for the use of both Houses of Congress" was approved by Congress. It provided for a room for the Library of Congress, the establishment of suitable rules and regulations by the President of the Senate and the Speaker of the House, and the appointment of a librarian by the President. President Thomas Jefferson appointed the first Librarian of Congress three days later. He was the Clerk of the House, John Beckley of Virginia.

The first classification system used by the Library of Congress was by size: folios, quartos, octavos, and duodecimos. The books were further subarranged by accession numbers. By 1812 the first subject arrangement consisting of some eighteen classes was in use. This classification was based on that system used by Benjamin Franklin's Library Company of Philadelphia in 1789. The Library Company's scheme had its basis in the system of classification of Sir Francis Bacon and the system of classification of d'Alembert. The classes of the 1812 system were:

1. Sacred history;
2. Ecclesiastical history;
3. Civil history, including chronology, biography, antiquities, etc.;
4. Geography and topography; voyages and travels;
5. Law;
6. Ethics, or the moral system in general; theology and mythology;
7. Logic, rhetoric, and criticism;
8. Dictionaries, grammars and treatises on education;

9.   General and local politics; political economy, etc.;
10. Trade and commerce;
11. Military and naval tactics;
12. Agriculture, rural economy, etc.;
13. Natural history; natural and experimental philosophy, etc.;
14. Medicine, surgery, and chemistry;
15. Poetry, and the drama; works on fiction, wit, etc.
16. Arts and sciences, and miscellaneous literature;
17. Gazettes;
18. Maps, charts, and plans. [1]

The last two classes, "17. Gazettes;" and "18. Maps, charts, and plans" are not subject divisions but rather form divisions. Under each of the eighteen classes the books were subdivided by size and arranged alphabetically.

JEFFERSON'S SYSTEM

On August 24, 1814 the Library of Congress, as well as most of the Capitol, was burned by British soldiers. The majority of the collection was destroyed in the fire. Thomas Jefferson offered to sell his personal library to Congress. In 1815 Congress voted $23,950 to purchase the Jefferson library of 6487 books which were classified in Jefferson's own system. Forty-four main classes, or "chapters," comprised this system which was also based on the systems of Bacon and d'Alembert. The following summary shows not only the forty-four chapters but also Jefferson's subdivisions including his use of geographic subdivision.

"1. History, civil; ancient history. -- 2. Modern history, foreign, southern: General works, Italy, Rome, Florence, Naples, Venice, Spain, Portugal, France. Northern: General works, Lapland, Russia, Poland, Hungary, Sweden, Denmark, Prussia, Germany, Flanders, United Netherlands, Switzerland, Geneva, Turkey, Asia, Africa. -- 3. Modern history, British, Scotland, Ireland. -- 4. Modern history, American, Ante-Revolutionary: General, particular. Post-Revolutionary: General, particular. Newspapers. -- 5. History, ecclesiastical. -- 6. History, natural: physics, natural philosophy. -- 7. Agriculture. -- 8. Chem-

---

[1]William Dawson Johnston. History of the Library of Congress, 1800-1864. Washington: Govt. Print. Off., 1904. p. 49 and plate 29.

istry. -- 9. Surgery. -- 10. Medicine. -- 11. Natural history:
Animals, anatomy. -- 12. Natural history: Animals, zoology. -- 13. Natural history: Botany. -- 14. Natural history: Mineralogy. -- 15. History, natural: Occupations of
man, technical arts. -- 16. Philosophy, moral: Ethics,
(1) moral philosophy, (2) law of nature and nations. -- 17.
Religion. -- 18. Jurisprudence: Equity. -- 19. Jurisprudence: Common law, bodies of law, statutes, courts, entries, conveyancing, criminal law, tracts, reports. -- 20.
Jurisprudence: Law, merchant. -- 21. Jurisprudence: Law,
maritime. -- 22. Jurisprudence: Law, ecclesiastical. --
23. Jurisprudence: Foreign law. -- 24. Politics: General
theories of government, special governments. Ancient.
Modern. France: Monarchical, revolutionary, imperial,
her colonies. England: Constitution, Parliament, depen-
dencies. United States: Colonial, Revolutionary, recon-
stituted, States. Political economy: General, statistics,
commerce, finance. -- 25. Mathematics, pure: Arithmetic. --
26. Mathematics, pure: Geometry. -- 27. Physics-mathe-
matics: Mechanics, statics, dynamics, phonics, optics. --
28. Astronomy. -- 29. Geography, general: Europe, Asia,
Africa, America. -- 30. Fine arts: Architecture. -- 31.
Fine arts: Gardening, painting, sculpturing. -- 32. Fine
arts: Music. -- 33. Poetry, epic. -- 34. Romance, tales,
fables. -- 35. Pastorals, odes, elegies, etc. -- 36. Didac-
tic. -- 37. Tragedy. -- 38. Comedy. -- 39. Dialogue, epis-
tolary. -- 40. Logic, rhetoric, orations. -- 41. Criticism:
Theory. -- 42. Criticism: Bibliography. -- 43. Criticism.
Languages, general: Polyglot, Oriental, Greek, Latin,
Italian, Spanish, French, Northern, English, Welsh. -- 44.
Polygraphical. [2]

It should be pointed out that the Librarian of Congress, George
Watterston, did not use all of Jefferson's subdivisions. For example,
in "Chapter 2. Modern History: Foreign" Watterston arranged all the
books in this chapter into a single alphabet ignoring Jefferson's geographic subdivisions. [3] Jefferson's system with modifications was used
at the Library of Congress until the close of the nineteenth century.
Each successive librarian made changes in the system. Ainsworth
Rand Spofford, Librarian of Congress from 1864 to 1897, made

---

[2]Ibid., p. 145-146.
[3]Ibid., p. 148.

major adjustments in both the classification and the notation.

Originally a notation had been developed combining the chapter number and the book number in a fraction-like arrangement. For instance, $\frac{4}{27}$ would have meant Chapter 4, American history, book number 27.

> "An inserted book was numbered by adding a letter to the book number of the book next preceding, or by renumbering the entire class. For example, a Collection of papers relating to the history of Massachusetts being numbered 4/27, the Collections of the Massachusetts Historical Society when added to the Library were marked 4/27a. As many as a dozen or more insertions, arranged in order of accession, were sometimes made and numbered thus by the added letters ℓ, m, etc. "[4]

The notation was revised by Spofford so that the denominator was really a shelf number, not a book number. For example, 15/9456 might then mean Chapter 15, technology, shelf 9456, which was the shelf reserved for books on the subject of Inter-Ocean Canals. Canal and River improvements in general had the number: 15/9453. This meant Chapter 15, Technology, and shelf number 9453 for books on canal and river improvements in general. Obviously shelf 9453 precedes shelf 9456 just as the subordination of subject matter from general to specific does in this case. This device allowed far greater subdivisions within each chapter. This change meant that the notation denoted a fixed location, not a relative one. However, as the collection of the Library grew often the shelf number came to have only a subject meaning and not a locational one. [5]

THE NEW L. C. CLASSIFICATION

By the 1890's it was obvious that the Jeffersonian system was no longer adequate. The collection had grown from seven thousand books to nearly a million. The move to the new library building in 1897 made this fact painfully apparent. John Russell Young, the Librarian of Congress at that time, instructed James C. M. Hanson, the Head of the Catalogue Division, and Charles Martel, the Chief

---

[4]Ibid., p. 368.

[5]Leo E. LaMontagne. American Library Classification with Special Reference to the Library of Congress. Hamden, Conn.: Shoe String Press, 1961. p. 55-56.

Classifier, to study the possibilities of adopting a new classification system for the Library of Congress. In December of 1897 Young gave the following advice.

"As an inflexible rule, no method of classification should be favored which would disintegrate the general collection. The Library of Congress must ultimately be the universal library of the Republic. To that end the most magnificent library edifice in the world has been erected and is destined to be, it is to be hoped, the home of America's literary and artistic genius, supplemented and strengthened by that of all lands and all time. And now, when the work of organization is in a plastic condition, before what is done hardens and consolidates and becomes difficult of undoing, no step should be taken without considering not alone what is most convenient today, but what will be most useful a hundred years from today.

Therefore, in the work of classification, while each department maintains its respective character, the main purpose is the consolidation of the general library. What may have gone from its shelves to strengthen the medical or develop a law library, what may be contemplated in the way of a Congressional library of reference, can and should be replaced. But there must be no invasion of the general library's domain as one of universal reference. [6]

Hanson and Martel investigated the three major published classification schemes: Melvil Dewey's Decimal Classification, then in its fifth edition; the first six expansions of Charles Ammi Cutter's Expansive Classification; and, the Halle Schema of Otto Hartwig published in 1888. All three systems were considered and evaluated by Hanson and Martel. It is indeed regrettable that the Library of Congress could not adopt Dewey's Decimal Classification in 1898. A prime difficulty was Dewey's refusal to allow any major changes in his system; over a hundred libraries had adopted the Decimal Classification. Further, Martel criticised the Decimal Classification as a "system bound up in and made to fit the notation, and not the notation to fit the classification." [7] The Halle Schema was considered to be too strongly oriented in traditional German philosophi-

---

6David Chambers Mearns. The Story Up to Now, The Library of Congress, 1800-1946. Washington: Govt. Print. Off., 1947. p. 162.

7LaMontagne, op. cit., p. 224.

cal thought to be of use to the Library of Congress. However,
serious consideration was given to Cutter's Expansive Classification.
Cutter was quite helpful and ready to allow any necessary changes.
In 1929 Hanson wrote describing these early decisions concerning
the development of L. C. classification.

"The situation as to classification was fully appreciated
by men like Mr. Spofford and Mr. Hutcheson, and little or
no opposition was made, therefore, when plans for a new
system were submitted. No attempt will be made here to
present a detailed explanation of the new classification. It
will be sufficient to say Cutter's Expansive Classification
was selected as the chief guide, with, however, radical
modifications in the notation. For instance, one, or at
most two capital letters were to indicate classes, Arabic
numerals in integral, not decimal sequence, with gaps
(Springende Nummer) for subdivisions, and Cutter numbers
for individual books. It was Spofford who insisted on the
integral, not decimal, sequence of numbers. Mr. Spofford
was inexorably opposed to the decimal system, per se, and
his opposition was shared in part by other members of the
staff, including the chief of the Cataloging Division, who
felt that only by supplying a mixed notation and providing
many radical changes would it have been possible for the
Library of Congress to consider this system. "[8]

In 1898 Martel developed the first version of Class Z: Bibliography and Library Science from a revision of the seventh expansion of Cutter's Class Z: Book Arts. The following table shows
the close relationship of Cutter's Class Z and the new L. C. Class
Z. The L. C. Class Z omitted the following subclasses and subjects
contained in Cutter's Class Z: ZA, Authorship; ZB, Rhetoric;
ZC, Branches of literature; ZY, Literary history; and ZZ, Selection
of reading. These subjects were to be classed in the general literature schedule PN.

---

[8] J. C. M. Hanson. "The Library of Congress and its New Catalogue: Some Unwritten History, " In Essays Offered to Herbert
Putnam by His Colleagues and Friends on his Thirtieth Anniversary
as Librarian of Congress: 5 April 1929. New Haven: Yale University Press, 1929. p. 186-187.

CUTTER	L. C.
Z BOOK ARTS	Z BIBLIOGRAPHY AND LIBRARY SCIENCE

Production ZA-ZK

ZA Authorship

ZB Rhetoric

ZC Branches of literature

                                                     4-8 History of books and bookmaking

ZD Writing: Paleography   40-115 Writing

ZE Manuscripts   41-42 Autographs

ZF Shorthand, Stenography   43-48 Calligraphy. Penmanship.

ZG Penmanship, Calligraphy   49-51 Typewriting

                                            53-100 Shorthand

                                        105-115 Paleography

ZH Printing   116-550 Book industries and trade

ZI-ZJ Incunabula and Block-books   116-265 Printing

ZK Binding.   266-275 Binding

Distribution ZL-ZM

ZL Publishing and bookselling   278-550 Publishing and bookselling

ZM Book Buying

                                        551-661 Copyright. Intellectual property

Storage and Use ZN-ZS   665-997 Libraries and library science

ZN Private libraries

ZP-ZS Public libraries

Description and Use ZT-ZZ   1001-8999 Bibliography

ZT Publications

ZU Bibliography in general

ZV Anonymous and Pseudonymous books	1041-1107 Anonyms and pseudonyms
ZW Subject and class bibliographies	1201-4941 National bibliography
	5051-7999 Subject bibliography
ZX National bibliography	8001-8999 Personal bibliography
ZY Literary history	
ZZ Selection of reading	

Class Z: Bibliography and Library Science was chosen as the first schedule to develop as it would contain the bibliographical works necessary for the reclassification project. Although Cutter's Expansive Classification was used in Class Z, most of the later classes represent original developments.

When Herbert Putnam became Librarian of Congress in 1899, he strongly supported the plans for reclassification. He wrote,

> "The present classification of the Library is but a slight expansion of that adopted by Thomas Jefferson in 1815 for his library of 6,700 volumes. It is meager, rigid, inelastic, and unsuited to a library of a million volumes. The entire library must be reclassified."[9]

The Outlines of the New L. C. Classification

Before Hanson came to the Library of Congress, he had worked with Cutter's Expansive Classification at the University of Wisconsin Library. Cutter's outline of classes consisted basically of subject classes using a single letter. The single letters were to be expanded by adding one or two additional letters. Hanson's revision or adaptation of the Expansive Classification used the single letters but expanded them numerically to form the notation. This resulted in the mixed notation of letters and numbers which was to be used for L. C. Classification.

---

[9]U. S. Library of Congress. Annual Report of the Librarian of Congress. Washington: Govt. Print. Off., 1899. p. 29.

Cutter's outline was:	Hanson's first outline was:	
A General works.	A 1-200	Polygraphy; Encyclopedia; General Periodicals;Societies.
B Philosophy.	A 201-3000	Philosophy.
BR Religion.	A 3001-B9999	Religion; Theology; Church history.
C Christianity.		
D Historical sciences.	C 1-9999	Biography; and studies auxiliary to history.
E Biography	D 1-9999	General history; periods; and local (except America).
F History	E-F	America; history and geography.
G Geography and travel.	G	Geography; general; and allied studies (e.g. Anthropology and Ethnology).
H Social sciences	H 1-2000	Political science.
I Demotics, Sociology.	H 2001-9999	Law.
J Civics.	I 1-8000	Sociology.
K Legislation.	I 8001-9999	Women; Societies; clubs, etc.
	J 1-2000	Sports; amusements.
	J 2001-9999	Music.
	K	Fine arts.
L Sciences and Arts.	L-M	Philology & Literature.
M Natural history.		
N Botany.	N	Science; Mathematics; Astronomy; Physics; Chemistry.
O Zoology.	O	Natural history; general; Geology.
	P	Zoology; Botany.
Q Medicine.	Q	Medicine.
R Useful arts. Technology.	R	Useful arts; Agriculture.

S	Constructive arts.	S	Manufactures.
T	Fabricative arts.	T	Engineering.
U	Art of War.	U	Military, Naval science; light houses; life saving; fire extinction.
V	Recreative arts. Music.	V-Y	Special collections.
W	Fine arts.		
X	Language.		
Y	Literature.		
Z	Book arts.	Z	Bibliography (Book arts).

The only major change in the order of the <u>Expansive Classification</u> in Hanson's revision was placing the arts--fine arts, music, and literature between the social sciences and the sciences. In 1903 Hanson further perfected this outline as the basis for the new L. C. classification; the nearly final form of the outline was completed the following year. It is interesting to note the final expansion of classes A and B. In Hanson's first outline A1-200 was designed for Polygraphic works, A201-3000 for Philosophy and A3001-B9999 for Religion. In the 1903 outline Philosophy was reduced by 300 numbers--Philosophy started with A501 instead of A201. In the 1904 outline Polygraphy was alloted a separate Class - A, and Philosophy and Religion combined into the separate Class - B. These changes in the 1904 outline represent the decision to use double instead of single letters as were used for the first classes of L. C. classification (Classes Z and E-F).

The 1903 outline was:		The 1904 outline was:	
A(in part)	Polygraphy. General works.	A	General works. Polygraphy.
A501-3000	Philosophy.	B	Philosophy.
A3001-B	Religion.	BL-BX	Religion.
C	Biography; Studies auxiliary to History.	C	History--Auxiliary sciences.
D	History (except America).	D	History & topography (except America).

E-F	America. History and Geography.	E	America General and U. S. General History.
		F	U. S. Local and America Outside U. S. History.
G	Geography; & allied studies: Anthropology; etc.	G	Geography, Anthropology, Sports.
H-J-K	Social science; Economics, Political science.	H	Social sciences.
		J	Political sciences.
L	Law	K	Law.
M	Education. Sports. Amusements.	L	Education.
N	Architecture. Graphic Arts.	M	Music.
P	Music.	N	Fine arts.
Q	Philology and Literature.	P	Language and Literature.
R	Science.	Q	Science.
S	Natural history.	R	Medicine.
T	Botany. Zoology.	S	Agriculture.
U	Medicine.	T	Technology.
V	Useful arts. Agriculture;	U	Military science.
W	Engineering. Military and Naval science.	V	Naval science.
Z	Bibliography.	Z	Bibliography.

Individual Schedules

Subject specialists at the Library of Congress developed each of the individual schedules consulting bibliographies, treatises, comprehensive histories and the existing classification schemes in initially determining the scope and content of an individual class and subclass. The arrangement of the books often established the final pattern for the sequence. The specialists worked on individual subclasses independently with an editor in charge of the whole schedule. For example, Clarence Perley was the editor of <u>Class C: The Auxiliary Sciences of History</u>. He prepared the subclasses CC, CN, and CT. J.D. Wolcott developed subclasses CB, CJ, and CR. Julian Leavitt worked with Wolcott on subclass CB. Subclasses CD and CE were prepared by Alfred Schmidt. Charles Martel and Malma A. Gilkey developed subclass CS. Subclass CN was not included in the first edition of the schedule in 1915 and was not published until 1942.

The approach used in the development of L.C. classification is discussed by Richard S. Angell, former Chief of the Subject Cataloging Division, in an article in <u>Law Library Journal.</u>

"While in general outline and sequence of topics it has affinity with earlier systems, the Library's schedules basically represent a fresh start in the design of a system for its own particular purposes. The schedules were developed one by one, by specialists working under a central direction, but with considerable independence. They were built up for the most part inductively, that is, by taking account of the collections of the Library as they existed and as they were expected to develop because of the Library's needs for comprehensive collections in all fields of knowledge.

From these origins and impulses the Library of Congress classification has developed into a comprehensive practical system for the arrangement and management of collections of books. With one obvious exception [i.e., Class K. Law] it is a complete system, embracing all of the areas of human knowledge, the various components of this universe of knowledge having been allocated to the respective schedules. The objective in the partitioning of this universe is to secure well-defined areas corresponding to the concepts by which the separate fields are taught and expounded, and on which developmental research is based. Within each area the objective is to provide an orderly and apprehendable arrangement of the volumes in an array which will make direct access to the collections useful and meaningful to qualified students and scholars, and helpful to the staff in the control and servicing of items wanted for reference or circulation. To the extent that this partitioning is successful the classification as a whole becomes a seamless garment in that each of the parts exist basically for its place in the whole structure. At the same time the size and scope of the collections give each of the parts a considerable independence and self-sufficiency within its own field. This is particularly true of the manner in which certain common elements of a general classification scheme are treated in each of the parts of ours. Geographical and chronological arrangements, for example, are framed in accordance with the needs of each subject field; that is, they are not carried out by means of a single division table as is the case in certain other classifications. This feature of the schedules has been both criticized and praised; criticized for resulting in extremely detailed and bulky individual schedules, praised for the freedom allowed in each schedule for development according to its subject field's own intrinsic structure. "10

The main unifying factor in all the classes is the notation consisting of double letters, cardinal numbers, and Cutter numbers, however this was not consistent until the development of Class D in 1902. Class D was the first schedule to use double letters instead of single letters as had been used in Classes Z and E-F. The publication of the individual schedules began in 1901 with Class E-F. By June 1, 1904, the classification of classes D, E-F, M, Q, R, S, T, U, and Z had been completed. Classes A, C, G, H, and V were in the process of development.

SUMMARY

This chapter has briefly surveyed the basic outlines of the classification systems used at the Library of Congress prior to the development of the present Library of Congress Classification system. The inherent weaknesses in the Jeffersonian system have been demonstrated. The reasons for the development of a new system for the Library of Congress were the weaknesses of that older system as well as the great physical growth of the Library's collections. As a result of study of available classification schemes and systems of notation, and the dissatisfaction with decimal notation in particular, Library of Congress proceeded with planning for its own unique classification system. Charles Ammi Cutter's Expansive Classification was used to develop the first class in the new system,

---

10Richard S. Angell. "Development of Class K at the Library of Congress, " Law Library Journal, 57:353-354, November 1964.

Class Z: Bibliography and Library Science, and was a basis for
the general outline of all the classes. A mixed notation of letters
and numbers was found to satisfy the requirements of the new classification.

BIBLIOGRAPHY

HISTORY OF THE LIBRARY OF CONGRESS CLASSIFICATION

Johnston, William Dawson. History of the Library of Congress,
    1800-1864. Washington: Govt. Print. Off., 1904.
    This volume is the first and only volume of a planned compre-
    hensive history of the Library of Congress. The succeeding
    volumes were never completed or published.

Lacy, Dan. "Library of Congress: A Sesquincentenary Review, "
    Library Quarterly, 20:157-179; 235-58, July and October 1950.
    This two-part article presents many helpful facts about the
    history of the Library of Congress.

LaMontagne, Leo E. American Library Classification with Special
    Reference to the Library of Congress. Hamden, Conn.: Shoe
    String Press, 1961.
    Pages 27-62 deal with early American classification schemes
    and especially those at the Library of Congress. Based on
    primary sources.

Mearns, David Chambers. The Story Up to Now, The Library of
    Congress, 1800-1946. Washington: Govt. Print. Off., 1947.
    This work is a reprint of the first section of the 1946 Annual
    Report of the Librarian of Congress. (Pp. 13-227 in the 1946
    Report.) Although it is far less detailed than Johnston, it does
    provide information on the history of the classification systems
    including the development of the present Library of Congress
    system.

Spofford, Ainsworth Rand. A Book for All Readers; Designed as an
    Aid to the Collection, Use and Preservation of Books and the
    Formulation of Public and Private Libraries. 3d ed., rev.
    New York: Putnam, 1909.
    This book by one of the most important Librarians of Congress
    includes a section on classification of books, pp. 362-372.
    Spofford makes some reference to the development of L. C.
    classification as well as comments on other classification
    systems.

U.S. Library of Congress. Alphabetical Catalogue of the Library of Congress.Authors. Washington: Govt. Print. Off., 1864.
This is the first printed author catalog of the Library of Congress. It includes an interesting preface by Spofford.

U.S. Library of Congress. Catalogue of the Library of Congress. Index of Subjects. Washington: Govt. Print. Off., 1869. 2v.
This is the second major printed catalog to be issued by Spofford and also includes a useful preface.

U.S. Library of Congress. Catalogue of the Library of the United States; To Which Is Annexed a Copious Index, Alphabetically Arranged. Washington: Printed by Jonathan Elliot, 1815.
This is the first Library of Congress printed catalog to be arranged using the Jeffersonian Classification system. It was edited by George Watterston.

U.S. Library of Congress. Jefferson Collection. Catalogue of the Library of Thomas Jefferson. Compiled with annotations by E. Millicent Sowerby. Washington: The Library of Congress, 1952-59. 5v.
This catalog lists the original Jefferson collection purchased by the Library of Congress. It is arranged in Jefferson's forty-four chapters. The introduction to the first volume contains additional information on the Jefferson collection and its organization.

SUPPLEMENTAL READINGS ON EARLY AVAILABLE SCHEMES

(With Particular Emphasis on Cutter's Expansive Classification)

Aldred, Thomas. "The Expansive Classification, " Library Association Record, 7:207-19, 1905.
Discussion of Cutter's system from a British viewpoint.

American Library Association. Catalogue of the A.L.A. Library: Five Thousand Volumes for a Popular Library. Washington: Govt. Print. Off., 1893.
Pp. 145-256 show entries arranged according to the Expansive Classification. Sample pages of author and subject indexes are also included.

American Library Association. <u>A. L. A. Catalog</u>, 8,000 Volumes
   for a Popular Library, With Notes, 1904. Prepared by the
   New York State Library and the Library of Congress under the
   Auspices of the American Library Association Publishing Board.
   Editor: Melvil Dewey. Associate editors: May Seymour and
   Mrs. H. L. Elmendorf. Part 1: Classed. Part 2: Dictionary.
   Washington: Govt. Print. Off., 1904.
   Pp. 5-7 contain an explanation and outline of the <u>Expansive</u>
   <u>Classification</u>. The entire first part consists of a two column
   class number approach with the Dewey Decimal number on the
   left of the entry and Cutter Expansive number on the right.
   This work can be used as an interesting comparison of the two
   systems.

Bliss, Henry Evelyn. <u>The Organization of Knowledge in Libraries,</u>
   <u>and the Subject-Approach to Books</u>. New York: The H. W. Wilson Co., 1934.
   Pp. 230-241 are thoughtful criticisms of the <u>Expansive Classi-</u>
   <u>fication</u>.

Boston Athenaeum. <u>How to Get Books,</u> with an Explanation of the
   New Way of Marking Books, by Charles Ammi Cutter. Boston:
   Rockwell and Churchill, 1882.
   This and the following eight entries represent a part of Cutter's
   work on classification in general and his Expansive system in
   particular.

Cutter, Charles Ammi. "Classification on the Shelves," <u>Library</u>
   <u>Journal,</u> 4:234-243, July-August 1879.
   This article written while Cutter was Librarian at the Boston
   Athenaeum includes an account of the new scheme prepared for
   use at the Library. Cutter cites the value of relative classification instead of fixed location. He also comments on both the
   Decimal system of Dewey and his own Expansive system.

_____. "The Expansive Classification." In <u>Transactions and</u>
   <u>Proceedings</u> of the Second International Library Conference,
   London, July 13-16, 1897. London: Printed for Members of
   the Conference by Morrison & Giblex of Edinburgh, 1898. Pp.
   84-88.
   This exposition of the Expansive system serves as an excellent
   introduction to that system. A synopsis for a special scheme
   for Shakespeare is included.

Cutter, Charles Ammi. Expansive Classification. Part 1: The
First Six Classifications. Boston: C.A. Cutter, 1891-1893.
This is the only completed work by Cutter on his classification
system. The first six expansions are included with instructions
for the use of each.

_____. Expansive Classification. Part 2: Seventh Classifi-
cation. Ed. by W.P. Cutter. Boston (Northampton, Mass.): 1896-
1911. 2v. with suppl. pages.
Much of the seventh expansion was completed by Cutter's
nephew, William P. Cutter, after the elder Cutter's death.
This work was issued in parts and is difficult to describe biblio-
graphically.

_____. Explanation of the Cutter-Sanborn Author-Marks
Three-Figure Tables. Rev. by Kate Amery Jones. Northampton, Mass.: Kingsburg Press, 1935.

_____. Local List. Boston: C.A. Cutter, 189?

_____. Subject Divisions under Countries instead of Country
Divisions under Subjects. Boston: C.A. Cutter, 189?

_____. "Suitability of the Expansive Classification to College
and Reference Libraries," Library Journal, 24:C41-49, July
1899.
This is an interesting discussion by Cutter with examples of
the uses and especially the notation of his system. He also included some comments on the Decimal system.

Cutter, William Parker. Charles Ammi Cutter. Chicago: American Library Association, 1931.

Dewey, Melvil. Decimal Classification and Relativ Index for
Libraries, Clippings, Notes, etc. 5th ed. Boston: Library
Bureau, 1894.
This is the edition of Dewey's Decimal Classification that was
available for consideration by Hanson and Martel.

Eaton, Thelma. "The Development of Classification in America, "
The Role of Classification in the Modern American Library.
Papers presented at an Institute Conducted by the University of
Illinois Graduate School of Library Science, November 1-4,
1959. Champaign, Ill.: Illini Union Bookstore, 1959. Pp. 8-30.
This is a short but sound summary of the history of American
library classification.

Halle. Universität. Bibliothek. Schema des Realkatalogs. Leipzig: O. Harrassowitz, 1888.
This is the Halle Schema primarily developed by Otto Harwig. It as well as Dewey's fifth edition were considered and rejected by Hanson and Martel.

Lamb, Eliza. "The Expansive Classification in Use, " Library Quarterly, 4:265-269, April 1934.
The use of the Expansive Classification in the twentieth century at the University of Wisconsin Libraries is presented in this article.

LaMontagne, Leo E. American Library Classification with Special Reference to the Library of Congress. Hamden, Conn.: Shoe String Press, 1961.
Pp. 204-220 deal with the available classification systems in 1898.

Phillips, W. Howard. A Primer of Book Classification. 5th ed. London: Association of Assistant Librarians, 1961.
Pp. 83-94 cover the Expansive Classification.

Sayers, W. C. Berwick. Canons of Classification, Applied to "The Subject, " "The Expansive, " "The Decimal, " and "The Library of Congress" Classifications. A Study in Bibliographical Classification Method. London: Grafton, 1915.
The Expansive Classification is discussed on pp. 67-93.

_____. An Introduction to Library Classification: Theoretical, Historical and Practical with Readings, Exercises and Examination Papers. 9th ed. London: Grafton, 1954.
Pp. 93-99 deal with the Expansive Classification.

_____. A Manual of Classification for Librarians and Bibliographers. 3d ed., rev. with some corrections. London: Andre Deutsch, 1959.
Another similar presentation of the Expansive Classification on pp. 141-150.

Tauber, Maurice F. and Edith Wise. Classification Systems. Vol. 1, pt. 4 of The State of Library Art. Edited by Ralph R. Shaw. New Brunswick, N. J.: Graduate School of Library Service, Rutgers--The State University, 1961.
Pp. 108-139 give a complete survey of material about the Expansive Classification.

A SELECTED LIST OF
ADDITIONAL EARLY CLASSIFICATION SCHEMES

Edmands, John. New System of Classification and Scheme for Numbering Books, Applied to the Mercantile Library of Philadelphia. Philadelphia: Grant, Faires & Rodgers, printers, 1883.

Fletcher, William I. Library Classification. Reprinted, with alterations, additions, and an index from his "Public Libraries in America." Boston: Roberts Bros., 1894.

Harris, William T. Essay on the System of Classification. St. Louis: Missouri Democrat and Job Printing House, 1870. This is a reprint from the Catalogue, Classified and Alphabetical, of the Books of the St. Louis Public School Library, St. Louis: Missouri Democrat and Job Printing House, 1870, p. ix-xvi, which also contains Harris' "System of Classification."

Perkins, Fred. B. A Rational Classification of Literature for Shelving and Cataloging Books in a Library. Rev. ed. San Francisco: Francis, Valentine & Co., printers, 1882.

Schleiermacher, A. A. E. Bibliographisches System der Gesammten Wissenschaftskunde, mit einer Anleitung zum Ordnen von Bibliotheken... Braunschweig: Vieweg, 1852.

Shurtleff, Nathaniel B. A Decimal System for the Arrangement and Administration of Libraries. Boston: Priv. print., 1856. This is a decimal notation for the fixed location of materials, which was used at the Boston Public Library.

Smith, Lloyd P. On the Classification of Books. A Paper Read Before the American Library Association, May, 1882. Boston: Library Bureau, 1882.

Steffenhagen, Emil. Die Ordnungsprincipien der Universitäts-Bibliothek Kiel... Burg: Hopfer, 1888.

CHAPTER 2.

GENERAL CHARACTERISTICS OF L. C. CLASSIFICATION

THE PURPOSE FOR L. C. CLASSIFICATION

The Library of Congress classification was originally designed and developed as an utilitarian system for the use of the Library of Congress only. L. C. classification was not based on any philosophical system for classifying knowledge. It was designed to classify the books of the Library of Congress collection and future expansions of the collections. Herbert Putnam emphasized practical consideration as a basis for the development of the L. C. classification when he wrote in 1901:

> "The system of classification thus far applied is one devised from a comparison of existing schemes (including the "decimal" and the "expansive"), and a consideration of the particular conditions in this Library, the character of its present and probable collections, and of its probable use. It is assumed that the departments of history, political and social science, and certain others will be unusually large. It is assumed that investigators will be more freely admitted to the shelves.
> "The system devised has not sought to follow strictly the scientific order of subjects. It has sought rather convenient sequence of the various groups, considering them as groups of books, not as groups of mere subjects. "[1]

This system was not intended for use by any library other than the Library of Congress. As L. C. classification was being developed, no attempt was made to create a perfect general classification system which could be used by all major American libraries. The original attitude of the Library of Congress may be discerned in the following statement taken from the Annual Report of 1916.

> "In contrast with the card catalogue of the Library which, owing to the sale of the printed cards is a matter of general concern to libraries, the classification of our collections was assumed to be of concern solely to ourselves--that is to the efficient administration of this

---

[1]Herbert Putnam. "Manual: Constitution, Organization, Methods, etc., " In Report of the Librarian of Congress for the Fiscal Year Ending June 30, 1901. Washington: Govt. Print. Off., 1901. p. 23

Library within itself. Upon this assumption the scheme
adopted has been devised with reference (1) to the character and probable development of our own collections,
(2) to its operation by our own staff, (3) to the character
and habits of our own readers, and (4) to the usages in
vogue here, a distinguishing feature of which is the freedom of access to the shelves granted to serious investi-
gators.

"With these considerations the resultant scheme,
while organic in the sense that certain fundamentals were
the basis of each schedule, is unsymmetrical, since each
schedule was devised with reference to its own utilities
(as applied to that particular group of material) rather
than with reference to its proportionate part in an integral whole.

"There was therefore no expectation that the scheme
would be adopted by other libraries; much less was there
any profession that it would be suited to their needs. It
is, moreover, still incomplete, and various schedules
sufficiently advanced for our own use are yet unavailable
in printed form.

"Under the circumstances the number of other libraries
that are already adopting it in whole or in part is somewhat surprising. "[2]

Many of the problems in the use of L. C. classification result from
its having been designed and developed for a single library with
specific services.

THE FORMAT OF L. C. CLASSIFICATION

The Individual Schedules

The schedules for L. C. classification comprise 29 individual
volumes for the main classes and subclasses. A full set of schedules
contains about 7, 000 pages and costs over $60. 00. The individual
schedules are:

---

[2]U. S. Library of Congress. Report of the Librarian of Congress and Report of the Superintendent of the Library Grounds for
the fiscal year ending June 30, 1916. Washington: Govt. Print.
Off., 1916. p. 103.

A: General works, Polygraphy.

B, pt. 1, B-BJ: Philosophy.

B, pt. 2, BL-BX: Religion.

C: Auxiliary - Sciences of History.

D: General and Old World History.

E-F: American History.

G: Geography, Anthropology, Folklore, Manners and Customs, Recreation.

H: Social Sciences.

J: Political Science.

KF: Law of the United States.

L: Education.

M: Music and Books on Music.

N: Fine Arts.

P-PA: Philology, Linguistics, Classical Philology, Classical Literature.

PB-PH: Modern European Languages.

PG, in part: Russian Literature.

PJ-PM: Languages and Literatures of Asia, Africa, Oceania, America, Mixed Languages, Artificial Languages.

PN, PR, PS, PZ: Literature (General), English and American Literature, Fiction in English, Juvenile Literature.

PQ, pt. 1: French Literature.

PQ, pt. 2: Italian, Spanish, and Portuguese Literatures.

PT, pt. 1: German Literature.

PT, pt. 2: Dutch and Scandinavian Literatures.

Q: Science.

R: Medicine.

S: Agriculture, Plant and Animal Industry, Fish Culture, and Fisheries, Hunting Sports.

T: Technology.

U: Military Science.

V: Naval Science.

Z: Bibliography and Library Science.

Besides these 29 schedules, there are presently in use two supplements, one partial index, and the outline of the classes. The supplements are for 1) PA covering Byzantine and modern Greek literature and 2) T, Technology. The partial index is for subclasses P-PM covering only languages and dialects. A total of 33 physical volumes comprises the L. C. schedules.

The individual schedules are kept current by 1) L. C. Classification--Additions and Changes, which is published quarterly by the Library of Congress, 2) the addition of supplementary pages of Additions and Changes to the later printing of an individual schedule, and 3) periodic new editions of the individual schedules. Both the quarterly Additions and Changes and the supplementary pages are printed on leaves, i. e. with alternate pages blank, to allow the possibility of clipping and tabbing into the original schedules. The new edition of an individual schedule include all additions and changes in the main sequence of the schedule. Class Q is already in its fifth edition. Classes T and Z are in fourth editions. Classes A, E-F, G, H, L, N, R, S, and U are all in third editions. The remaining classes are all in second editions with the exception of the entire Class P which still is in its first edition.

Format of Each Schedule

Each schedule has a similar if not identical format. The usual elements making up each schedule are 1) a prefatory note, containing a brief history of the schedule as well as concise remarks on the scope of the schedule (see Figure 1); 2) a synopsis, consisting of a list of all double letters covered in the schedule (see Figure 2); 3) an outline, in greater detail than the synopsis of the portion of the classification covered in the schedule (see Figure 3); 4) the schedule, containing the main classification tables (see Figure 4); 5) any necessary auxiliary tables (see Figure 5); 6) a detailed index (see Figure 6); and 7) any supplementary pages of additions and changes to the schedule (see Figure 7). All 29 schedules do not have auxiliary tables; some do not have an outline (e. g. Subclass PN, PR, PS, PZ); and some do not have an index (e. g. Subclass PQ, pt. 1 or pt. 2). Usually, if there is no index to a schedule, there is an extensive outline at the beginning of the schedule.

FORM OF THE NOTATION

L. C. call numbers, just as Dewey Decimal Classification call numbers, consist in general of two principal elements, a class number and an author number, to which may be added symbols designating a particular title and a particular edition. For example, the third edition of Richard D. Altick and Andrew Wright's Selective Bibliography for the Study of English and American Literature has the following call numbers in L. C. classification and Decimal Classification.

	L. C. Classification	Decimal Classification
Class number:	Z2011	016. 82
Author number:	. A4	A468s
Publication date used to indicate later edition	1967	1967

The main classes in L. C. are designated by single capital letters, the subclasses by two capital letters (except in classes E-F and Z) and the divisions and subdivisions by integral numbers in ordinary sequence ranging from 1 to 9999, which may be extended decimally. In the example above, the class number "Z2011" in L. C. means a general bibliography of English literature as does the Decimal Classification number "016. 82. " See also the following card.

Additional numbers used in an L. C. call number consist of one or two Cutter or author numbers. A Cutter number consists of an initial letter followed by Arabic numerals. In the example above ". A4" is the author number in L. C. while "A468" is the author number if the work is classed in the Decimal Classification.

Z --------- The main class letter for bibliography.
2011 ----- The subdivision by integral numbers meaning general bibliography of English literature.
. A4------- The Cutter number for author, Atlick.
1967 ------ The date of publication used to indicate edition other than the first edition.

This is an example of a simple L. C. call number in which the class number and author number are easily separable. (See card on next page.)

Altick, Richard Daniel, 1915–
    Selective bibliography for the study of English and
American literature, by Richard D. Altick and Andrew
Wright. 3d ed. New York, Macmillan [1967]

    xii, 152 p. 21 cm.

    Alternate pages blank (p. 11–115)

    1. English literature — Study and teaching — Bibl. 2. American
literature—Study and teaching—Bibl.   I. Wright, Andrew H.,
joint author. II. Title.

Z2011.A4   1967   016.82   67–13598

Library of Congress   [5]

Occasionally in L. C. call numbers these Cutter numbers
will be used for a further subdivision of the class number. This
is a particularly frequent device for a simple alphabetical arrangement of countries, regions, cities, topics, etc. This more complex use of L. C. notation is shown in the next card.

Jackson, Holbrook, 1874–1948, *comp.*
    Bookman's holiday, a recreation for booklovers, designed
by Holbrook Jackson. London, Faber & Faber limited [1945]

    264 p. 19½ cm.

    "This anthology shows what writers of books think of their prede-
cessors, their contemporaries, and themselves."—Pref.
    "First published in Mcmxlv."
    American edition (New York, Farrar, Straus and company) has
title: Bookman's pleasure.
    "Bibliography: Books from which quotations have been made": p.
246–255.

    1. Authors.   I. Title.

PN6071.A9J3   928   45—9031

Library of Congress   [a60i½]

PN---------- The Subclass number of double letters meaning General or World literature.

6071 -------- The subdivision by integral numbers meaning Literary collections to be subarranged by subject, A-Z.

.A9 --------- The first Cutter number used for further subdivision meaning the specific subject, "authors."

J3 ---------- The second Cutter number for the author, Jackson.

In this case the class number continues through the first Cutter number and the author number does not begin until "J3." In a few exceptional cases, both Cutter numbers may be used for further subdivisions of the class number. This characteristic of L. C. notation may confuse the classifier accustomed to Decimal Classification class numbers and Cutter-Sanborn author numbers with work marks. When both Cutter numbers are used as further subdivisions of the subject, the shelflisting of L. C. numbers becomes a process more closely related to the classification than the shelflisting process in the Decimal Classification.

In the foregoing examples the first Cutter number was preceded by a decimal point. This is consistent with the Library of Congress practice. The use of this decimal point before the first element of the Cutter number may be traced to Cutter's own use of Cutter numbers. The remainder of the notation in the previous examples does not follow the normal Library of Congress practice. The reason for this variation is to analyze the call number graphically. The proper representation of the notation at the Library of Congress is to present the class letter or letters on one line with the integral number. Any decimal extension of the integral number would follow on a separate line to avoid the possibility of confusion should the decimal point be accidentally dropped. The next line is introduced by the decimal point for the Cutter number or numbers which usually fill only one line even if there are two Cutter numbers. Finally the date may be the last element on a separate line. This practice is followed at the Library of Congress for the representation of the call number on the catalog card. The representation of the call number on the spine of the book is the same except that the first line is divided into two lines with the class letter or letters on the first line and the integral number on the second. The following two examples demonstrate the Library of Congress representation of the call number on the catalog card and book label.

CALL NUMBER MARKING USED BY LIBRARY OF CONGRESS

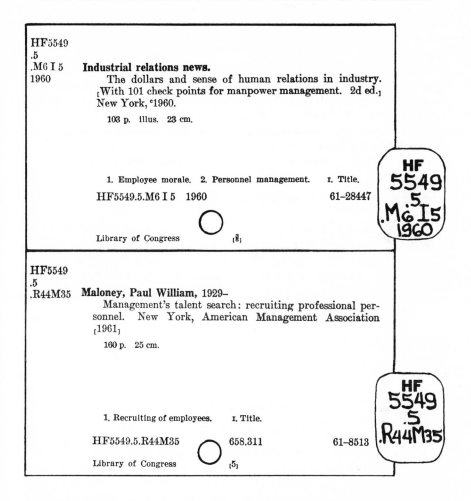

Many libraries do not follow this same representation of the notation. For example, some libraries do not use the introductory decimal point for the Cutter numbers. A discussion of one library's
solution to this particular problem may be found in Dàniel Gore's
"Further Observations on the Use of LC Classification" listed in
the bibliography of this chapter.

THE GENERAL PRINCIPLE OF ARRANGEMENT
WITHIN THE CLASSES

Just as L. C. classification has a recurring external format of
schedules, there is another unifying element in the internal form

for arrangement within the classes, subclasses, or under subjects. This internal form, the general principle of arrangement within the classes, is often called "Martel's Seven Points." Each of the individual subject specialists made use of these seven points or appropriate parts of them. They are 1) General form divisions: Periodicals, Societies, Collections, Dictionaries, etc.; 2) Theory, Philosophy; 3) History; 4) Treatises, General works; 5) Law, Relation, State relations; 6) Study and Teaching; and 7) Special subjects and subdivisions of subjects progressing from the more general to the specific and as far as possible in logical order. Under individual subjects, this general principle of arrangement occurs although the exact sequence may differ in individual cases.

General Form Divisions

In addition to periodicals, societies, collections and dictionaries, general form divisions may consist of congresses, exhibitions, museums, yearbooks, documents, or any general form division peculiar to a specific class or subclass. An example of this is shown in the following extract from the beginning of subclass **CR** (See also Figure 8 - Heraldry).

HERALDRY   CR

    1 Periodicals. Societies.

    Collected works.

    4   Several authors.

    5   Individual authors.

    7   Congresses, conventions, etc.

    9   Exhibitions.

    11   Directories.

    13   Dictionaries. Encyclopedias.

Although all the general form divisions usually precede all other divisions, this is not an absolute rule. For instance, "CN 70 Dictionaries, Terminology" is separated from the other general form divisions by the elements "CN 40, Philosophy"; "CN 50, Study and teaching"; and "CN 55-62, History." (See Figure 9.)

Theory, Philosophy

This second element of the general principle of arrangement is used primarily in the main classes and subclasses. It is often only a single number such as "CN 40, Philosophy, Theory" (see Figure 9). However, this element, just as all the other elements, may be expanded to many numbers in some instances. The theory and philosophy of literature, PN 45-58, receives 14 numbers (see Figure 10). This particular element may be compared to the standard subdivision ".01" in the Decimal Classification.

History

The history element of a class or subject is most commonly divided chronologically. This may be discerned in subclass JV 6021-6033 for the history of emigration and immigration (see also Figure 11).

	History
6021	General.
	By period.
	Under each: (1) General.
	(2) Special.
6023-4	Ancient.
6026-7	Medieval to 1800.
6029-30	19th century.
6032-3	20th century.

"Early to 1800" and "1800 —— " are the most common chronological divisions. "History" and the following element, "Treatises, General works, " are often combined in actual usage. An example of this combination may be seen in AM 4-9 for history, treatises and general works about museums (see also Figure 12).

AM	Museums
4	Early works (to 1800).
5	General treatises.
7	General special. (Educational aspects, relations, etc.)

8	Children's museums.

9	Minor. Pamphlets, etc.

Both of these elements, "History" and "Treatises," make use of the terms "General" and "General special." "General" is usually used to mean comprehensive works on a particular class, subclass, or subject. "General special" means general or comprehensive works treated from a particular point of view, or in a particular relation or aspect. The phrase "General special" is not being used in the newly developing Class K, Law, but rather the phrase "particular aspects" is used. The following examples in the section on treatises show various uses of these terms. A classic example of "general special" in world history would be "A Child's History of the World."

Treatises, General Works

This element is used for comprehensive works covering a particular class, subclass or subject. The terminology of this element may be "Treatises," "General works," or "General." Often this element is subdivided chronologically. Also this element may be combined with the foregoing element, "History," as already demonstrated. The term, "general," is often used in sequence with the previously defined term, "general special." CN 74-90 is an example of this (see also Figure 9).

CN	EPIGRAPHY
	General works. Introductions and manuals.
74	Early works to 1800.
75	Later works, 1801-
	General special. Special aspects, relations, etc.
77	Relation to archeology, history, etc.
80	Relation to religion.
85	Other.
90	Minor works. Addresses, essays, lectures.

Occasionally the terms "Epitomes," "Outlines" and "Minor works" are also used in this sequence. An epitome may be defined as an annotated outline or chronology. An outline frequently is used to mean a skeletal structure. A minor work may be used to mean a work covering a comprehensive subject but not in a comprehensive fashion. (See Figures 8, 11, and 12 for examples of these uses.) Pamphlets are usually classed as minor works.

Law, Regulation, State Relations

This particular element is most widely used in the social sciences. It demonstrates the tendency of L. C. as well as the Decimal Classification to class legal material with the subject covered or regulated by the law and not as a separate class. However, this element may disappear or be substantially reduced as Class K: Law is completed. An example of the usage of this element may be seen in emigration and immigration laws, JV 6045-6049 (see also Figure 11).

> Law.

6045   General collections

6049   International law.

Study and Teaching

This element often occurs as a single number as it does in "CN 50, Study and teaching" of epigraphy (see Figure 9). Just as in the case of "Theory, Philosophy, " "Study and Teaching" may be said to parallel a standard subdivision in the Decimal Classification, ".07. " Occasionally "Study and Teaching" will use more than a single number as in the case of "PR 31-55, Study and teaching of English literature, " in which the whole number PR55 is devoted solely to biographies of teachers of English literature (see Figure 13). In one instance, "MT 1-950, " study and teaching of music, an entire subclass is devoted to this element (see Figure 14).

Subjects and Subdivisions of Subjects

This last element describes the bulk of the individual developments or expansions of classes, subclasses and subjects. In as far as possible a logical order is employed. "JN 1291-1361, " the numbers for civil and political rights in Scotland, may be seen as an example of this. The logical subdivisions of this particular subject are Citizenship, Naturalization, Suffrage, Electoral system, Contested elections, and Corrupt practices. Obviously one subdivision naturally or logically precedes the other. For example, one cannot have a contested election until an electoral system is present. (See Figure 15.) When a logical order cannot be discerned, an alphabetical arrangement is employed.

AUTHOR NUMBERS

With the possible exception of certain numbers in subclass "PZ, Fiction in English and Juvenile Literature, " L. C. notation does not use Cutter-Sanborn tables for author or Cutter numbers. As L. C. is a very close classification, the use of three figure Cutter-Sanborn numbers would cause the notation to contain unnecessary elements. The table for L. C. author or Cutter numbers is designed in a very simple fashion. It allows the easy assignment of one or two figures to the initial letter of the author's name. The following explanation of L. C. author numbers is given by the L. C. Processing Department.

"Library of Congress call numbers consist in general of two principal elements: class number and author number, to which are added as required symbols designating a particular work and a particular book. This statement offers a brief explanation of the Library's system of author numbers, or, more properly, of assigning the symbols by which names are designated and differentiated in call numbers.

"Library of Congress author symbols are composed of initial letters followed by Arabic numbers. The numbers are used decimally and are assigned on the basis of the tables given below in a manner that preserves the alphabetical order of names within a class.

1. After the initial letter S̲
for the second letter:	a	ch	e	hi		m o p	t		u
use number:	2	3	4	5		6	7-8		9

2. After the initial letters Q̲u̲
for the third letter:	a	e	i	o	r	y
use number:	3	4	5	6	7	9

3. After other initial consonants
for second letter:	a	e	i	o	r	u
use number:	3	4	5	6	7	8

4. After initial vowels
for second letter:	b	d	l m	n	p	r	s t
use number:	2	3	4	5	6	7	8

"Letters not included in the foregoing tables are assigned the next higher or lower number as required by previous assignments in the particular class.

The following examples illustrate the application of these tables:

1. Names beginning with the letter S:

Sabine	. S15	Seaton	. S4	Steel	. S7
Saint	. S2	Shank	. S45	Storch	. S75
Schaefer	. S3	Shipley	. S5	Sturges	. S8
Schwedel	. S35	Smith	. S6	Sullivan	. S9

2. Names beginning with the letters Qu:

Quabbe	. Q3	Quick	. Q5	Qureshi	. Q7
Queener	. Q4	Quoist	. Q6	Quynn	. Q9

3. Names beginning with other consonants:

Carter	. C3	Cinelli	. C5	Crocket	. C7
Cecil	. C4	Corbett	. C6	Croft	. C73
Childs	. C45	Cox	. C65	Cullen	. C8

4. Names beginning with vowels:

Abernathy	. A2	Ames	. A5	Arundel	. A78
Adams	. A3	Appleby	. A6	Atwater	. A87
Aldrich	. A4	Archer	. A7	Austin	. A9

"Since the tables provide only a general framework for the assignment of author numbers, it should be noted that the symbol for a particular name is constant only within a single class. "

The user of these tables must realize that L. C. practice does not always strictly follow these tables. For instance, the British Museum, is cuttered in "AM 101" as ". B8" not as ". B7, " the proper number according to the table. Also the user should be advised to take care in the use of either "1" or "9" in Cutter numbers. Either of these numbers, if used, can result in unnecessary decimal extensions. In general the preceding table should be used in original classing only when absolutely necessary. It is always preferable to discern the author or Cutter number actually used by the Library of Congress.

YEAR OF EDITION

One fairly common L. C. practice for all editions of a work after the first edition is to use the date of publication for an additional element in the notation. If two editions are published in the same year, a lower case letter "a" is assigned to the date of the

second publication received at the Library of Congress. If a third
publication is issued the same year, a "b" could be assigned to the
date of that work, etc. The following examples demonstrate the
possibility of two editions of a work being published the same year--
one in London and the other in New York.

Macmillan, Harold, 1894–
  Winds of change, 1914–1939. London, Melbourne ₍etc.₎
Macmillan, 1966.

  viii, 664 p. 16 plates (incl. ports.) 22½ cm. 55/-

                  (B 66–16645)

  Tables on endpapers.
  Bibliographical footnotes.

  1. Gt. Brit.—Pol. & govt.—20th cent. 2. Gt. Brit.—For. rel.—20th
cent. ɪ. Title.

  DA566.9.M33A3 1966   942.0820924 (B)   66–74717

  Library of Congress   ₍3₎

YEAR OF EDITION 1966

Macmillan, Harold, 1894–
  Winds of change, 1914–1939. ₍1st U. S. ed.₎ New York,
Harper & Row ₍1966₎

  vi, 584 p. illus., ports. 24 cm.

  First vol. of the author's memoirs.
  Bibliographical footnotes.

  1. Gt. Brit.—Pol. & govt.—20th cent. 2. Gt. Brit.—For. rel.—20th
cent. ɪ. Title.

  DA566.9.M33A3 1966a   66—21710
          942.0820924 (B)

  Library of Congress   ₍67w7₎

YEAR OF EDITION 1966a

WORKMARKS

Workmarks are used when absolutely necessary. Several numbers in subclass PZ make use of workmarks consisting of a capital letter for the title of the book. In many instances, this capital letter will be followed by one or more lower case letters. Sometimes these second letters are taken from the title, but occasionally they are simply devised to retain the alphabetical order of an author's works. The following examples demonstrate this use of workmarks.

Huxley, Aldous Leonard, 1894–
  Crome yellow, by Aldous Huxley. New York, George H.
Doran company [c1922]

  307 p. 19½ cm.

  I. Title.

  PZ3.H981Cr   22—6512

  Library of Congress   [60i1]

PZ---------- The subclass number of double letters meaning
             Fiction in English and Juvenile Literature.

3 ---------- The subdivision by integral numbers meaning
             Fiction in English by individual authors publishing prior to 1950.

.H981 ------- The Cutter number for author, Huxley.

Cr ---------- The workmarks for the title, Crome Yellow.

> **De Jong, Meindert,** 1910–
> Far out the long canal. Pictures by Nancy Grossman.
> New York, Harper & Row ₍1964₎
>
> 231 p. illus. 23 cm.
>
> ɪ. Title.
>
> PZ7.D3675Far   64–20947
>
> Library of Congress   ₍7–1₎

PZ---------- The subclass number of double letters meaning
             Fiction in English and Juvenile Literature.

7 ----------- The subdivision by integral numbers meaning
             General modern juvenile literature in English.

.D3675 ------ The Cutter number for author, De Jong.

Far --------- The workmarks for the title, Far out the long
             canal.

> **Phipson, Joan.**
> Threat to the Barkers. Illustrated by Margaret Horder.
> ₍1st American ed.₎ New York, Harcourt, Brace & World
> ₍1965, ᶜ1963₎
>
> 219 p. illus. 21 cm.
>
> ɪ. Title.
>
> PZ7.P55204Th 2   65–10962
>
> Library of Congress   ₍5₎

PZ---------- The subclass number of double letters meaning Fiction in English and Juvenile Literature.

7 ----------- The subdivision by integral numbers meaning General modern juvenile literature in English.

.P55204 ----- The Cutter number for author, Phipson.

Th2 --------- The workmarks for the title, Threat to the Barkers, with the use of "2" to indicate a later or different edition than the first edition.

"DIVIDE LIKE" NOTES

In order to save space in the printed schedules, L.C. classification occasionally uses "divide like" notes or "arrange like" notes. These notes are far simpler to use than the similar device employed in the Decimal Classification--especially in Edition 17. In L.C. "divide like" notes refer from one example to another example within the physical schedules and do not refer from one schedule to another. An example may be found in AG 5-91, the range of numbers for dictionaries and minor encyclopedias. "AG 5-91: Arranged like AE 5-91." Besides this device, L.C. schedules have many other helpful devices such as very clear scope notes (notes explaining the scope or type of material for inclusion), many cross references and other useful examples.

GEOGRAPHIC DIVISION

The geographic division in L.C. schedules follows one of two general patterns. Either continents and countries are arranged in a "logical" order or arranged alphabetically. Major geographic areas are generally arranged in the following logical order.

America.

North America.

United States.

British North America. Canada.

Mexico.

Central America.

West Indies.

South America.

Europe.

Great Britain.

Continental Countries.

Asia.

Africa.

Australia and New Zealand.

Pacific Islands.

Arctic regions.

Antarctic regions.

Within each region further subdivision is made either logically or alphabetically. The alphabetical geographic division is used when one number is assigned to the geographic division, e. g. "By country, A-Z. "

METHODS FOR EXPANSION OF L. C. CLASSIFICATION

There are five methods for possible expansion of L. C. classification.

1. By using the unused letters I, O, W, X, and Y. (It should be noted that the letter W has been used by the National Library of Medicine for its classification schedule for medicine which may be used by libraries adopting L. C. if Class R is not used.)

2. By adding a third capital letter or even a fourth to the existing double letters, e. g. CNA, CNB, CNC, etc. This device is presently being used in subclass KF for state law. This use is discussed in Chapter 5.

3. By the assignment of the unused numbers and double letters in the present schedules.

4. By extending the present numbers decimally.

5. By further use of Cutter numbers.

Only the last three methods of expansion have been generally used by the Library of Congress. The newly developed subclass KF is an exception to this general pattern. Obviously the first two methods would cause major reclassification within the L. C. schedules and hence have not been used.

BIBLIOGRAPHY

GENERAL ARTICLES AND WORKS ON L. C. CLASSIFICATION

Angell, Richard S. "On the Future of the Library of Congress Classification, " Classification Research. Proceedings of the Second International Study Conference held at Hotel Prins Hamlet, Elsinore, Denmark, 14th to 18th September 1964. Edited by Pauline Atherton. Copenhagen: Munksgaard, 1965. Pp. 101-112.
This is a recent statement by the then Chief of the Subject Cataloging Division summarizing the scope, notation, principle of class construction and provisions for revision of L. C. classification. Various modern problems of classification are discussed.

Davison, Keith. Theory of Classification; An Examination Guidebook. London: Clive Bingley, 1966.
Pp. 18-20 offer a short general summary of L. C. classification.

Doyle, Irene M. "Library of Congress Classification for the Academic Library, " The Role of Classification in the Modern American Library. Papers Presented at an Institute Conducted by the University of Illinois Graduate School of Library Science, November 1-4, 1959. Champaign, Ill.: Illini Union Bookstore, 1959. Pp. 76-92.
This article discusses the adoption and use of L. C. classification at the University of Wisconsin Libraries, the long time home of the Expansive Classification.

Hanson, J. C. M. "The Library of Congress and its New Catalogue: Some Unwritten History, " Essays Offered to Herbert Putnam by his Colleagues and Friends on his Thirtieth Anniversary as Librarian of Congress: 5 April 1929. Edited by William Warner Bishop and Andrew Keogh. New Haven: Yale University Press, 1929. Pp. 178-194.
This article contains much essential information about the beginnings of L. C. classification as recorded by one of its founders.

_____. "Library of Congress Classification for College Libraries, " Library Journal, 46:151-154, February 15, 1921.
Hanson discusses the advantages and disadvantages of the use of L. C. classification by college libraries.

50

Hawkes, A. J. "Library of Congress Classification, " Library Association Record, 16:188-189, April 15, 1914.
This is a synopsis of a paper by a British librarian who was using L. C. classification in its early days.

Hicks, Frederick C. "Library of Congress Classification and its Printed Catalogue Cards, " Library Journal, 31:255-256, June 1906.
Hicks, the Librarian of the U. S. Naval War College at Newport, R. I., discusses the reasons for using L. C. classification at the U. S. Naval War College Library in 1906.

Hoage, A. Annette Lewis. "The Library of Congress Classification in the United States: A Survey of Opinions and Practices, with Attention to Problems of Structure and Application. " Unpublished Doctoral dissertation, Columbia University, 1961.
This 233 page work is one of the three books devoted mainly to Library of Congress Classification. The other two are LaMontagne's American Library Classification and Catherine Grout's Explanation of the Tables Used in the Schedules of the Library of Congress Classification. Mrs. Hoage's work is now available in a University Microfilms edition. Chapters on "Development and Application of the Schedules, " "Opinions of the Classification, " "Acceptance of the Classification, " "Use of the Classification by Patrons, " and a description of the classification in the "Appendixes" are included in this important work. This should be carefully read by all students of L. C. classification.

LaMontagne, Leo E. American Library Classification with Special Reference to the Library of Congress. Hamden, Conn.: Shoe String Press, 1961. Pp. 221-333 present a complete study of the background, theory and structure of L. C. classification.

"Library of Congress Classification, " Library World, 17:45, July 1914.
This is simply an outline of the schedules available in 1914 and their prices.

_____. _____. 18:355-359, June 1916.
This second article in Library World contains short summaries and a few critical remarks on Classes A, C, GR, GT, HT, PN-PZ.

Mann, Margaret. Introduction to Cataloging and the Classification
of Books. 2d ed.Chicago: American Library Association, 1943.
Chapter V, "The Cutter Expansive and Library of Congress
Classification Systems," contains a simple introduction to L. C.
classification (pp. 70-85) with many suggestions for further
study.

Martel, Charles. "Classification," Report of the Librarian of
Congress, and Report of the Superintendent of the Library
Buildings and Grounds for the fiscal year ending June 30, 1911.
Washington: Govt. Print. Off., 1911. Pp. 58-64.
Martel presents the basic objectives and purposes of L. C.
classification.

_____. "Classification: a Brief Conspectus of Present
Day Library Practice," Library Journal, 36:410-416, August
1911.
Pp. 414-416 contain a brief summary of the structure of L. C.
classification.

_____. "Classification: Present Tendencies," Library
Journal, 29:C132-134, December 1904.
This article on "present tendencies in classification" written
in 1904 makes no reference to L. C. classification. Obviously
in 1904 the development of L. C. classification was not considered to be of major interest to other libraries.

_____. "Library of Congress Classification," ALA
Bulletin, 5:230-232, July 1911.
This is virtually the same summary of L. C. as contained in
the previously cited "Classification: a Brief Conspectus of
Present Day Library Practice."

_____. "The Library of Congress Classification,"
Essays Offered to Herbert Putnam by his Colleagues and
Friends on his Thirtieth Anniversary as Librarian of Congress:
5 April 1929. Edited by William Warner Bishop and Andrew
Keogh. New Haven: Yale University Press, 1929. Pp. 327-
332.
This is an attempt by Martel to justify the practical develop-
ment of L. C. classification.

Metcalfe, John. Subject Classifying and Indexing of Libraries and Literature. New York: Scarecrow Press, 1959.
Pp. 113-117 are a brief modern analysis of L. C. classification with seven points of comparison to the Decimal Classification and other systems listed.

Mills, Jack. A Modern Outline of Library Classification. London: Chapman and Hall, 1960.
Pp. 89-102 are a careful summary of L. C. classification by a scholar of faceted classification. This is an excellent analysis.

Needham, C. D. Organizing Knowledge in Libraries; An Introduction to Classification and Cataloguing. London: Andre Deutsch, 1965.
Pp. 109-113 present a brief summary of L. C. classification.

Perley, Clarence W. "Recent Developments in the Library of Congress Classification," Proceedings of the Catalog Section, American Library Association, Washington, D. C., Conference May 13-18, 1929. Chicago: Catalog Section, American Library Association, 1929.
One of the editors of the classification schedules presents a short historical note on L. C. classification in 1929. This article also appeared in an abbreviated form in ALA Bulletin, 23:300-301, August 1929.

Phillips, W. Howard. A Primer of Book Classification. 5th ed. London: Association of Assistant Librarians, 1961.
Pp. 96-109 present another brief summary of L. C. classification.

Roberts, M. A. The Library of Congress in Relation to Research. Washington: Govt. Print. Off., 1939.
Pp. 33-34 is a brief introductory summary of L. C. classification. Miss Mann quotes it in her "Explanation of the system" on pp. 72-73 of her Introduction to Cataloging and the Classification of Books.

Robertson, David Allen. "The LC Classification as an Aid to Research," Proceedings of the Catalog Section, American Library Association, Washington, D. C., Conference May 13-18, 1929. Chicago: Catalog Section, American Library Association, 1929. This is a short paper advocating the use of L. C. classification instead of the Decimal Classification in university libraries.

Sahaya, S. "Library of Congress and its Classification, " Modern
Librarian, 15:82-86, 1945.
This is a discussion of L. C. classification by an Indian librar-
ian.

Savage, Ernest Albert. Manual of Book Classification and Display
for Public Libraries. London: Allen & Unwin and the Library
Association, 1946.
Savage advocates the "Principles of Book Classification" of
E. Wyndham Hulme and thus the use of L. C. classification.
(Pp. 15-52.)

Sayers, W. C. Berwick. Canons of Classification, Applied to "The
Subject, " "The Expansive, " "The Decimal, " and "The Library
of Congress" Classifications; A Study in Bibliographical Classification Method. London: Grafton, 1915.
Pp. 127-161 represent the first writing on L. C. classification
by this famous British scholar of classification. This material
is revised and expanded in each of the following entries.

_____. An Introduction to Library Classification;
Theoretical, Historical, and Practical with Readings, Exercises and Examination Papers. 9th ed. London: Grafton, 1958.
Pp. 99-114 present a general introductory summary of L. C.
classification typical of British examination guide books.

_____. A Manual of Classification for Librarians and
Bibliographers. 3d ed., rev. London: Andre Deutsch, 1963.
Pp. 151-174 present one of the better discussions and summaries of L. C. classification. It should be read by all students
of L. C. classification. Pp. 333-335 contain Sayers' bibliography for L. C. classification.

Smither, Reginald Ernest. "Library of Congress Classification, "
Library World, 16:130-136, November 1913.
This article includes brief sections on history, description, a
critical survey, and notation of L. C. classification. Smither
is critical of the lack of a scientific or logical approach to the
L. C. outline.

54

Tauber, Maurice F. and Edith Wise. Classification Systems. Vol.
1, pt. 3 of The State of Library Art. Edited by Ralph R. Shaw.
New Brunswick, N.J.: Graduate School of Library Science,
Rutgers--The State University, 1961.
Pp. 140-188 give a complete bibliographical survey of writings
about L. C. classification with pertinent sections of quotations.

Tauber, Maurice F. Technical Services in Libraries. New York:
Columbia University Press, 1953.
Pp. 200-208 give another summary introduction to L. C. classification. This introduction is one of the most helpful to the
student of L. C. classification.

U. S. Library of Congress. Annual Report of the Librarian of Congress. Washington: Govt. Print. Off., 1901—.
Each of the annual Reports contain sections on the classification.

_____. The Library of Congress and its Activities.
Washington: Govt. Print. Off., 1926.
In both this and the following entry are brief official statements
on L. C. classification.

_____. The Library of Congress and its Work. Wash-
ington: Govt. Print. Off., 1907.

_____. "Manual: Constitution, Organization, Methods,
etc., " Report of the Librarian of Congress for the Fiscal Year
Ending June 30, 1901. Washington: Govt. Print. Off., 1901.
Pp. 177-357.
Herbert Putnam presents many valuable policy statements in
this manual.

_____. Catalog Division. Card Section. "An Account
of the Catalogs, Classifications, and Card Distribution Work
of the Library of Congress, " Bulletin, No. 7, June 15, 1904.
There are useful historical facts in this publication.

"United States Library of Congress Classification, " Library
Association Record, 8:663-664, 1906.
This is another brief review of the L. C. outline and selected
schedules.

Wilson, M. "Library of Congress Classification, " Australian
Institute of Librarian's Proceedings, 2:113-117, 1939.

Wynar, Bohdan S. Introduction to Cataloging and Classification.
3d ed. Rochester, N. Y.: Libraries Unlimited, 1967.
Pp. 207-222 presents one of the more complete summaries of
L. C. classification.

GENERAL SPECIAL ARTICLES ON L. C. CLASSIFICATION

Ambartsumian, Z. N. "Russian View of Library of Congress Classification, " Library of Congress Information Bulletin, 7:12-13,
September 7-13, 1948.

Bushnell, G. H. "Notes by a British Librarian on the Library of
Congress Classification Scheme, " Special Libraries, 24:41-48,
March 1933.

Hoage, A. Annette L. "Librarians Rate L. C. Classification, "
Special Libraries, 53:484-485, October 1962.
This is an abstract of the findings of one section of Mrs. Hoage's
dissertation.

_____. "Patron Use of the L. C. Classification, "
Library Resources & Technical Services, 6:247-249, Summer
1962.
This article represents the findings of another part of Mrs.
Hoage's dissertation.

Hulme, E. Wyndham. "Principles of Book Classification, " Readings
in Library Cataloguing. Edited and introduced by R. K. Olding.
Hamden, Conn.: Shoe String Press, 1966. Pp. 108-140.
Hulme represented a different theoretical position on classification to that of Bliss and Sayers. He strongly advocates the
use of L. C. classification in opposition to the use of philosophi-
cally based systems. Olding includes a three page biographical
sketch, pp. 105-107, on Hulme. The original publication of
"Principles of Book Classification" was Library Association
Record, 13:354-358, 389-394, 444-449, 1911; 14:39-46, 174-
181, 216-221, 1912. Also this was reprinted as A. A. L. Re-
prints, No. 1, London: The Association of Assistant Librarians,
1950.

"LC Card Division to Distribute Classification Schedules, " Library
Journal, 90:4312, October 15, 1965.

Mann, Margaret. "Use of Library of Congress Classification."
　　Chicago: 1927. (mimeographed)
　　This is the first use study of L. C. classification.

Mogk, H. "Das System der Kongressbibliothek in Washington,"
　　Beiträge zur Sachkatalogisieurung. O. S. Runge, ed. Samm-
　　lung bibliothekswissenschaftlicher Arbeiten, no. 45, ser. 2,
　　no. 28. Leipzig: Harrassowitz, 1937. Pp. 51-62.

NOTATION

Gore, Daniel. "Further Observations on the Use of LC Classifica-
　　tion," Library Resources & Technical Services, 10:519-524,
　　Fall 1966.
　　Mr. Gore advises the use of a lower-case "x" at the end of all
　　locally originated L. C. call numbers to avoid any possible
　　duplication with Library of Congress classification numbers.
　　He also recommends the moving of the first Cutter number's
　　decimal point from in front of the capital letter to beyond the
　　first decimal number, e. g. "Q1M5. 5x".

U. S. Library of Congress. Author Notation in the Library of Con-
　　gress. By Anna Cantrell Laws. Washington: Govt. Print.
　　Off., 1937.
　　This is a valuable work for analyzing call numbers, however
　　it is dated and some of the practices described are no longer
　　used.

Figure 1

PREFATORY NOTE

The additions and changes in the classification of the social sciences in this third edition of Class H reflect the changing world of economic and social fact and theory between World War I and the middle of the twentieth century. The provisions for the first World War and the reconstruction period following it are paralleled by class numbers for the second World War and the reconstruction now in progress. In addition, class numbers for many other topics not included in the second edition have been provided, as well as many notes and references to facilitate the use of the schedules.

In the preparation of the original schedules use was made of published systems of classification, bibliographies, and catalogs, as well as of an outline scheme drawn up by Dr. Roland P. Falkner, and suggestions from the Harvard University Library. The application to the collections in the Library, necessitating many additions and great extension of detail, was made by Mr. Charles Martel, then Chief Classifier, assisted by Mr. William Dawson Johnston, Mr. Luis Perez, and Mr. Edwin Wiley. Schedules HS and HT were prepared by Mr. George M. Churchill, who was in charge of Class H from 1907 to 1920. These schedules were based to a large extent on the material in the Library of Congress, although other published classification systems and bibliographies were consulted. The scope of Class HT was intentionally restricted to the general literature of the strictly sociological aspect of the groups included, hence the unusually large number of "see" references.

The second edition, published in 1920, contained no fundamental changes from the first edition of 1910. New sections and individual class numbers had been added as the literature required, including HT, which had been issued separately in 1915. These additions, together with modernized geographical tables and numerous changes in terminology made in the interest of clarity, constituted the new matter in that edition.

Classifiers in charge of Class H since the publication of the second edition in 1920 were Mr. C. K. Jones, Mr. Leo E. La Montagne, and Mr. Philip Krichbaum.

The editorial work on the present edition was carried out by the Editor of Classification Schedules, Miss L. Belle Voegelein.

DAVID JUDSON HAYKIN,
Chief of the Subject Cataloging Division.

LUTHER HARRIS EVANS,
    Librarian of Congress,
        Washington, October 20, 1949.

Figure 2

SYNOPSIS

SOCIAL SCIENCES

H GENERAL WORKS
HA STATISTICS

ECONOMICS

HB ECONOMIC THEORY
HC—HD ECONOMIC HISTORY AND CONDITIONS
HC   NATIONAL PRODUCTION AND ECONOMIC
      CONDITIONS (BY COUNTRY)
HD   AGRICULTURE AND INDUSTRY
      LAND
      AGRICULTURE
      CORPORATIONS
      LABOR
      INDUSTRIES
HE TRANSPORTATION AND COMMUNICATION
HF COMMERCE, INCLUDING TARIFF POLICY
HG FINANCE (GENERAL). PRIVATE FINANCE
      MONEY
      BANKING
      INSURANCE
HJ PUBLIC FINANCE

SOCIOLOGY

HM GENERAL WORKS. THEORY
HN SOCIAL HISTORY AND CONDITIONS. SOCIAL PROBLEMS
      SOCIAL REFORM
HQ—HT SOCIAL GROUPS
HQ   FAMILY. MARRIAGE. WOMAN
HS   SOCIETIES: SECRET, BENEVOLENT, ETC. CLUBS
HT   COMMUNITIES. CLASSES. RACES
HV SOCIAL PATHOLOGY. SOCIAL AND PUBLIC WELFARE
      CRIMINOLOGY
HX SOCIALISM. COMMUNISM. ANARCHISM

Figure 3

OUTLINE

SOCIAL SCIENCES

GENERAL

H
1–8	Periodicals.
9	Yearbooks.
10–19	Societies.
21–29	Congresses. Exhibitions.
31–39	Collections.
41–49	Encyclopedias.
51–53	History.
57–59	Biography.
61	Theory. Method.
62–69	Study and teaching: Museums. Schools. Debates.
71–95	General works.

STATISTICS

HA
1–23	General.
29–33	Theory. Method.
35	Study and teaching.
36–40	Organization.
41–48	Annuals. General works. Albums, etc.
155–173	Universal statistics.
175–4010	By country.

ECONOMIC THEORY

HB
1–9	Periodicals.
21	Congresses. Exhibitions.
31–55	Collections.
61	Encyclopedias.
71	Economics as a science.
72	Relation to philosophy, religion, ethics.
73	Relation to politics and law.
74	Relation to other special topics, A–Z.
75–129	History (including biography).
151–179	Treatises. Compends.
195–199	General special.
201–205	Value.
221–236	Price.
251	Wealth.
301	Labor and wages (cf. HD 4801–8942, Laboring classes).
401	Rent and land (cf. HD 101–2206, Land and agriculture).
501	Capital. Saving.
531–549	Interest. Usury.

Figure 4

SOCIAL SCIENCES (GENERAL)

H

Periodicals.
All periodicals of a general, more or less mixed character,
i. e., most of the serials called "Political," "Social," or
"Economic" journals. Special periodicals are to be classified with the subject in HA, HB, etc. In case of doubt
prefer H 1–8.

1 Polyglot. American and English.
.A1–2, Polyglot; .A3–Z, American and English.

3 French.
5 German.
7 Italian.
8 Other.
9 Yearbooks.
Societies.
Cf. HA 1; HB 1–9; HM 9; HN 54–55; HS; HV, etc.; also JK
674, Civil service reform; JS 302–303, Civic reform associations.

10 International.
11 American and English.
13 French.
15 German.
17 Italian.
19 Other.
Congresses. Exhibitions.
Cf. HA 9–12; HB 21; etc.
21 International.
22 American and English.
23 French.
25 German.
27 Italian.
29 Other. By country, A–Z.
Collections.
31 Monographs by various authors.
33 Collected works of individual authors.
35 Essays, papers, etc.
39 Pamphlets.
41–49 Encyclopedias. Dictionaries.
Arranged like H 11–19.
Cf. note at head of H 1–8.

Figure 5

TABLE OF CITIES IN THE UNITED STATES

Akron	A2	Fall River	F2
Albany	A3	Fort Wayne	F7
Allegheny	A35	Frankfort	F8
Annapolis	A4		
Atlanta	A7	Galveston	G2
Augusta	A9	Grand Rapids	G7
Austin	A95	Guthrie	G8
Baltimore	B2	Harrisburg	H2
Baton Rouge	B3	Hartford	H3
Bismarck	B63	Helena, Mont	H4
Boise City	B66	Hoboken	H6
Boston	B7	Holyoke	H7
Bridgeport	B78	Houston	H8
Brooklyn	B8		
Buffalo	B9	Indianapolis	I4
Cambridge	C2	Jackson, Miss	J2
Camden	C22	Jacksonville	J3
Charleston, S. C.	C3	Jefferson City	J4
Charleston, W. Va	C32	Jersey City	J5
Cheyenne	C38		
Chicago	C4	Kansas City	K2
Cincinnati	C5		
Cleveland	C6	Lawrence	L4
Columbia, S. C.	C68	Lincoln	L65
Columbus	C7	Little Rock	L67
Dallas	D2	Los Angeles	L7
Dayton	D3	Louisville	L8
Denver	D4	Lowell	L9
Des Moines	D5	Lynn	L97
Detroit	D6		
Dover	D7	Madison	M18
Dubuque	D8	Manchester	M2
Duluth	D88	Memphis	M4
		Milwaukee	M5
Elizabeth	E4	Minneapolis	M6
Erie	E6	Mobile	M7
Evansville	E9	Montgomery, Ala	M75

Figure 6

INDEX

Figure 7

ADDITIONS AND CHANGES TO JANUARY 1964

HD

8039		*(Below, add to or revise* "**Selected List.**"*)*—Con.

.M2	Machinists. Machinery industry.
.M78	Motion-picture industry. p. 81
.P375	Peat industry.
.P385	Pecan shellers.
	Pedicab drivers, *see* Rickshaw men.
.P65	Poldermen.
.P659	Porters.
	Porters, Railroad, *see* .R36.
.P88	Public utility workers. p. 82
	Radio operators, *see* .T25–27.
	Railroad employees.
.R315	Construction workers.
.R317	Dining-car employees.
.R48	Rice workers.
.R5	Rickshaw men. Pedicab drivers.
.R6	Road construction workers.
.R65	Road maintenance workers.
.S2	Salt workers.
.S3	Sawmill workers.
.S34	School employees.
	Teachers, maintenance employees, cafeteria workers, etc.
.S36	Scientific instrument industry workers.
.S45	Service industries.
	Cf. .B3, Barbers; .L3, Laundry workers; etc. HD 9980–9990, Service industries (General).
.S48	Shellac workers.
.T24	Telecommunication workers. p. 83
	Telegraphers. Radio operators.
.T25	Commercial.
.T3	Telephone employees. (Not "operators.")
.W8	Wreckers.

8065　　*(Change to* "8064.") p. 84

8101–8942　　*(Change ninth line of table below to* "Later, 1849–1945." *Insert new line. Change* "Note 1" *to* "Note 2." *Insert new note.)* p. 86

20 nos.	10 nos.	3 nos.	
(11)	6.5	3.5	1945–

Note 1. For Israel use: 8761.P3.

Figure 8

HERALDRY

Heraldry combined with genealogy classed with CS.

CR

1   Periodicals. Societies.
     Collected works.
4   Several authors.
5   Individual authors.
7   Congresses, conventions, etc.
9   Exhibitions.
11   Directories.
13   Dictionaries. Encyclopedias.
     Science, technique, theory, etc.
         History, *see* CR151–159.
     General works.
19   To 1800.
         1801–
21   Treatises.
23   Manuals.
27   Minor. Pamphlets, etc.
         General special. Special aspects, relations, etc.
29   Symbolism.
31   Heraldry and art, architecture, etc.
33   Heraldry and literature.
         Heraldry in Shakespeare, Scott, etc.
         Prefer the special author in PR, PQ, etc.
             e. g. PR3069.H4 for Shakespeare.
     Special.
41   Special branches, charges, etc., A–Z.
             e. g. Chess, collar, counter-charge, crest, crosses,
             doge's cap, double-headed eagle, fish, flowers (fleur-
             de-lis, rose, etc.), furs, goedendag, hatching, hatch-
             ments, helmets, heralds, linden, lion, liveries, marks
             of cadency, masons' marks, merchants' marks, mer-
             maids, pomegranate, rebus, rest, signboards, tinc-
             tures, trademarks, triquetra, unicorn, urchin, water
             bouget, white horse, wreaths.

         Printers' marks, *see* Z235–236.
(43)   Armorial bindings and bookplates, *see* Z266–276
             and Z993–996.
(45)   Armorial china, *see* NK4374.

Figure 9

EPIGRAPHY

Cf. Cuneiform writing, PJ3191–3225.
  Epitaphs, PN6288.5–6298.
  Genealogy, CS.
  Hieroglyphics, P211, PJ1091–1097.
  Petroglyphs, GN799.P4.
  Picture writing of the American
    Indians, E98.P6.
  Seals, CD5001–6471.

CN
1   Periodicals.   Societies.
15   Congresses.
20   Collected works (History and criticism).
25   Museums, libraries and other institutions, A–Z.
        e. g. .N3 Naples.   Museo nazionale.
               .R7 Rome.   Museo capitolino.
        For inscriptions in special languages, prefer CN355, 515,
           etc.
30   Private collections.
        Prefer inscriptions in special languages.
40   Philosophy.   Theory.
50   Study and teaching.
55   History of epigraphy.
        Prefer P–PM, Philology, Assyriology, Egyptology, etc.
     Biography of epigraphists.
        Prefer the special language.
61   Collective.
62   Individual, A–Z.
        Champollion, see PJ1064.C6.
70   Dictionaries.   Terminology.
     General works.   Introductions and manuals.
74   Early works to 1800.
75   Later works, 1801–
     General special.   Special aspects, relations, etc.
77   Relation to archeology, history, etc.
80   Relation to religion.
85   Other.
90   Minor works.   Addresses, essays, lectures.
95   Technique.   Methods.
97   Photographic methods.
99   Forgeries of inscriptions.

66

Figure 10

LITERATURE

41   ENCYCLOPEDIAS. DICTIONARIES.
      e. g. Vapereau, Dictionnaire universel des littératures.
      Cf. PN 451–481, Biography.

43   Minor.
      Including works not in dictionary form:
      Notes and queries, Curiosities of literature, etc.

  Theory. Philosophy. Esthetics.
      Cf. BH; N 70–79; PN 80–99, 101+, 1031+, 1631+, etc.

45   General works. Ideals, form and content, etc.

  General special. Relation to and treatment of
    special elements, problems, and subjects.

46   Inspiration.

47   Life.

48   Nature.
      Cf. PQ 145.3, 473; PR 143, 508; etc.
      See also PN 56.F5, Fishing, piscatory literature;
      PN 56.G3, Gardens.

49   Philosophy, ethics, religion, etc.
      Cf. PN 1077, Poetry; PN 1647–1649, Drama; PN 3347–
      3351, Prose.

50   Relation to history.

51   Relation to sociology, economics, political science,
    etc. (Social ideals, forces, etc., in literature.)

52   Relation to education.

53   Relation to art.

54   Relation to language.

55   Relation to science.

56   Other special, A–Z.
      e. g. .F5, Fishing, piscatory literature.
           .G3, Gardens.
           .I4, Idealism (including realism and idealism,
               and general esthetic discussions of
               idealism, realism, naturalism, roman-
               ticism, etc.).
               For history of movements, see PN 599
               605.
               Cf. PN 56.R3, PN 56.R7.
           .M7, Mountains.
          (.N2) Naturalism, see Realism.
           .R3, Realism. Naturalism.[1]
           .R7, Romanticism.[1]
           .S8, Supernatural.
           .S9, Symbolism.
          (.W6) Women.
               Cf. PN 481. Feminine influence in lit-
               erature.

---

[1] Prefer history, e. g. PN 769.R7, Romanticism in the 19th century.

Figure 10a

LITERATURE

Theory. Philosophy. Esthetics.
General special—Continued.
57 Individual characters in literature, A–Z.
e. g. .A1, Collective.
Cf. PN 1103, Poetry; PN 1711, Drama;
PN 3411, Fiction.
.A2, Female characters.
.A6, Arthur and Arthurian legends.
.C2, Cæsar.
.D7, Don Juan.
.F3, Faust.
.G3, Galahad.
.G7, Grail.
.G8, Griselda.
.H4, Helen of Troy.
.J8, Judith.
.P3, Parsifal.
.S6, Sohrab and Rustum.
.T3, Tannhäuser.
.T8, Tristan and Isolde.
58 Essays.
Cf. PN 88–94, Criticism; PN 500–519, Collections.
Books and reading, see Z 1003.
Cf. PN 81–99, 510–519; Z 1055.
STUDY AND TEACHING.
Cf. LB 1527, 1575, 1631, 2365; LC 1001-1021.
59 General.
61 General special.
By period.
63 Ancient.
64 Middle ages.
65 Renaissance.
66 17th–18th century.
67 19th century.
68 20th century.
By country.
Prefer PQ–PV.
70 United States.
71 Other countries, A–Z.
72 By school, A–Z.
Prefer PQ–PV.
Criticism.
80 Periodicals.
Theory. Canons.
Cf. PN 1031–1035, Poetry.
PN 3335, Fiction.
81 General works.
85 Minor works. Essays, lectures, etc.

Figure 11

EMIGRATION AND IMMIGRATION

JV

Periodicals.
6001   American.
6002   English.
6003   French.
6004   German.
6005   Italian.
6006   Other.
6008   **Associations** (International).
6011   **Congresses** (International).
      Collections.
6014   Monographs.
6018   Documents. General only. Special with countries in
        JV 6409, etc.
      History.
        General works on emigration and immigration here.
6021   General.
      By period.
        Under each:
          (1) General.
          (2) Special
6023–4   Ancient.
6026–7   Medieval to 1800.
6029–30 19th century.
6032–3   20th century.
      Treatises.
6035   General.
      Special.
6038   Relations to the state.
        Cf. JV 6045.
6041   Minor works. Pamphlets, etc.
      Law.
6045   General collections.
6049   International law.
        Cf. JX 4231.

Figure 12

MUSEUMS

MUSEOGRAPHY AND MUSEOLOGY

Cf. N400–490; QH61–71; T391–999.

AM
1   Periodicals, societies, collections, etc.
      Only publications devoted to the interests of museums, methodology, description, etc.
      Serials or collections of scientific contributions, memoirs, etc., on other subjects, in AC, AS, B–Z.

4   Early works (to 1800).
5   General treatises.
7   General special.
      Educational aspects, relations, etc.
8   Children's museums.
9   Minor. Pamphlets, etc.

Museography.

10–99   By country.
      Under each country (Three numbers):
        (1) General.
        (2) States, provinces, etc.
        (3) Cities, towns, etc.
      Under each country (Two numbers):
        (1) .A1   Periodicals. Societies.
            .A2   General.
            .A3–Z   Provinces, etc.
        (2)   Cities, towns, etc.
      Under each country (One number):
        (1) .A2   General.
        (2) .A3–Z   Local.

10   America.
11–13   United States.
21–22   British America. Canada.
23–24   Mexico.
25–27   Central America.
29–31   West Indies.
33–35   South America.
40   Europe.
41–43   Great Britain.
44–45   Austria-Hungary.
46–48   France.
49–51   Germany.

Figure 13

ENGLISH LITERATURE.

PR	Literary history and criticism.
1	Periodicals.
3	Yearbooks.
5	Societies.
7	Congresses.
	Collections of monographs, studies, etc.,
	For texts, sources, anthologies, etc. see PR 1101–1508.
	For collected essays, studies, etc., of individual authors, see PR 99.
13	Serials.
14	Minor collections. Festchrifts, etc.
19	Encyclopedias. Dictionaries.
21	Theory and principles of the study of English literature.
25	Relation to English history.
27	History (of literary history).
29	Biography of historians of English literature.
	Study and teaching.
31	Collections.
33	General works. Treatises, etc.
34	Outlines, syllabi, etc., see PR 87.
35	General special.
	By period.
41	Middle ages to 1600.
43	17th–18th centuries.
45	19th century.
47	20th century.
51	By country, A–Z.
53	By school, A–Z.
55	Biography (of teachers of English literature).
	Criticism.
	Favor PN 80–99.
57	Treatises.
59	Minor works.
61	Addresses, essays, lectures.
63	History.
65	Special topics.
	e. g. Book reviewing.

Figure 14

SYNOPSIS

(121)

Figure 15

SCOTLAND.
 Government. Administration.
  The Legislative. Parliament—Continued.
   History.
1263   General.
    By period.
1265   Early, to 1054.
1267   Medieval, to 1707.
1269   Modern, 1707–.
    Special topics.
1273   Prerogatives.
1277   Representation.
1279   Privileges of members.
1281   Procedure.
1282   Private bill legislation.
      e. g. General orders under the private legislation procedure.
   Judiciary.
1283   General.
1285   Special.
  Civil and political rights.
   Citizenship.
    Cf. JN 901–1097; JX 4211–4399.
1291   General.
1295   Law.
1299   Special topics.
   Naturalization.
1305   General.
1309   Law.
1311   Special topics.
   Suffrage.
    General.
1321   Documents.
1325   History.
1329   Other.
1333   Special.
   Electoral system.
1341   General.
1346   Law, by date.
1351   **Contested elections.**
1361   **Corrupt practices.**
1371 **Political parties.**

CHAPTER 3.

SPECIAL PROBLEMS IN THE USE OF L. C. CLASSIFICATION

AUXILIARY TABLES

In order to reduce the total number of pages in individual schedules, detailed subdivisions of subjects are often treated by the use of auxiliary tables. These may be short, simple tables within the schedule itself or long, complex tables at the end of the schedule or subclass. There are five different types of auxiliary tables:

1) Form Tables.

2) Geographic tables.

3) Chronological tables.

4) Subject subdivision tables.

5) Combination tables.

Form Tables

The subdivisions of these tables follow various forms, e. g. "General Form divisions" or literary forms. These tables are usually used when geographic or chronological subdivision is not needed or has already been extensively employed. Examples of "form tables" may be found in the tables for individual authors and the tables for individual philosophers in subclasses PQ, PR, PS, PT, and B. Figure 16 is an example of one of these tables.

Geographic Tables

Geographic tables use the two types of geographic division discussed in Chapter Two: 1) the logical arrangement and 2) the alphabetical arrangement. The schedule for Class H has excellent examples of both of these types of division. There are the "Tables of Geographical Divisions, " which contain ten different numerical arrangements based on the logical order of geographic division. (Figure 17 is the first page of this six page table.) Following this table in Class H is the "Table of Countries in One Alphabet, " which may be used when the instructions within the schedule call for geographic division alphabetically. Such geographic division is often introduced by the phrase, "By country, A-Z." This table is simply a list of the countries likely to occur in any geographic division. Each country, arranged alphabetically, has been assigned one or more Cutter numbers. (Figure 18 is the first page of this two page table.) This table is called a "floating table," i.e. it may be used in any schedule whenever the direction to subdivide "By country, A-Z" is given. The following table in Class H, "Notation for States and Other Subdivisions under Countries," may be used to extend this table (see Figure 19 for the first page of this two page table). Other "floating tables" in H are the "Table of States" (in the United States) and the "Table of Cities in the United States" (see Figures 20 and 21 for the first pages of each of these two page tables). Examples of other geographic tables include geographic tables in Class N, including a table of "Art Cities" and a "List of English Counties" (see Figures 22 and 23).

Chronological Tables

Usually found under the historical division of a subject, chronological tables are simple tables of subdivision by date. These tables nearly always occur within the schedules and are usually very brief. Examples may be found in JN 5251-5299 (see Figure 24) or HJ 2391-2442 (see Figure 25 for the first page of this two page example).

Subject Subdivision Tables

The further division of a subject may be done by the use of auxiliary tables. However, it should be observed that there are very few pure subject subdivision tables using a logical arrangement. Usually subject subdivision tables are simply alphabetical lists with Cutter numbers for the subdivisions of a subject (see Figure 26).

Combination Tables

The most common type of auxiliary table consists of a combination of two or more of the other types of tables. Form, Subject and Geographic tables are often combined. Similarly some chronological subdivisions may occur in a combination table. The "Table for Arrangement of Works under Foreign Countries" in subclass PN for journalism may be examined as a combination table containing all of these elements. Figure 27 should be carefully studied for the following observations: under the "20 nos." column the first four numbers "1-4" represent a form table; the next four numbers "5-8" are chronological dividers; numbers "12 and 13" are examples of both form and subject divisions; number "14", "Special topics, A-Z, " is another subject subdivision; numbers "16-19, " "Local, " are geographic subdivision; and number "20", "Special magazines and other periodicals, A-Z, " is another example of form division.

The use of these auxiliary tables is discussed with examples from actual Library of Congress practice in Chapter 4 of this guide.

Subject Division under Country

Often in L. C. classification, especially in the social sciences, subject division under country is used instead of country division under subject. In the Decimal Classification a subject is usually subdivided fully before adding any geographic division; in L. C., however, a class or subclass may be divided geographically and then have further subdivisions. An example of this is the division of "Constitutional History and Administration" in Class J: Political Science. Subdivisions by country occur before further subdivisions of the subject, i. e. subclasses JK, United States; JL, British America, Latin America; JN, Europe; and JQ, Asia, Africa, Australia, etc. This process of subdividing a subject first by country and then using specific subject divisions appropriate to that country may be called "collocating" by country.

Shelf List Numbers

Within the L. C. schedules, there are often integral numbers in the ordinary sequence which are enclosed in parentheses. These are called "shelf list" numbers. The parentheses mean that this number is not used by the Library of Congress but exists as an added entry in the card shelf list at the Library of Congress. In subclass CT, Biography, there are many examples of these shelf list numbers (see Figure 28). Shelf list numbers can be used by any library preferring them to the recommended L. C. number. If these numbers are used by other libraries it should be fully realized that L. C. printed cards will have to be reclassified.

SPECIAL USES OF CUTTER NUMBERS

Official or Reserved Cutter Numbers

An official or reserved Cutter number is the reservation of an individual Cutter number or range of Cutter numbers to be used for a specific subdivision of a subject. ".A1, " ".A2, " ".A1-5, " or ".A4-9" are all examples of typical Cutter numbers and ranges of Cutter numbers which may be used as official Cutter numbers. They are used extensively in Classes H and J for the publications of government organizations, societies and other corporate bodies.

e. g.　HA　Statistics.

　　　　　　　United States.

　730　　　　　Cities, A-Z.

　　　　　　　Under each:　.A1-5　Official.

　　　　　　　　　　　　　.A6-Z　Nonofficial.

Although this example and many other instances in the social sciences use reserved Cutter numbers for official or authorized material, the use of reserved Cutter numbers is not limited to official publications. The reservation of any Cutter number for a specific purpose conforms with the definition of official Cutter numbers.

Double Cutter Numbers

As has been stated already in the section of Chapter 2 on notation, the L. C. call number may have one or two (but usually no more) Cutter numbers. Double Cutter numbers are the use of two Cutter numbers for a particular book or subject. Often the first number completes the classification and the second number stands for the author's name. Occassionally, both Cutter numbers may be used to subdivide the subject. In such cases it may be necessary to add a distinguishing feature to the second Cutter to stand for the author's name.

e. g.　HC　Economic History and Conditions.

　　　　　　20th century.

　57　　　　　Reconstruction, 1919-1939.

.A15A-Z	Periodicals and societies.
	Documents.
.A2	League of Nations.
.A3A-Z	Individual countries.

In the above example, ".A15A-Z" and ".A3A-Z" are both instances of the use of double Cutter numbers. ".A15," ".A2," and ".A3," are all examples of official or reserved Cutter numbers.

Successive Cutter Numbers

Successive Cutter numbers are numbers in an established succession or order used to subdivide further a single Cutter number. A constant successive Cutter number may be defined as a successive Cutter number whose succession or sequence to be used in further subdivision is strictly established. "AM 101, Individual museums, A-Z" is an example of constant successive Cutter numbers.

e. g.	AM	Museums.
	101	Individual museums, A-Z.

Alphabetically by name.

Under each (using successive Cutter numbers):

(0)	Collections, etc.
(1)	Acts of incorporation, statutes, by-laws, rules, and regulations. By date.
(2)	Administration. List of officers, etc.
(2. 5)	Examinations.
(3)	Annual reports.
(4)	Other serials: Periodicals, collections, memoirs, etc.
(4. 5)	Other minor official reports. By date.
(5)	Guidebooks, catalogs. By date.
(5. 2)	Special minor exhibits. By date.

(6)   History.

(6.5)   Descriptive works (official). By date.

(7)   General works (nonofficial).

(9)   Miscellaneous printed matter, circulars, announcements. By date.

e. g. . B80-89 British Museum.

From this table the uses of the following successive Cutter numbers may be analyzed.

1) The British Museum, A Guide to its Public Services, 1962.

AM-----The double letters meaning museums.

101-----The integral number meaning individual museums.

Cutter number   . B85 ---The successive Cutter number
for Brit. Museum   meaning guidebooks.

1962----The date of publication as required in the table of successive Cutter numbers.

In this example ". B8" is the Cutter number meaning the British Museum. The successive element for guidebooks "5" is added to or rather attached to the Cutter number for the British Museum, ". B8. " The resulting number is ". B85. "

2) A Guide to the Exhibition Gallaries of the British Museum. With an introduction by E. Maunde Thompson, 1909.

AM-----The double letters meaning museums.

101-----The integral number meaning individual museums.

Cutter number   . B85 ---The successive Cutter number
for Brit. Museum   meaning guidebooks.

T5 -----The second Cutter number used for the author of the introduction, Thompson.

Again in this example ".B8" is the Cutter number meaning the British Museum. The successive element for guidebooks "5" is again added to the Cutter number for the British Museum, resulting in the complete first Cutter number, ".B85." In this case a second Cutter number for the author of the introduction is used.

3) Statutes and Rules for the British Museum, 1932.

> AM-----The double letters meaning museums.
>
> 101-----The integral number meaning individual museums.

Cutter number   .B81 ---The successive Cutter number
for Brit. Museum   meaning statutes.

> 1932----The date of publication as required in the table of successive Cutter numbers.

".B8" is the Cutter number meaning the British Museum. The successive element for acts of incorporation, statutes, by-laws, rules and regulations "1" is attached to this Cutter number for the British Museum, resulting in the number ".B81."

4) H. C. Shelley's British Museum: Its History and Treasures, 1911.

> AM-----The double letters meaning museums.
>
> 101-----The integral number meaning individual museums.

Cutter number   .B87 ---The successive Cutter number
for Brit. Museum   meaning nonofficial general works.

> S6------The second Cutter number used for the author, Shelley.

".B8" is the Cutter number meaning the British Museum. The successive element for nonofficial general works "7" is attached to this Cutter number for the British Museum, resulting in the number ".B87." Again in this case a second Cutter is available and may be used as this one is for the author of the work.

Variable successive Cutter numbers occur far more frequently than constant ones. Variables may be a part of a larger auxiliary table, or form a small table themselves. This type of successive Cutter number is literally variable. A short sequence of numbers is given in an established order or sequence, e.g. (1), (2), (3). See also Figure 29. The numbers shown in the tables, e.g. (1), (2), (3) are not always followed exactly; what is important is the pattern of numerical sequence. The following chart illustrates possible patterns.

(1)		4		3		7		0
(2)	or	5	or	4	or	8	or	1
(3)		6		5		9		2

The last example in this succession, i.e. "0-1-2" is most important for the classifier to recognize, as the first element of the sequence, "0", will disappear in actual use. This sequence of three in the form of "0-1-2" is frequently used. Table XI "Separate works with Cutter numbers" from the tables of "Subdivisions under Individual authors" is shown below as an example of the use of this type of successive Cutter number (see also Figure 29).

XI   Separate works with Cutter numbers.

(Cutter no.)

(1)   . x date   Texts.

      . xA-Z   Translations, by language.

(2)   Adaptations, dramatizations, etc.

(3)   . xA-Z   Criticism.

> NOTE.   In Table XI, (1), (2), and (3), . x represents successive Cutter numbers, as for example: . F6, . F7, . F8 or . F66, . F67, . F68.
> In the case of works where division (2) is inapplicable the numbers may be modified by using two Cutter numbers only, as . F4, . F5 or . F4, . F41.

In the note to this table it should be pointed out that ". F" represents a Cutter number for the title of a work beginning with "F. " In the case of ". F66, " ". F67, " and ". F68, " the ". F" represents a Cutter number standing for the title of a work probably having the initial letters "Fo" as for example "Fourscore. " This table cannot be applied without first establishing the Cutter number sequence being used for an individual work at the Library of Congress.

Herman Melville's novel Moby Dick may be used as an example.

1) The Limited Edition Club publication of Moby Dick, 1943.

PS----- The double letters meaning American literature.

2384 --- The integral number for individual works of the author, Herman Melville.

Cutter number for Moby Dick   . M6 --- The lack of any successive Cutter number indicating that this is the text of the work.

1943 --- The date of publication as required in the table.

". M6" is the Cutter number for the title of Melville's novel Moby Dick. It may be assumed at this point that variation of the "1-2-3" being used is "0-1-2"; however, this is only an assumption and must be proved by further establishment of the sequence. This further establishment may be done by verifying other elements involved in Table XI, i. e. translations, adaptations, and criticism.

2) A translation of Moby Dick in Hebrew.

PS----- The double letters meaning American literature.

2384 --- The integral number for individual works of the author, Herman Melville.

Cutter number for Moby Dick   . M6 --- The lack of any successive Cutter number indicating that this is one form of the text of the work.

H4----- The second Cutter number used for the language of the translation, Hebrew.

This example is consistent with the assumption that the variation of the sequence is "0-1-2. "

3) William Gleim's The Meaning of Moby Dick, 1962.

PS----- The double letters meaning American literature.

2384 --- The integral number for individual works of the author, Herman Melville.

Cutter number   .M6|2--- The successive Cutter number
for Moby Dick   meaning criticism.

                        G5 ----- The second Cutter number used
                                for the author of the criticism,
                                Gleim.

This example proves the original assumption that the variation of the sequence being used is "0-1-2." If the text of Moby Dick is ".M6" and criticism of Moby Dick is ".M62," then obviously the text is really cuttered ".M60" with the "0" dropped as the meaningless last element of a decimal extension. This method should be employed in any instance when variable successive Cutter numbers are used.

Often variable successive Cutter numbers will be used without explanatory notes as are given in Table XI. A general rule is to use successive Cutter numbers when there is no other way to subdivide one number or a Cutter number into three or more parts. Also the establishment of the sequence will assist the classifier in determining the use of successive Cutter numbers. The classification of individual parts of Chaucer's Canterbury Tales may be used as an example (see also Figure 30).

e. g.   PR   English Literature

           Chaucer, Geoffrey.

             Canterbury Tales.

               Texts.

1865   By date.

1866   By editor.

1867   Selections.

1868   Special parts, A-Z.

                Under each:

                  Text.

                     (1)   By date.

                     (2)   By editor.

                     (3)   Criticism.

     1870   Translations, by language, A-Z.

In the above example "PR 1868, Special parts, A-Z, " must be subdivided into three divisions: "(1) By date; (2) By editor; and (3)

Criticism. " Obviously integral numbers cannot be used as there
are not three available integral numbers--the number "1870" precludes any development such as 1868 for (1), 1869 for (2), and 1870
for (3). In this case it is necessary to use successive Cutter numbers. Even though there are no instructions to use them, the classifier must recognize that successive Cutter numbers must be used.
The establishing of the sequence of successive Cutter numbers may
be accomplished by verifying an individual part of the Canterbury
Tales.

1) Pardoner's Tale, edited by Carleton Brown, 1935.

PR----- The double letters meaning English literature.

1868 --- The integral number for individual parts of the
Canterbury Tales.

. P2 ---- The Cutter number for the title of individual part.

B7 ----- The second Cutter number for editor, Brown.

2) Betty Kantor's The Sin of Pride in "The Pardoner's Tale, "
1962.

PR----- The double letters meaning English literature.

1868 --- The integral number for individual parts of the
Canterbury Tales.

. P3 ---- The Cutter number for the title of the individual
part, adjusted into the sequence.

K3 ----- The second Cutter number for author, Kantor.

In this case the verification establishes the sequence as "1-2-3"
which does not appear to be a variation from the given sequence of
"1-2-3. " However this verification is incomplete without a text of
the Pardoner's Tale classified by the Library of Congress to meet
the requirements of the first element of the succession. Such a
text might well use ". P2 date" as its Cutter number as this would
be distinctive from an edited text such as the first example ". P2B7. "

Besides the attachments of successive Cutter numbers to single
Cutter numbers, a Cutter number may be extended decimally to
place a very similar work beside a book with the original single
Cutter number. Dependent supplements provide typical examples
of decimal extension. See card below.

South Dakota. School of Mines and Technology, *Rapid City. Library.*
    Master, professional, and senior theses and class reports, South Dakota School of Mines and Technology, 1904–1965. Compiled by the Library staff. Rapid City, South Dakota School of Mines and Technology, 1966.
    iii, 64 l. 28 cm.
    ———— Key word index. Rapid City, South Dakota School of Mines and Technology, 1966.
    95 l. 28 cm.

                       Z6736.S582

    1. Mineral industries—Bibl.   I. Title.

Z6736.S58   016.6   67–63167

Library of Congress   [3]

In this case the independent work, Master, Professional, and Senior Theses and Class Reports, South Dakota School of Mines and Technology, 1904-1965, compiled by the Library Staff, is classed "Z 6736 . S58"; its dependent Key Word Index is classed "Z 6736 . S582. " The Cutter number of the independent work is extended decimally to "2" to place the two works together on the shelf. There are similar decimal extensions used for translations of individual works and other closely related material.

SUPPLEMENTARY AIDS TO THE USE OF
LIBRARY OF CONGRESS CLASSIFICATION

An Index to L. C. Classification

    Although most individual L. C. schedules include detailed indices, there is no general index to the entire classification. In 1947 work toward a general index was begun by the Library of Congress. All existing individual indices were cut and mounted on cards; Class K: Law, was not included as this schedule is still in process of completion. It was decided to wait until Class K was completed to publish the general index. This index would consist of over 1, 400 pages containing more than 140, 000 entries. Presently the L. C. Subject Headings list may be used as a general index to the classification. This is not a completely satisfactory device. However, most subject headings in the L. C. Subject Headings list do have the related L. C. classification number as a part of the heading's entry in the list. In addition, there are other possible substitutes for a general index. Some libraries use the Index to the Classed Catalog of the Boston University Libraries which, though helpful, is not a complete index to L. C. classification. Another similar publication is the Subject and Name Index of Books Contained in the Libraries of the Edinburg Public Library. This work has the same limitations as the Boston Index. In addition to the above mentioned indices, there are some indices of limited scope produced for internal use by libraries or library schools. Complete bibliographic descriptions of all of these possible substitute indices are given in the bibliography at the end of this chapter.

A Manual to L. C. Classification

There is no manual issued by the Library of Congress explaining the classification. One was begun by Cecil K. Jones and Leo LaMontagne but was never completed. Leo LaMontagne's American Library Classification with Special Reference to the Library of Congress contains many helpful statements on the history, theory and use of L. C. classification. This book is particularly valuable as it contains many citations from material available only in Library of Congress departmental reports, etc. All students of classification should carefully read this book. Catherine W. Grout's Explanation of the Tables Used in the Schedules of the Library of Congress Classification, 1940 is useful as a manual on the auxiliary tables. However, Miss Grout did not cover all the auxiliary tables. Also, many of her examples are taken from earlier editions of the Library of Congress Classification schedules and are thus somewhat dated and occasionally invalid. There are additional sources in various books on classification as included in the bibliography at the end of Chapter 2.

Abridgments of L. C. Classification

Although there is no standard abridgment of L. C. classification as there is of the Decimal Classification in the Abridged Decimal Classification, there are a few abridgments of individual parts of L. C. classification schedules. The bibliography at the end of this chapter lists some of these abridgments.

Use of L. C. Printed Cards

One major factor influencing many libraries to convert to L. C. classification is the existence of the complete L. C. call number on the L. C. printed cards. This L. C. number has a great advantage over the suggested Decimal Classification number on the L. C. printed card. The Decimal Classification number is only a class number and not a whole call number. One disadvantage of complete acceptance of the whole L. C. call number is the problem of assigning original Cutter numbers to those works for which L. C. cards have not been printed; obviously a complete Library of Congress shelf list is not available to libraries using L. C. classification. Further, all L. C. call numbers should be carefully checked before being automatically accepted. Typographical errors do occur; some material may need to be reclassified. The classifier will find the Library of Congress Catalog of Books Represented by Library of Congress Printed Cards, its successor, the National Union Catalog, and the Library of Congress Catalog, Books: Subjects invaluable aids in establishing and verifying actual Library of Congress classifying practice.

BIBLIOGRAPHY

General Works Pertaining to this Chapter

(see also Bibliography to Chapter 2)

Grout, Catherine W. Explanation of the Tables Used in the Schedules of the Library of Congress Classification, Accompanied by an Historical and Explanatory Introduction. New York: Columbia University, School of Library Service, 1940.
This basic work is available presently in a University Microfilms edition. For a review of this see Andrew D. Osborn's "The L. C. Classification," Library Journal, 66:300, April 1, 1941.

Hoage, A. Annette Lewis. "The Library of Congress Classification in the United States: A Survey of Opinions and Practices, with Attention to Problems of Structure and Application." Unpublished Doctoral dissertation, Columbia University, 1961.
(See annotation to this work in the Bibliography to Chapter 2.)

LaMontagne, Leo E. American Library Classification with Special
Reference to the Library of Congress. Hamden, Conn.: Shoe
String Press, 1961.

Indexes

Boston University. Libraries. Index to the Classed Catalog of the
Boston University Libraries; A Relative Index Based on the
Library of Congress Classification. Compiled by Mary Darrah
Herrick. 2d ed., rev. and enl. Boston: G. K. Hall, 1964. 2v.

Dewton, J. L. "Subject Index According to Library of Congress
Classification," Library of Congress Information Bulletin,
8:12-13, December 27, 1949-January 2, 1950.

Edinburgh. Public Library. Subject and Name Index of Books Contained in the Libraries. 3d ed. Edinburgh: Published by Edinburgh Public Libraries Committee, 1949.

Nitecki, Andre. Index to the Library of Congress Classification
Outline. Syracuse: Syracuse University, School of Library
Science, 1967.

U. S. Library of Congress. Subject Cataloging Division. Subject
Headings Used in the Dictionary Catalogs of the Library of
Congress. 7th ed. Washington: Govt. Print. Off., 1966.

Abridgments

Rovelstad, Betsey. "Condensation of the Library of Congress M
Classification." ₍n. p. ₎: 1953.
This is an abridgment of Class M: Music which was reprinted
in 1963 as Supplement No. 34 to Music Library Association's
Notes.

Perry, F. C. "The Library of Congress Classification Adapted for
School Libraries," School Library Review, 7:68-73, 1938.
This is an adaptation of Classes D, G, H, J and P.

Tiffy, Ethel. "Library of Congress Classification Simplified for
Use in the Smaller College Library." Unpublished Master's
thesis, Columbia University, 1935.
This is simply an abridgment of the history Classes C, D, and
E-F. An abstract of this thesis appears in the ALA Cataloging
and Classification Yearbook, 5:95, 1936.

Printed Cards

U. S. Library of Congress. Catalog of Books Represented by Library
of Congress Printed Cards... Ann Arbor, Mich.: Edwards,
1942-1955. 191v. (Title varies.)

_____. The National Union Catalog.: a Cumulative
Author List Representing Library of Congress Printed Cards
and Titles Reported by Other American Libraries. Jan. 1956—.
Washington: Govt. Print. Off., 1956—.
(Title varies.)

_____. Library of Congress Catalog, Books: Subjects,
1950-1954. Ann Arbor, Mich.: Edwards, 1955. 20v.

_____. _____, 1955-1959. Paterson, N.J.:
Pageant Books, 1960. 22v.

_____. _____, 1960-1964. Ann Arbor,
Mich.: Edwards, 1965. 25v.

_____. _____, 1965— Washington: Govt.
Print. Off., 1965—

Figure 16

SUBDIVISIONS UNDER INDIVIDUAL AUTHORS

VIII[b] (1 no.)	IX[b] (Cutter no.)	Authors with one number or Cutter number.
		Collected works.
.A1	.x	By date.
.A11–14	.xA11–14	By editor.
.A15	.xA15	Collected novels.
.A16	.xA16	Essays, miscellanies, etc.
.A17	.xA17	Collected poems.
.A19	.xA19	Collected plays.
.A3–Z29	.xA3–Z29	Separate works.
		Translations.
.Z3–39	.xZ3–39	English.
.Z4–49	.xZ4–49	French.
.Z6–69	.xZ6–69	Other. By language.
.Z7–79	.xZ7–79	Adaptations, imitations, dramatizations, etc.
		(By title).
.Z8–9	.xZ8–9	Biography and criticism.

X (1 no.)	X[a] (1 no.)	Separate works with one number. Use Table X[a] for works after 1600.
		Texts.
.A1	.A1	By date.
.A11–2	.A2A–Z	By editor.
	.A3	School texts.
		Translations.
.A21–39		Modern versions of medieval works.
.A4–49	.A4–49	French.
.A5–59	.A5–59	German.
.A6–69	.A6–69	Other languages. By language.
.A7–Z	.A7–Z	Criticism.

Figure 17

TABLES OF GEOGRAPHICAL DIVISIONS

The first number in curves (100), (200), etc., below the Roman numeral at head of column indicates the total number of divisions comprised in that table; the second number in curves (1), (2), (5; 10), etc., indicates the number of subdivisions assigned to any one country in a given table.

May be modified to meet the requirements of special subjects, where different order and different distribution of numbers is desired.

I	II	III	IV		V	VI	VII	VIII	IX	X
(100)	(200)	(300)	(400)		(130)	(200)	(830)	(840)	(420)	(1000)
(1)	(2)	(2)	(4)		(1; 4)	(2; 5)	(5; 10)	(10; 20)	(5; 10)	(5;10)
1	1	1	1	America	1	1	------	------	------	11
2	3	3	3	North America	2	2	------	------	------	21
3	5	5	5	United States	3-6	3	------	------	------	31
4	7	8	9	Northeastern (New England).	---------	------	------	------	------	41
5	9	11	13	Atlantic	---------	------	------	------	------	51
6	11	14	17	South (Gulf, etc.)	---------	------	------	------	------	61
7	13	17	21	Central	---------	------	------	------	------	71
8	15	20	25	Lake region (St. Lawrence Valley).	---------	------	------	------	------	81
9	17	23	29	Mississippi Valley and West.	---------	------	------	------	------	91
10	19	26	33	Southwest (south of Missouri and west of the Mississippi River.	---------	------	------	------	------	101
11	21	29	37	Northwest, and Rocky Mountains.	---------	------	------	------	------	111
12	23	32	41	Pacific coast	---------	------	------	------	------	121
----	----	----		Colonial possessions	---------	------	------	------	------	-----
13	25	35	45	States, A–W (see p. 537)	---------	8	------	------	------	131
14	27	38	49	Cities, A–Z (see p. 539)	---------	9	------	------	------	141
15	29	41	53	Canada, British N. A	7-10	10	11-20	1-10	1-10	151
----	----	----		Provinces, A–Z	---------	------	------	------	------	-----

Alberta.	Newfoundland.
Assiniboia.	Northwest Territories.
Athabasca.	Nova Scotia.
British Columbia.	Ontario (Upper Canada).
Franklin.	Prince Edward Island.
Keewatin.	Quebec (Lower Canada).
Labrador.	Saskatchewan.
Mackenzie.	Ungava.
Manitoba.	Yukon.
New Brunswick.	

I	II	III	IV		V	VI	VII	VIII	IX	X
16	31	44	57	Mexico	11	12	21	11	11	161
----	----	----		States, A–Z	---------	------	------	------	------	-----
17.A1-5	33	47	61	Central America	13.A1-5	14	31	21	16	171
17.A6-Z	35	48	65	British Honduras	13.A6-Z	------	36	26	19	181
18	37	49	69	Costa Rica	14	------	41	31	21	191
19	39	52	73	Guatemala	15	------	51	41	26	201
20	40	55	75	Honduras	16	------	61	51	31	211
21	41	57	77	Nicaragua	17	------	71	61	36	216
22	42	59	79	Panama	18	------	81	71	41	221
22.5	43.5	61	80	Panama Canal Zone	18.5	------	86	76	45 5	226
23	44.	62	81	Salvador	19	------	91	81	46	231
I	II	III	IV		V	VI	VII	VIII	IX	X

Figure 18

TABLE OF COUNTRIES IN ONE ALPHABET

Abyssinia, *see* Ethiopia.		Hawaii	H3
Afghanistan	A3	Holland, *see* Netherlands.	
Algeria	A4	Honduras	H7
Arabia	A6	Hungary	H8
Argentine Republic	A7	Iceland	I2
Australia [1]	A8	India	I4
Austria [1]	A9	Iran, *see* Persia.	
Belgium	B3	Iraq	I7
Bolivia	B6	Ireland, *see* Great Britain.[1]	
Brazil	B7	Italy	I8
British Guiana	B74	Japan	J3
British Honduras	B75	Korea	K8
Bulgaria	B8	Liberia	L5
Burma	B9	Luxemburg	L9
Canada [1]	C2 or C2–3	Mexico	M6
Chile	C5	Montenegro	M7
China	C6	Morocco	M8
Colombia	C7	Netherlands	N4
Costa Rica	C8	New Zealand	N45
Cuba	C9	Nicaragua	N5
Czechoslovak Republic	C95	Norway	N7
Denmark	D4	Palestine	P15
Dutch East Indies	D7	Panama	P2
Dutch Guiana	D8	Paraguay	P3
Ecuador	E2	Persia	P4
Egypt	E3	Peru	P5
Ethiopia	E8	Philippine Islands	P6
Finland	F5	Poland	P7
France	F8	Portugal	P8
French Guiana	F9	Puerto Rico	P9
Germany [1]	G3 or G2–4	Rumania	R8
Great Britain [1]	G7 or G5–8	Russia	R9
Greece [1]	G8 or G9	Salvador	S1
Guatemala [1]	G9 or G95	Santo Domingo	S2
Guiana (General)	G96	Scandinavia (General)	S3
Haiti	H2	Scotland, *see* Great Britain.[1]	

---

[1] For subarrangement, *see* "Notation for subdivisions under countries," p. 535–536.

Figure 19

NOTATION FOR SUBDIVISIONS UNDER COUNTRIES

Applies where more than one Cutter number is needed for a country.
May be modified to suit the requirements of special subjects, or of sections
where entries are already made.   Cf. H D 6473.

	Australia and New Zealand.
.A8	General.
.A82	New South Wales.
.A83	New Zealand.
.A84	North Australia.
.A85	Queensland.
.A86	South Australia.
.A87	Tasmania.
.A88	Victoria.
.A89	Western Australia.
	Austria. Austro-Hungarian Empire.
.A9	General.
.A91–94	Period divisions.
	e. g. .A94 1900–
	Austria.
.A95	Lower.
.A956	Upper.
.A96	Bohemia.
.A967	Galicia.
.A97	Hungary.
.A98	Moravia.
.A986	Styria.
.A987	Transylvania.
.A99	Tyrol.
	Canada and Newfoundland.
.C2	General.
.C21–25	Period divisions.
	e. g. .C24 1867–
.C26	British Columbia.
.C28	Manitoba.
.C3	New Brunswick.
.C31	Newfoundland.
.C32	Nova Scotia.
.C34	Ontario.
.C36	Prince Edward Island.

Figure 20

TABLE OF STATES [1]

I Cutter no.		II 1 no.	III [2] 2 nos.
A2	Alabama	1	1
A4	Alaska	2	3
A6	Arizona	3	5
A8	Arkansas	4	7
C2	California	5	9
C6	Colorado	6	11
C8	Connecticut	7	13
D2	Dakota (prefer S8 South Dakota)	8	15
D3	Delaware	9	17
D6	District of Columbia	10	19
F6	Florida	11	21
G4	Georgia	12	23
I2	Idaho	13	25
I3	Illinois	14	27
I4	Indian Territory	15	29
I6	Indiana	16	31
I8	Iowa	17	33
K2	Kansas	18	35
K4	Kentucky	19	37
L8	Louisiana	20	39
M2	Maine	21	41
M3	Maryland	22	43
M4	Massachusetts	23	45
M5	Michigan	24	47
M6	Minnesota	25	49
M7	Mississippi	26	51
M8	Missouri	27	53
M9	Montana	28	55
N2	Nebraska	29	57
N3	Nevada	30	59
N4	New Hampshire	31	61
N5	New Jersey	32	63
N6	New Mexico	33	65
N7	New York	34	67

---

[1] For regions, *see* arrangement under HC 107.

[2] For example: Alabama, 1–2; Wyoming, 103–104.

94

Figure 21

TABLE OF CITIES IN THE UNITED STATES

Akron	A2	Fall River	F2
Albany	A3	Fort Wayne	F7
Allegheny	A35	Frankfort	F8
Annapolis	A4		
Atlanta	A7	Galveston	G2
Augusta	A9	Grand Rapids	G7
Austin	A95	Guthrie	G8
Baltimore	B2	Harrisburg	H2
Baton Rouge	B3	Hartford	H3
Bismarck	B63	Helena, Mont	H4
Boise City	B66	Hoboken	H6
Boston	B7	Holyoke	H7
Bridgeport	B78	Houston	H8
Brooklyn	B8		
Buffalo	B9	Indianapolis	I4
Cambridge	C2	Jackson, Miss	J2
Camden	C22	Jacksonville	J3
Charleston, S. C	C3	Jefferson City	J4
Charleston, W. Va	C32	Jersey City	J5
Cheyenne	C38		
Chicago	C4	Kansas City	K2
Cincinnati	C5		
Cleveland	C6	Lawrence	L4
Columbia, S. C	C68	Lincoln	L65
Columbus	C7	Little Rock	L67
		Los Angeles	L7
Dallas	D2	Louisville	L8
Dayton	D3	Lowell	L9
Denver	D4	Lynn	L97
Des Moines	D5		
Detroit	D6		
Dover	D7	Madison	M18
Dubuque	D8	Manchester	M2
Duluth	D88	Memphis	M4
		Milwaukee	M5
Elizabeth	E4	Minneapolis	M6
Erie	E6	Mobile	M7
Evansville	E9	Montgomery, Ala	M75

Figure 22

FINE ARTS—GENERAL

ART CITIES

Amsterdam	N 6950	Madrid	N 7110
Angoulême	6851.A6	Mantua	6921.M3
Antwerp	6971.A6	Messina	6921.M5
Assisi	6921.A8	Milan	6921.M6
Athens	6900	Moscow	6997.M7
Ancient	5650	Munich	6886.M9
Augsburg	6886.A9		
		Nancy	6851.N2
Basel	7151.B3	Naples	6921.N2
Beaune	6851.B4	Nîmes	6851.N7
Bologna	6921.B7	Nuremberg	6886.N9
Berlin	6885		
Bruges	6971.B8	Padua	6921.P2
Brunswick	6886.B8	Palermo	6921.P3
Brussels	6970	Paris	6850
Budapest	6836.B9	Pisa	6921.P6
		Poitiers	6851.P7
Cairo	7383	Pompeii	5770–1
Christiania	7070	Prague	6836.P8
Cologne	6886.C7		
Constantinople	7170	Ravenna	6921.R3
Copenhagen	7020	Rome	6920
Cordova	7111.C7	Rouen	6851.R8
Cracow	6836.C8		
		St. Petersburg	6996
Dantzig	6886.D2	Seville	7111.S5
Dijon	6851.D5	Siena	6921.S6
		Stockholm	7090
Florence	6921.F7	Strassburg	6886.S8
		Syracuse	6921.S9
Genoa	6921.G4		
Ghent	6971.G4	Toledo	7111.T6
Granada	7111.G8	Tours	6851.T7
Grenoble	6851.G8	Tunis	7389.T9
		Turin	6921.T7
Hague	6951.H2		
Hildesheim	6886.H6	Venice	6921.V5
		Verona	6921.V6
Lisbon	7130	Versailles	6851.V5
Liverpool	6771.L7	Vienna	6835
London	6770		

Figure 23

LIST OF ENGLISH COUNTIES

B4	Bedfordshire.		M6	Middlesex.
B5	Berkshire.		M8	Monmouthshire.
B9	Buckinghamshire.			
			N5	Norfolk.
C2	Cambridgeshire.		N6	Northamptonshire.
C5	Cheshire.		N7	Northumberland.
C7	Cornwall.		N8	Nottinghamshire.
C9	Cumberland.			
			O9	Oxfordshire.
D4	Derbyshire.			
D5	Devonshire.		R9	Rutlandshire.
D7	Dorsetshire.			
D9	Durham.		S3	Shropshire.
			S5	Somersetshire.
E8	Essex.		S6	Staffordshire.
			S7	Suffolk.
G5	Gloucestershire.		S8	Surrey.
			S9	Sussex.
H2	Hampshire (Hants).			
H5	Herefordshire.		W3	Warwickshire.
H9	Huntingdonshire.		W5	Westmoreland.
			W7	Wiltshire.
K3	Kent.		W9	Worcestershire.
L2	Lancashire.		Y5	Yorkshire.
L5	Leicestershire.			
L7	Lincolnshire.			

Figure 24

ITALY.

(For ancient Rome, see JC 81–88.)

5201	**Periodicals.**
	Manuals.
5203	Nonofficial.
5204	Official.
	Collections (Constitutions, etc.).
5208	General collections.
	Special constitutions, see period.
	Constitutional history.
5211	Comprehensive works.
5213	Compends.
5215	Miscellany.
	By period.
5221	Early to French Revolution (ca. 1793).
5223	Earliest to 768/843 (Charlemagne, Treaty of Verdun).
5225	Northern Italy (Langobardia).
5227	Southern Italy.
5231	768/843 to ca. 1268 (Italy and the Empire).
5235	Ca. 1268 to ca. 1495 (Development of city states).
5240	Ca. 1495 to ca. 1793 (Foreign influence).
	Special states and regions.

Under each:
(1) General.
(2) 769/843 to ca. 1268.
(3) ca. 1268 to ca. 1495.
(4) ca. 1495 to ca. 1793.

5251–5254	Piedmont. Savoy.
5256–5259	Liguria: Genoa.
5261–5264	Lombardy: Milan.
5266–5269	Venice.
5271–5274	Romagna. Emilia.
	Including Modena and Parma.
5276–5279	Tuscany: Florence.
5281–5284	Rome. Marches. Umbria.
5286–5289	Naples. Sicily.
5291–5294	Sardinia. Corsica.
5299	Other, A–Z.

98

Figure 25

Revenue. Taxation.
  By country.
    United States—Continued.
      General works. History.
        Including practice.

2362	General.
2368	Early to 1789.
2369	1789–1815.
2370	1815–1860.
2371	1861–1865/70.
2372	Confederate States.

          Cf. HJ 3255–3257, Tax law and legislation.

2373	1865/70–1900.
2375	1898 (War revenue act).
2377	1901–
2379	War revenue acts, 1914–1918.

          Arranged like HJ 4652.

2380	Defense and war revenue acts, 1938–1946.

          Arranged like HJ 4652.

2383	Facetiae, satire, etc.
2385	States collectively.
	Regions.

        Under each:
          .A1   General works. History.
          .A3   Early.
          .A4   1830/40–1900.
          .A6–Z8 1901–
          .Z9   Special.

2386	New England and Atlantic States.
2387	South.
2388	Middle West.
2389	Pacific.
2391–2442	States individually.

        Under each:
             General works. History.
         .A2   General.
             Early to 1800.
         .A29   Documents.
         .A3   Other.
             1801–1860.
         .A39   Documents.
         .A4   Other.
             1861–1865/70.
         .A49   Documents.
         .A5   Other.
             1865/70–1900.
         .A59   Documents.
         .A6   Other.

Figure 26

QD   CHEMISTRY   QD

181   Special elements.
          Alphabetically by chemical symbol of principal element.
          Under QD 181 are classified all works on the origin, properties,
             preparation, reactions, and analytical chemistry of individual
             elements and their inorganic compounds, excluding determina-
             tions of atomic weights (QD 464).
          .A1   = A.   Argon.
          .A2   = Ac.   Actinium.
          .A3   = Ag.   Silver (Argentum).
          .A4   = Al.   Aluminum.
          .A5   = Am.   Americium.
                             Antimony, see .S3.
          .A7   = As.   Arsenic.
          .A8   = At.   Astatine.
          .A9   = Au.   Gold (Aurum).
          .B1   = B.   Boron.
          .B2   = Ba.   Barium.
          .B4   = Be.   Beryllium (Glucinum).
          .B5   = Bi.   Bismuth.
                             Boron, see .B1.
          .B7   = Br.   Bromine.
          .C1   = C.   Carbon.
          .C15   = CN.   Cyanogen.
          .C2   = Ca.   Calcium.
          .C3   = Cd.   Cadmium.
                             Cassiopeium, see .L8.
                             Celtium, see .H5.
          .C4   = Ce.   Cerium.
          .C5   = Cl.   Chlorine.
          .C55   = Cm.   Curium.
          .C6   = Co.   Cobalt.
          .C7   = Cr.   Chromium.
          .C8   = Cs.   Cesium.
                             Columbium, see .N3.
          .C9   = Cu.   Copper.
          .D1   = D.   Deuterium.
                             Didymium, see .N4.
          .D8   = Dy.   Dysprosium.
          .E6   = Er.   Erbium.
          .E8   = Eu.   Europium.
          .F1   = F.   Fluorine.
          .F4   = Fe.   Iron (Ferrum).
          .F7   = Fr.   Francium.
          .G2   = Ga.   Gallium.
          .G4   = Gd.   Gadolinium.
          .G5   = Ge.   Germanium.
                             Glucinum, see .B4.
                             Gold, see .A9.
                             Hydrargyrum, see .H6.
          .H1   = H.   Hydrogen.
          .H4   = He.   Helium.
          .H5   = Hf.   Hafnium (Celtium).
          .H55   = Ho.   Holmium.

Figure 27

TABLE FOR ARRANGEMENT OF WORKS UNDER FOREIGN COUNTRIES

20 nos.	10 nos.	
		Periodicals, see PN 4701–4705.
	1	Societies, Conferences, Collections.
1		Societies.
2		Conferences. Congresses.
3		Collections.
		History and other general works.
4	2	Comprehensive.
5	3	Early.
	4	Recent.
6		18th century.
7		19th century.
8		20th century.
	6	Biography of editors, journalists, etc.
12	.A1–5	Collective.
13	.A6–Z	Individual, A–Z.
14	7	Special topics, A–Z.
		(.L5) Literary reviews. Prefer PQ–PV.
		Local.
16		By region, A–Z.
17	8	By state, province, etc., A–Z.
		Under each:
		(1) Collections.
		(2) History and other general.
19	9	By place, A–Z.
		Under each, using successive Cutter numbers:
		(1) Collections.
		(2) History and other general.
		(3) Special newspapers, A–Z.
20	10	Special magazines and other periodicals, A–Z.
		(For newspapers, see 19 and 9.)

5 nos.	1 no.	
1	.A2–5	Societies, Conferences, Collections.
2	.A6A–Z	History and other general works.
3.A1–5	.A7A1	Biography—Collective.
3.A6–Z	.A7A3–Z	Biography—Individual.
4	.A8–Z5	Local, A–Z.
5	.Z6A–Z	Special journals, A–Z.

Figure 28

BIOGRAPHY BY SUBJECT

Biography of women—Continued.

3700	Asia.
3710	China.
3720	India.
3730	Japan.
3750	Africa.
3770	British Africa.
3800	Australia and New Zealand.
3830	Pacific islands.
	Cf. CT4150.
3910	**Encyclopedists.**
(3950)	Museum officials.
	Journalists, *see* CT8350, 8547, 8557, etc.
(3990)	**Academicians. Scholars. Savants.**
	For scholars eminent in more than one of the special subjects following.
.A2	Collective.
.A3–Z	Individual.
(4150)	**Philosophy.**
(4160)	Ancient, *see* B, PA, PJ–PL.
(4180)	American.
(4190)	Dutch.
(4200)	English.
(4210)	French.
(4220)	German.
(4230)	Italian.
(4240)	Scandinavian.
(4250)	Slavic.
(4260)	Spanish and Portuguese.
(4270)	Swiss.
(4280)	Other.
	Religion. Theology.
(4350)	General.
(4360)	Christian.
(4370)	Missions.
(4380)	Lives of the Saints.
(4390)	Early Christian. Fathers of the Church.
(4400)	Eastern Church. Greek and Russo-Greek.
(4450)	**Roman Catholic Church.**
(4460)	Lives of the Popes.
(4470)	Lives of the Cardinals.
(4480)	Other clerics (Archbishops, bishops, abbés, etc.).

Figure 29

SUBDIVISIONS UNDER INDIVIDUAL AUTHORS

XI (Cutter no.)	Separate works with Cutter numbers.

(1).x date
.xA–Z
 	
(2)
(3).xA–Z
	Texts.
	Translations, by language.
	  .A3–39, Modern versions in same language.
	  .A4–Z, Other languages.
	Adaptations, dramatizations, etc.
	Criticism.
	   Note. In Table XI, (1), (2), and (3), .x represents successive Cutter numbers, as, for example: .F6, .F7, .F8 or .F66, .F67, .F68.
	   In the case of works where division (2) is inapplicable the numbers may be modified by using two Cutter numbers only, as .F4, .F5 or .F4, .F41.

XII (2 nos.)	Authors with two numbers.

(1).A1
.A2–49
 	
.A5–Z
(2).A–Z
	Collected editions.
	  By date.
	  By editor.
	    (If there are many different editions, .A2A–Z may be used instead of .A2–49.)
	Separate works. By title.
	Biography and criticism.

XII* (2 nos.)	Single works with two numbers.

(1).A1
.A2–59
.A6–Z
(2)
	Texts.
	  By date.
	  By editor.
	Parts, by title.
	Criticism.

Figure 30

Anglo-Norman period. Early English.
Individual authors and works—Continued.

1829	Au-Ay.
	Ayenbite of inwyt, see Michel of Northgate.
1831	Bacon, John.
1833	Barbour, John (VIII).
1834	Barb-Bes.
1836	Bestiary (X).
1837	Bes-Blz.
	Blind Harry, see Henry, the minstrel.
1840.B5	Bokenham, Osbern.
1841	Bradwardine, Thomas.
1843	Canute song (X).
1845	Capgrave, John.
1847-1848	Caxton, William (XII).
1849.C4	Chandos, the herald.
.C6	Charles, count of Angoulême, duke of Orléans.
	Cf. PQ 1553.C5.
	DC 102.8.O7.

Chaucer, Geoffrey.

Collected works.

1850	Original editions and reprints, by date.
1851	Editions with commentary, by editor, A-Z.
1852	Selections. Anthologies.
1853	Minor poems. Collected fragments.
1854	Translations, by language, subarranged by translator.
1855	Adaptations, modernization, etc.
	For the Canterbury tales, see PR 1872.

Separate works.

1856-1857	Anelida and Arcite.
1859-1860	Boethius's De consolatione philosophiae.
1862-1863	Book of the Dutchess.
	Canterbury tales.
	Texts.
1865	By date.
1866	By editor.
1867	Selections.
1868	Special parts, A-Z.
	Under each:
	Text.
	(1) By date.
	(2) By editor.
	(3) Criticism.
1870	Translations, by language, A-Z.
1872	Miscellaneous: Adaptations; Versions for children, etc.
(1873)	Indexes, see PR 1903.
	Criticism.
1874	General.
1875	Special, by subject, A-Z.

CHAPTER 4

EXAMPLES OF THE USE OF TABLES

The following examples are designed to give the reader a general understanding of the use of tables in Library of Congress classification. These tables vary in length and complexity depending on each particular situation. The simpler tables will occur within the schedules while the more complex tables occur following the schedules in the form of auxiliary tables. All of these tables, both simple and complex, may be mastered by following the same standard pattern. First, the classifier must determine the range of integral numbers to be applied to a table. Second, the appropriate table must be discerned. Third, the appropriate integral number must be fitted into the subdivisions proscribed by the appropriate table. These three steps will be demonstrated in the following examples of simple tables within the schedules, simple auxiliary tables, complex tables for individual authors in literature, and complex tables of geographic divisions in the social sciences.

SIMPLE TABLES WITHIN THE SCHEDULES

Tables are often used to subdivide the geographic divisions of a particular subject. The tables referred to in Chapter 3, Figures 17-23 are examples of such divisions. The following discussion of AM 10-99, the numbers assigned to the geographic division of the subject museography, explains the use of simple tables within the schedules (see Figure 31). The three tables within the schedules to be used to subdivide the geographic numbers are for: three number countries, two number countries and one number countries. A section of Figure 31 is reproduced below to show these three tables.

Museography.

AM
10-99   By country.

Under each country (Three numbers):

(1)   General.

(2)   States, provinces, etc.

(3)   Cities, towns, etc.

Under each country (Two numbers):

(1)   . A1   Periodicals.

      . A2   General.

      . A3-Z Provinces, etc.

(2)   Cities, towns, etc.

Under each country (One number):

(1)   . A2   General.

      . A3-Z Local.

Following these tables are the specific geographic divisions indicating the range of integral numbers to be used for each division. A part of the table of numbers from Figure 31 is reproduced below:

AM	10	America
	11-13	United States
	21-22	British America. Canada
	23-24	Mexico

Three Number Countries

As shown in the table above, AM 11-13 is assigned to the United States. This means that the United States, in this case, is a three number country. AM 11-13 is the range of numbers to be used for works on museography in the United States. Without a table the classifier could not discern how to subdivide this range. By using the appropriate table from Figure 31, the classifier can easily locate the correct subdivisions. As the United States is a three number country, the first table (for three number countries) should be applied. The range of numbers for United States is shown below matched to the table for three number countries.

AM 11 -- (1) General

     12 -- (2) States, provinces, etc.

     13 -- (3) Cities, towns, etc.

A general work on museography in the United States will use the first number, AM 11. For instance the Museums Directory of the United States and Canada is classed as "AM 11 . M8. " "AM 11"

means a general work on museography of the United States and
". M8" is the Cutter number for the main entry which in this case
is the title.

Museums Directory of the United States and Canada.

AM-----The double letters for the subclass, Museums.

11------The integral number meaning a general work on
the museography of the United States.

. M8 -----The Cutter number for the main entry, Museums
Directory...

A work on museography in one of the states of the United States
would use the second number in the table as applied to the range of
numbers for the United States, AM 11-13. The second number is
AM 12. Similarly, the third number AM 13 would be used for a
work on museography in one of the cities in the United States. For
example, the Tennessee Association of Museums' List of Museums
in the State of Tennessee is classed as "AM 12 . T4T4. " As Tennessee is one of the states of the United States, the second number AM
12 is used. The first Cutter number ". T4" stands for the specific
state, in this case, Tennessee. The second Cutter number "T4"
stands for the main entry, Tennessee Association of Museums.
The same process as applied to the United States may be applied to
any country or geographic division with a range of three numbers in
the subject museography.

Tennessee Association of Museums' List of Museums in
the State of Tennessee.

AM-----The double letters for the subclass, Museums.

12------The integral number meaning a work on the
museography of one of the states of the United
States.

. T4 ----The first Cutter number for the specific state,
Tennessee.

T4 -----The second Cutter number for the main entry,
Tennessee Association of Museums.

It must be noted that both states and cities for three number
countries are arranged alphabetically as a natural further subdivision. This instruction is not given by the table but it is an obviously necessary one. The beginner may wish to annotate this

table to read:

> Under each country (Three numbers):
>
> (1)   General.
>
> (2)   States, provinces, etc., A-Z.
>
> (3)   Cities, towns, etc., A-Z.

The lack of such instructions within the tables may seem discouraging to the beginner. However, if the beginner will consult a similar work already classed using a particular table, any further subdivisions will become apparent. In fact, the beginner should always be advised to ascertain how the Library of Congress has classed similar material before assigning an original call number.

Two Number Countries

A similar process may be used with two number and one number ranges. For example, Fernando Castelo-Branco's The Museums of Lisbon is a work of museography dealing with a city in Portugal. Portugal's geographic division, in this case, is combined with Spain's. Spain-Portugal has a range of numbers AM 65-66. See Figure 31a. This means that Spain-Portugal is to be treated as a two number geographic division which will use the second table-- for two number countries. See Figure 31 and below.

> Under each country (Two numbers):
>
> (1)   .A1   Periodicals. Societies.
>
>   .A2   General
>
>   .A3-Z Provinces, etc.
>
> (2)   Cities, towns, etc.

This table clearly indicates "(2) Cities, towns, etc. " which means that the second number within the range of integral numbers must be used for works of museography of cities or other local areas. The number for Lisbon would be "AM 66 . L5. " "AM 66" means a city in Spain or Portugal, while ". L5" means Lisbon. This call number is completed by the use of the second Cutter number for the main entry, Castelo-Branco, or "C3. " The complete number for The Museums of Lisbon by Castelo-Branco is "AM 66 . L5C3. "

Fernando Castelo-Branco's <u>The Museums of Lisbon</u>

AM-----The double letters for the subclass, Museums.

66------The integral number meaning a work on museography of one of the cities in the geographic area of Spain-Portugal.

.L5 ----The first Cutter number for the specific city, Lisbon.

C3 -----The second Cutter number for the main entry, Castelo-Branco.

<u>One Number Countries</u>

A one number country which uses this third table is Norway. See Figures 31, 31a and below.

Under each country (One number):

(1) .A2   General

(2) .A3-Z Local

The number for Norway is AM 63. In this case the further subdivisions employ the use of reserved Cutter numbers. Thus, AM 63 .A2 would be used for general works on museography in Norway.

"A general directory of the museums of Norway."

AM-----The double letters for the subclass, Museums.

63------The integral number meaning a work on some aspect of the museography of Norway.

.A2------The first Cutter number meaning a general work on the museography of Norway.

___-----The second Cutter number to be used for the main entry of such a work.

Works on museography at the local level employ the range of Cutter numbers .A3-Z. This means that instead of alphabetically subdividing from A-Z, as in other instances, the classifier cannot use .A1 or .A2 but must <u>start</u> the range with .A3. Any locality beginning with the letter "A" must be cuttered from the base .A3. Localities beginning with letters other than "A" are cuttered as usual. For instance, Oslo, Norway would be .O8 which is within the range of .A3-Z. A work on museography in Oslo would be classed "AM 63 .O8.

"A directory of the museums of Oslo, Norway. "

AM-----The double letters for the subclass, Museums.

63------The integral number meaning a work on some aspect of the museography of Norway.

. 08-----The first Cutter number meaning a local work on museography of Norway, the locality being Oslo.

___ -----The second Cutter number to be used for the main entry.

Cutter Number Countries

A final example of the use of this set of tables in museography is the instance of Cutter number countries. These are countries which receive only a Cutter number for their distinctive element. For example, AM 70 is for "Other European countries, A-Z. " One such country is Hungary which appears no where separately in the geographic divisions and must use AM 70. The Cutter number for Hungary may be verified as ".H8" (See Figure 18). A directory of museums in Hungary entitled Magyar Muzeumok is classed "AM 70 .H8M3. " In this case the tables were not used at all. "AM 70" means "Other European countries, A-Z"; ".H8" is Hungary; and "M3" is Cuttering for the main entry, "Magyar. "

Magyar Muzeumok, a directory of museums in Hungary.

AM-----The double letters for the subclass, Museums.

70 ------The integral number meaning a work on some aspect of the museography of the other European countries.

. H8 ----The first Cutter number meaning the specific country, Hungary.

M3 -----The second Cutter number for the main entry, Magyar. . .

SIMPLE AUXILIARY TABLES

The auxiliary tables used to subdivide the grographic divisions for Yearbooks, Almanacs, Directories in AY 410-1725 may be used as examples of simple auxiliary tables. There are three tables at the end of subclass AY (Figure 32) to be used to subdivide the geographic numbers for almanacs and yearbooks of foreign countries. These three tables are for ten number countries, two number countries and one number or Cutter number countries. These tables are used only for foreign countries as the numbers for United States yearbooks and almanacs are worked out fully in the schedules. This is often the case with subdivisions for geographic division; the United States is given more numbers and does not use auxiliary tables.

Ten Number Countries

The use of the table for ten number countries is simply a matter of carefully matching the sequence of numbers in the table with the integral numbers assigned to the geographic divisions. For instance, the schedule for subclass AY assigns the range AY 890-899 to Italy for yearbooks, almanacs and directories. In order to use these ten numbers for Italy one must use the auxiliary table for ten number countries at the end of the subclass AY. This table is reproduced below. See also Figure 32.

Table I (Ten numbers)

Early (to 1800).

(0)		Collections, by date of first volume.
(1)	.A-Z5	Serial, by title or editor.
	.Z7	Other, by date.
(2)		Yearbooks (without almanacs).

1800—

(3)	Collections.
(4)	General, by title or editor.
(5)	Newspaper, etc., by name of place, sub-arranged by title.
(6)	Other.
(7)	Almanacs in foreign languages, by languages, A-Z.
(8)	Special, By subject, A-Z.
(9)	Local, by place, A-Z.

The range of ten numbers for Italy (890-899) must be matched with the range of ten numbers in this table (0-9). As the table begins with the same last digit as the base number for Italy, there is no problem in directly matching the numbers. Thus, AY 895 would be an Italian newspaper yearbook; AY 892 would be an early Italian yearbook without almanacs; or, AY 899 would be a local Italian almanac. In each case the last digits are simply matched. For example, the Almanacco d'Italia is classed as a general Italian almanac "AY 894 . A58. " The ". A58" is the Cutter number for the main entry, which in this case is the title, Almanacco d'Italia.

Almanacco d'Italia, a general Italian almanac.

AY----- The double letters for the subclass, Yearbooks.

894 ---- The integral number meaning a general Italian almanac.

. A58 --- The first Cutter number for the main entry, Alamancco...

Another example is a Jewish almanac published in Germany entitled Jüdischer Almanach. Germany's range of numbers is AY 850-860 with AY 859 for states and AY 860 for places. Except for these last two numbers, Germany may use the table for ten number countries even though it is really an eleven number country. The Jewish almanac is a special almanac and should receive the ninth number in the table which is "8". (Please note that the first number in the table is "0".) The call number for this book, Jüdischer Almanach, is "AY 858 .J4J8. " "AY 858" means a special German Almanac; ".J4" is the Cutter number for the special subject, Jews; and, "J8" is the Cutter number for the title, Jüdischer Almanach.

Jüdischer Almanach, a Jewish almanac published in Germany.

AY----- The double letters for the subclass, Yearbooks.

858 ---- The integral number meaning a special German almanac.

. J4 ---- The first Cutter number for the special subject, Jews.

J8 ----- The second Cutter number for the main entry, Jüdischer...

Two Number Countries

The auxiliary tables for two number tables (Table II) and for one number or Cutter number countries (Table III) are used in a similar fashion. (Table II is shown below; see also Figure 32).

Table II (Two numbers)

(1)   Collections and general.

(2)   Local, by place, A-Z.

For instance, New Zealand has two numbers for almanacs, yearbooks and directories "AY 1651" and "AY 1652." The table for two number countries (Table II) is used to determine the individual assignments of each number. The first number, AY 1651, is used for collections and general almanacs, yearbooks or directories of New Zealand. The second number, AY 1652, is used for local almanacs, yearbooks or directories of New Zealand, subdivided by place, A-Z.

One Number or Cutter Number Countries

A one number or Cutter number geographic division should be used with the appropriate division auxiliary table for one number or Cutter number countries, Table III. (See also Figure 32).

Table III (One number or Cutter number)

(1) .A2   Collections.

(2) .A3   Serial.

(3) .A4-Z   Local, by place.

The subdivisions of this table are derived through the use of reserved Cutter numbers as is usually the case when one number or a Cutter number is to have subdivisions. The use of this table is directly parallel to the application of the table for one number countries under AM 10-99 in museography which was discussed in the first section of this chapter.

However, it is important to observe that Table III is not always used for subdivisions of almanacs, yearbooks or directories at the Library of Congress; direct cuttering for the main entry may be substituted. For example, Iran is a one number country, AY 1185. The Library of Congress classes the Iran Almanac and Book of Facts, an annual publication, as "AY 1185 . I7. "

Iran Almanac and Book of Facts

AY----- The double letters for the subclass, Yearbooks.

1185 --- The integral number meaning Iran.

. I7----- The first Cutter number for the main entry,
Iran. . .

Obviously the ". I7" is the Cutter number for the main entry, which is, in this case, the title. The classifier directly cuttered for the main entry and did not use Table III. If one applies Table III, the "I7" could be interpreted as a locality within Iran whose name begins with an "Ir. " Table III was not used in this case. Use of the table would yield the following number "AY 1185 . A3I7. " The table shows ". A3" would be used as this is an annual publication of general, not local, nature.

There is a similar pattern at the library of Congress for the classing of Cutter number countries. For example, Poland is a Cutter number country under "AY 1039 Other European, A-Z. " Poland's Cutter number is ". P7" (See Figure 18). A Polish directory, Deutscher Kalendar im Generalgovernement, is classed "AY 1039 . P7D4. " "D4" is simply the Cutter number for the main entry, which is, in this case, the title. Table III was not used.

Deutscher Kalendar im Generalgovernement, a Polish
directory.

AY----- The double letters for the subclass, Yearbooks.

1039 --- The integral number meaning "Other European"
countries.

. P7 ---- The first Cutter number for the specific country,
Poland.

D4 ----- The second Cutter number for the main entry,
Deutscher. . .

The classifier should always verify whether or not a particular table of subdivisions is being used in a particular instance at the Library of Congress. Often in the case of further subdivisions of one number, or a Cutter number, appropriate tables are not used by the Library of Congress. If the further subdivisions can be gained by cuttering immediately for the main entry thus avoiding the use of a table, this may be done providing it is consistent with specific Library of Congress usage.

COMPLEX TABLES FOR INDIVIDUAL AUTHORS IN LITERATURE

There are twenty-three different form tables for use with individual authors in subclasses PR, English literature, and PS,
American literature. A form table must be used for all individual
authors. Only in a few cases are these tables worked out within
the schedules--e. g. William Shakespeare. These auxiliary tables
are designed for both individual authors and separate works. Each
author is assigned a certain range of numbers appropriate to the
amount of material written by and about him. There are tables for
authors assigned ninety-eight numbers (although none yet exist),
forty-eight numbers, eighteen numbers, eight numbers, five numbers, four numbers, one number, or only a Cutter number. Separate works with eight, five, two, one and Cutter numbers have
auxiliary tables as do anonymous literary works.

Authors with Forty-eight Numbers

Robert Browning is a nineteenth century English author with a
range of forty-eight numbers. In the appropriate schedule for subclass PR, English literature, Browning's range of numbers is given
as:

"PR
4205-4248   Browning, Robert (II). "

However, within the Additions and Changes section of the schedule,
Browning's first number is given as PR 4200, which allows him his
full forty-eight number range. This example is chosen to demonstrate the need to use the Additions and Changes section of each
schedule. In the original schedule, "PR 4205" is simply a typographical error. The classifer must always be alert for such possible errors both within the schedules and on the printed Library
of Congress cards.

Browning's section in the schedule includes a list of his separate works shown below. (See also Figure 33.)

Separate works.

4205   The blot on the scutcheon.

4206   Dramatic idyls.

4207   Dramatic lyrics.

4208   Dramatic romances.

4209	Dramatic personae.
4210	In a balcony.
4211	Jocoseria.
4212	King Victor and Prince Charles.
4213	Luria.
4214	Men and women.
4215	Paracelsus.
4216	Parleyings.
4217	Pauline.
4218	Pippa passes.
4219	Ring and the book.
4220	Sordello.
4221	Strafford.
4222	Other, A-Z.

The more important works are assigned a whole number, e. g. Pippa Passes PR 4218. The lesser works are assigned one number PR 4222, Other A-Z. However, to use Browning's entire range of forty-eight numbers, the appropriate auxiliary table must be found. Following Browning's name in the schedule is the instruction "(II)." This means that Table II, for forty-eight number authors, is used to class Browning's works. Following the schedule are auxiliary tables called "Table of Subdivisions under Individual Authors." The first tables are I and II for ninety-eight and forty-eight number authors respectively. The following is taken from the beginning of Table II. (See also Figure 34.)

Collected works.

0	or	50	Original editions, and reprints. By date.	
			To 1500:	A00-A99.
			1500-1599:	B00-B99.
			1600-1699:	C00-C99.
			1700-1799:	D00-D99.
			1800-1899:	E00-E99.
			1900-1999:	F00-F99.

1	51	Editions with commentary etc. By editor, A-Z.
2	52	Selected works. Minor works. Inedited works, fragments, etc.
3	53	Selections. Anthologies. Extracts.
4	54	Translations. By language; subarranged by translator.
5-22	55-72	Separate works, alphabetically by title.

The appropriate column for Table II must be chosen in relation to the last two digits of the first number of an author's range of numbers. Browning's numbers begin at PR 4200. The last two digits are "00." These match with the numbers in the first column of Table II, "0." They do not match with the second column which begins at "50." In contrast Lord Byron's range of numbers is PR 4350-4398. The last two digits of Byron's base number are "50." Hence, the second column of Table II would be used for Byron, while the first column is used for Browning.

An edition of the complete works of Browning without commentary published in 1910 is classed "PR 4200 . F10." "PR 4200 means an edition without commentary of the collected works of Browning. ". F10" is a date letter representing the year 1910. As shown in the table above (see also Figure 34), "F" equals "19" (1900-1999: F00-F99). This device retains the consistency of the notation; without it the call number would appear as "PR 4200 1910."

The Complete Works of Browning, 1910.

PR----- The double letters for the subclass, English literature.

4200 --- The integral number meaning an edition without commentary of the collected works of Robert Browning.

. F10 --- The first Cutter number meaning the date "1910."

An edited edition with commentary by Charlotte Porter of Browning's complete works is classed "PR 4201 . P6." "1" is the number in Table II, column 1, for "Editions with commentary." ". P6" is the Cutter number for the editor, Charlotte Porter.

The Complete Works of Browning, edited by Charlotte
Porter.

PR----- The double letters for the subclass, English
literature.

4201 --- The integral number meaning an edition with
commentary of the collected works of Robert
Browning.

.P6 ---- The first Cutter number for the author of the
commentary, Porter.

In neither example is there any reason for a second Cutter number.
Beginners may feel a desire to cutter for Browning or for title but
either would be redundant. The range of numbers used means
Browning and the class number means his complete works.

As Table II demonstrates, the separate works or individual
titles of a forty-eight number author are assigned as either "5-22"
or "55-72. " As Browning is using the first column, "5-22" is
appropriate. These numbers match with the numbers assigned to
Browning's separate works as given in the schedule. For instance,
Browning's The Ring and the Book is assigned "PR 4219. " In order
to complete this call number another table must be used. Table X
and Xa, "Separate Works with One Number, " is the appropriate
table. Table Xa is a modification of Table X for works written
after 1600. The Ring and the Book would use Table Xa as it was
written after 1600. (See also Figure 16.)

Table Xa

Texts.

.A1   By date.

.A2 A-Z   By editor.

.A3   School texts.

Translations.

.A4-49   French.

.A5-59   German.

.A6-69   Other languages. By language.

.A7-Z   Criticism.

An edition without commentary published in 1964 of the latter work
would be classed "PR 4219 . A1 1964"; an edited version by Charlotte

Porter would be "PR 4219 . A2P6. " "A2" meaning an edited version and "P6" the Cutter number for the editor's name, Porter. If Charlotte Porter had written a separate monograph devoted entirely to the interpretation of The Ring and the Book, it would be classed "PR 4219. P6. "

    Browning's The Ring and the Book, 1964.

        PR----- The double letters for the subclass, English literature.

        4219 --- The integral number meaning Browning's The Ring and the Book.

        . A1 ---- The first Cutter number meaning the text without commentary.

        1964 --- The date of publication as called for by the table.

    Browning's The Ring and the Book, edited by Charlotte Porter.

        PR----- The double letters for the subclass, English literature.

        4219 --- The integral number meaning Browning's The Ring and the Book.

        . A2 ---- The first Cutter number meaning the text with commentary.

        P6 ----- The second Cutter number for the commentator, Porter.

    "An Interpretation of Browning's The Ring and the Book" by Charlotte Porter.

        PR----- The double letters for the subclass, English literature.

        4219 --- The integral number meaning Browning's The Ring and the Book.

        . P6 ---- The first Cutter number for the main entry, Porter.

The shelf order of these three works would be:

PR	PR	PR
4219	4219	4219
. A1	. A2	. P6
1964	P6	

Criticism is given a range of Cutter numbers ". A7-Z" in Table X^a. The implications of the above operations are important. Although Browning is a forty-eight number author using Table II, any of his separate works require the application of a different table—Table X or X^a for works with one number and Table XI for works with a Cutter number. The use of these tables is important in order to keep all the works about an individual work close to the individual work. The part of Table II for biography and criticism of a forty-eight number author follows the part of the table for the works of the author. For instance literary dictionaries of a forty-eight number author use the following:

30   80   Dictionaries, Indexes, etc.

General encyclopedic dictionaries only.

Special dictionaries with subject.
e. g. Characters, see 78 (Table I);
39, 89 (Table II).

The entire page for this part of the table is reproduced in Figure 35.

Edward Berdoe's The Browning Cyclopedia is classed "PR 4230 . B4. " "30" is the appropriate number within Browning's range of numbers, 4200-4248. ". B4" is the Cutter number for the author of the work, in this case Berdoe.

Edward Berdoe's The Browning Cyclopedia.

PR----- The double letters for the subclass, English
literature.

4230 --- The integral number for a literary dictionary of
Robert Browning.

. B4 ----The first Cutter number for the main entry,
Berdoe.

Browning and the Christian Faith, a monograph by Berdoe, is classed "PR 4242 . R4B4. " The appropriate section in the table is:

42. A-Z 92. A-Z   Treatment and knowledge of special subjects.

The entire page for this section may be seen in Figure 36.

"PR 4242" means Browning's treatment and knowledge of a special subject, religion. ". R4" is the Cutter number for that special subject religion. "B4" is the Cutter number for Berdoe. In most cases the forty-eight number tables are simply a matter of matching the appropriate numbers with the author's range of numbers.

Edward Berdoe's <u>Browning and the Christian Faith</u>.

PR----- The double letters for the subclass, English literature.

4242 --- The integral number meaning Browning's treatment and knowledge of special subjects.

. R4 ---- The first Cutter number for the special subject, religion.

B4 ----- The second Cutter number for the main entry, Berdoe.

Authors With Eight or Eighteen Numbers

The tables for authors with eight or eighteen numbers may be treated similarly to the authors with forty-eight numbers. Table IV is for eight number authors and Table III is for eighteen number authors. Bernard Shaw is an example of an eight number author in English literature. He is assigned the range of numbers PR 5360-5368. It should be observed that both eight and eighteen number authors really have an additional number within their ranges. They are simply called eight or eighteen number authors as eight or eighteen is the last number in their range. Shaw's range of numbers and their specified assignments in the schedule are shown below. (See also Figure 37.)

PR
5360-5368   Shaw, George Bernard (IV[a]).

5360   Complete works (also collected dramas).

5361   Selections.

5362   Translations.

5363   Separate dramatic works, A-Z.

. A2,   The doctor's dilemma, etc.

.A25,   Misalliance, the dark lady of the
           sonnets, and Fanny's first play.

.A3,   Plays pleasant and unpleasant.

.A5,   Three plays for Puritans.

.A8-Z,   Separate dramas, A-Z.

Other works

5364   Collected.

5365   Separate, A-Z.

As Shaw is an eight number author and as "(IV^a)" appears following his name, Table IV is used in subdividing his range of nine numbers.[1] (See Figure 38.) Table IV^a is simply a single modification of Table IV. Date letters, as used in Table I and II, are to be used in Table III and IV when the author is assigned III^a or IV^a.

Table IV

Collected works.

0   By date.

1   By editor.

2   Selections.

3   Translations.

4. A-Z   Separate works.

         Under each:

         IV, see Table XI.

5   Apocryphal, spurious works, etc.

6. A1-19 Periodicals. Societies. Collections.

.A2-3   Dictionaries, indexes, etc.

---

[1] The choice of Shaw as an eight number author represents a combination of problems in using the numbers assigned within the schedules and in selecting the appropriate part of the tables for subdividing the numbers. Most of the numbers are assigned within the schedule rather than being determined from the table. Many authors have such variations where the schedule shows assigned numbers and the table is not fully utilized.

. A5- Z Biography and criticism

Criticism.

7 General.

8 Other, A- Z.
e. g. Language, grammar, style, etc.

Table IV is only used for three of the nine numbers assigned to
Shaw. If the numbers assigned to Shaw in the schedule (Figure 37)
are compared with Table IV (Figure 38), it should be observed that
the first six numbers (5360-5365) have been assigned within the
schedule for this specific author. Only numbers PR 5366, PR 5367
and PR 5368 --not described in the schedule-- require use of Table
IV for the assignment of subdivisions. Thus, classing is accomplished directly from the schedules as demonstrated in the following
example.

The Complete Plays of Bernard Shaw published in 1963 is
classed "PR 5360 . F63. " The schedule shows that "PR 5360" means
the complete works or collected dramas of Bernard Shaw. ". F63"
is the appropriate date letter from Table IV^a meaning "1963. "
Table IV is not used in this case as the number PR 5360 is fully
described in the schedules.

The Complete Plays of Bernard Shaw, 1963.

PR----- The double letters for the subclass, English
literature.

5360 --- The integral number meaning the collected
works or collected dramas of Bernard Shaw.

. F63 --- The first Cutter number meaning the date "1963. "

Three Plays for Puritans, the text of a separate work by Shaw, is
classed as "PR 5363 . A5. " Again this number is taken entirely
from the schedule. For further subdivisions of this number the
classifier must use Table XI, "Separate Works with Cutter Numbers. "
(See Figure 29.) This table was previously discussed in relation to
successive Cutter numbers in Chapter 3, p. 80.

Shaw's Three Plays for Puritans.

PR----- The double letters for the subclass, English
literature.

5363 --- The integral number meaning a separate dramatic
work by Shaw.

.A5---- The first Cutter number meaning <u>Three Plays</u>
<u>for Puritans</u>.

In this case which is, the text of the separate work, <u>Three Plays</u>
<u>for Puritans</u>, the date is the only element necessary to be added.
Frank Harris' biography of Shaw is classed in the seventh number in Table IV, which is "6". Within Shaw's range of numbers
this is "PR 5366. " Harris is cuttered ".H35" within the range of
Cutter numbers ".A5-Z. " The complete number is "PR 5366 .H35. "

Frank Harris' <u>Bernard Shaw</u>, a biography.

PR----- The double letters for the subclass, English
literature.

5366 --- The integral number meaning biographical works
about Bernard Shaw.

.H35 --- The first Cutter number for the author of the
biography, Harris.

"PR 5367 .B4" is the number assigned to Eric Bentley's critical study entitled <u>Bernard Shaw</u>. "7" is the appropriate number in
Table IV for general criticism and "PR 5367" is the corresponding
number within Shaw's range of numbers. ".B4" is the Cutter number for the main entry, Bentley.

Eric Bentley's <u>Bernard Shaw</u>, a critical study.

PR----- The double letters for the subclass, English
literature.

5367 --- The integral number meaning criticism of
Bernard Shaw.

.B4 ---- The first Cutter number for the author of the
criticism, Bentley.

Authors With One Number or a Cutter Number

Authors with only one number or a Cutter number must use an
auxiliary table composed of reserved Cutter numbers to achieve
form divisions similar to those of other authors. Tables VIII,
VIII^a and VIII^b are designed for authors with one number. Tables
IX, IX^a, and IX^b are for authors with only a Cutter number. (See
Figures 39 and 16.) Tables VIII and IX are intended for authors
who wrote very few works but have had a good deal of material

written about them.   Tables VIII^a and IX^a are used primarily for nineteenth and twentieth century authors.   Tables VIII^b and IX^b are rarely used at all.   Table IX^a may be used as an example of these tables. (See also Figure 39.)

Table IX^a

(x equals the Cutter number assigned)

Collected works.

. x	By date.
. xA11-14	By editor.
. xA15	Collected novels.
. xA16	Essays, Miscellanies, etc.
. xA17	Collected poems.
. xA19	Collected plays.

Translations.

. xA2-29	English. By translator.
. xA3-39	French. By translator.
. xA4-49	German. By translator.
. xA5-59	Other. By language.
. xA6-Z4	Separate works.
. xZ5-99	Biography and criticism.

The majority of the range of Cutter numbers, A-Z, is given to separate works, A6-Z4. Biography and criticism has only the end of the range, Z5-99.

Gertrude Stein, an American author, is an example of a Cutter number author. Her number is "PS 3537 . T323. " (See Figure 40.) "PS" means American literature; "PS 3537" is the number within American literature for modern authors whose last name begins with "S"; and ". T323" is the Cutter number for Stein based on the "-tein" part of the name as the "S" has already been designated in the number "3537. " Stein's novel, The Making of Americans, is classed "PS 3537 . T323M3. " In Table IX^a ". T323" equals "x" and "M3" is the Cutter number for the title of the novel, "Making. " This Cutter number is taken from the range of "A6-Z4" for separate works.

Gertrude Stein's The Making of Americans.

PS----- The double letters for the subclass, American literature.

3537 --- The integral number meaning modern American authors whose last name begins with the letter "S".

. T323-- The first Cutter number for Stein.

M3 ---- The second Cutter number for the title, Making...

The Autobiography of Alice B. Toklas, an autobiographical work by Miss Stein, is classed "PS 3537 . T323 Z525. " "Z525" is one of first numbers in the range of Cutter numbers for biography and criticism, "Z5-99. " This early number is chosen as autobiographical material regularly precedes biographical material. The "Z525" is merely a device to achieve this locational purpose. With another author in a similar circumstance a different number might be used to achieve the same result. There is no single number to be used for autobiographical work of Cutter number authors.

Stein's The Autobiography of Alice B. Toklas.

PS----- The double letters for the subclass, American literature.

3537 --- The integral number meaning modern American authors whose last name begins with the letter "S".

. T323-- The first Cutter number for Stein.

Z525--- The second Cutter number for autobiographical material.

A criticism of Stein by Donald Sutherland, Gertrude Stein: A Biography of Her Work, is classed "PS 3537 . T323 Z83. " The "Z83" represents the Cutter number for the main entry, Sutherland. "83" is chosen to place this work nearer the end of the alphabet as "S" is nearer the end of the alphabet. Of course, "83" does not regularly mean "Su. " It only means it in this particular case.

Donald Sutherland's Gertrude Stein: A Biography of Her Work.

PS----- The double letters for the subclass, American literature.

3537 --- The integral number meaning modern American authors whose last name begins with the letter "S".

. T323 -- The first Cutter number for Stein.

Z83 ---- The second Cutter number meaning a biography or criticism. (See the preceding discussion for the full meaning of this number.)

COMPLEX TABLES OF GEOGRAPHICAL DIVISIONS

Perhaps the most typographically complex auxiliary tables are the "Tables of Geographical Divisions" in Class H, Social Sciences. Ten tables make use of a single column of geographical locations. (See Figure 17.) The reader should carefully follow the examples given below with the classification schedule to acquaint himself with the typographical features of these tables. The use of these tables is further complicated by the fact that the subject subdivisions are represented by tables within the schedules. For instance, works dealing with labor in geographic areas other than the United States must be classed within the range of HD 8101-8942 using Table VIII. Following this statement of the range of numbers in the schedule is the table for subject subdivisions for twenty number countries, ten number countries and five number countries. A condensed form of this particular table is shown below. See Figures 41 and 42 for the two pages of Table VIII.

Table VIII

20 nos.	10 nos.	5 nos.	
			Documents.
(1)	(1)	(1)	General.
(2)			State.
(3)	(2)	(2)	Associations and periodicals.
(4)			Conferences.
(5)	(3)		Annuals
(6)			Directories.
(7)			Statistics.

20 nos.	10 nos.	5 nos.	
(8)	(4)	(3)	History (General).
			General works and history.
			By period.
(9)	(5)		Early to 1848.
(10)	(6)		Later, 1849-1945.
(11)	(6. 5)	(3. 5)	1945—
(13)	(7)		Biography, A-Z.
			. A1 Collective.
	(8)		Labor in politics.
(15)			General works.
(16)			Chartist movement (Great Britain).
(17)			Local, A-Z.
(18)	(8. 5)		Immigrant labor, by race, A-Z.
(19)	(9)	(4)	By state, A-Z.
(20)	(10)	(5)	By city, A-Z.

Twenty Number Countries

Before using Table VIII, however, the classifier must determine the range of geographic numbers available to the geographic
area in question. For instance, in Table VIII, Great Britain has a
range of numbers beginning with "281. " (See Figure 43.) The next
country in the column for Table VIII is Austria which begins with
"301". (See Figure 44.) This means that Great Britain has a range
of numbers from 281 to 301. Great Britain is thus a twenty number
country and her last number is "300. " These twenty numbers are
to be applied to the subject subdivisions for a twenty number geographic division. For example, a general historical work on British labor history entitled Essays in Labour History by Asa Briggs
is classed in the following fashion. As Great Britain is a twenty
number country in Table VIII beginning with number 281, the twenty
number column of the table for HD 8101-8942 is used. A general
historical work will use the eighth number in the table and hence
the eighth number in Great Britain's range of 281 through 300. The
eighth number in that range is 288. This number is then added to

the base number for labor in areas other than the United States.
This base is HD 8101. However, a footnote instructs the classifier
to add the country number directly to 8100. This gives the number
HD 8388. Cuttering for the main entry, Briggs, gives ". B7. " The
completed number is "HD 8388 . B7. "

> Asa Briggs' Essays in Labour History, (i. e., British
> Labor history).
>
> HD----- The double letters for the subclass, Economic
> history.
>
>> 8100---the base number for foreign labor as
>> given in the footnote.
>> 288---the adjusted country number meaning
>> _____ a general historical work on labor
>> 8388 in Great Britain.
>
> 8388 --- The integral number meaning a general histori-
> cal work on labor in Great Britain.
>
> . B7 ---- The first Cutter number for the main entry,
> Briggs.

Another example of this may be seen in Arthur Redford's
Labour Migration in England, 1800-1850, which is classed "HD
8389 . R4. " This is an "early to 1848" general work and history
and thus uses the ninth number in the subject table. The ninth
number in Great Britain's range is 289. When 289 is added to
8100, the base number for labor in areas other than the United
States, the result is 8389. This is the correct class number for
this work, "HD 8389. " ". R4" is simply cuttering for the main
entry.

> Arthur Redford's Labour Migration in England, 1800-1850.
>
> HD----- The double letters for the subclass, Economic
> history.
>
>> 8100---the base number for foreign labor as
>> given in the footnote.
>> 289---the adjusted country number meaning
>> _____ work on early British labor history.
>> 8389
>
> 8389 --- The integral number meaning a work on early
> British labor history.
>
> . R4 ---- The first Cutter number for the main entry,
> Redford.

Another example is the classification of The Age of Chartists, 1832-1854 by John Lawrence Le Breton Hammond. This work is classed "HD 8396 .H3." The sixteenth number in this case is for the Chartist movement in the subject table and the sixteenth number in Great Britain's range is 296. 296 added to 8100 gives HD 8396.

John Hammond's The Age of Chartists, 1832-1854.

HD-----The double letters for the subclass, Economic history.

      8100---the base number for foreign labor as given in the footnote.
      <u>296</u>---the adjusted country number meaning
      8396   the Chartist movement in Great Britain.

8396 ---The integral number meaning a work on the Chartist movement in Great Britain.

.H3 ----The first Cutter number for the main entry, Hammond.

Ten Number Countries

An example of a ten number geographic area is Europe. In Table VIII Europe has a range of 271 to 281. (See Figure 43.) A work on labor in relation to the Common Market by Val Schur entitled Labour in Britain and the Six is classed "HD 8376.5 .S35." This would be a current work on labor and would use the "6.5" number in the table for ten number countries. (See Figure 7.) This number adjusted to Europe's range of numbers is 276.5. 276.5 added to 8100 as directed by the footnote gives 8376.5. Again the Cutter number for author is ".S35." The completed number is "HD 8376.5 .S35."

Val Schur's Labour in Britain and the Six.

HD----- The double letters for the subclass, Economic history.

      8100---the base number for foreign labor as given in the footnote.
      <u>276.5</u>--the adjusted country number meaning
      8376.5   a work on current labor in Europe.

8376.5 - The integral number meaning a work on current labor in Europe.

.S35 --- The first Cutter number for the main entry, Schur.

Another example showing a further variation is the classification of Willard Beling's <u>Modernization and African Labor: A Tunisian Case Study</u>. Tunis is within the geographic division for French possessions in Africa. French possessions in Africa in Table VIII is 701 to 711 which equals ten numbers. (See Figure 45, 45a.) Tunis would be treated as a state in this geographic area. The ninth number for ten number countries is for states, A-Z. The ninth number in the range of numbers for French possessions in Africa is 709. This added to 8100 is 8809. The Cutter number for Tunis is ". T8" and a second Cutter number for the author is "B4. " The completed number is "HD 8809 . T8B4. "

> Willard Beling's <u>Modernization and African Labor: A Tunisian Case Study</u>.
>
> HD----- The double letters for the subclass, Economic history.
>
>   8100--the base number for foreign labor as given in the footnote.
>   709--the adjusted country number meaning
>   8809   French possessions in Africa.
>
> 8809 --- The integral number meaning a work concerned with labor in the French possessions in Africa.
>
> . T8 ---- The first Cutter number for an individual possession, Tunis.
>
> B4 ----- The second Cutter number for the main entry, Beling.

The tables in "H" present no great problems in use provided these steps are followed. First, the appropriate position in the schedule must be located. Second, the correct geographical table must be used. Third, the range of numbers within that table for a specific geographic area must be discerned. Fourth, that range of numbers must be applied to the appropriate table of subject subdivisions. Fifth, the adjusted geographic number must be added to the designated base number. This base number is usually given in a footnote. The classifier must always be careful to avoid simple errors in addition.

AN EXAMPLE OF A SPECIAL PROBLEM IN TABLE USE

The tables for individual oriental philosophers in subclass B represent a typical special problem in the use of tables. Two tables are given for Cutter number oriental philosophers. The first table is for three Cutter number philosophers (Figure 46) and the second table is for two Cutter number philosophers. (Figure 47.)

Individual philosophers, A-Z.

Under each (using successive Cutter numbers):

Three Cutter-number table.

(1)   Complete works.

(2)   Separate works. By title.

(3)   Biography, criticism, etc.

By author.

Two Cutter-number table.

(1)   .A1-3 Complete works.

.A4-Z Separate works.

(2)   .A-Z Biography, criticism, etc.

By author.

These tables are similar to many other tables which have already been discussed. The use of successive Cutter numbers creates no problem once the specific range of succession being applied by the Library of Congress is discerned. However, in discerning this range in this particular instance, an unusual development is found. These tables are not used for all oriental philosophers. For instance, Confucius and Hsun-tze are both worked out in the schedules and are neither three nor two number philosophers. The individual Chinese philosophers listed in the schedule are shown below. (See Figure 47.)

B 128 China.   Individual philosophers, A-Z.

Confucius.

.C6   Collections by two or more authors.

Translations.

.C7   English.

.C72   Latin.

.C75   Other, by language, A-Z.

.C8   Biography and criticism.

.H3 Han Fei.

    Hsun-tze.

.H65   Complete works.

.H66   Translations, By language, A-Z.
      Subarranged by translator.

.H67-69 Separate works (alphabetically).

.H7   Biography and criticism.

.K25 Kaibara, Ekken.

.K3   K'ang-hsi, emperor of China.

.M32 Mencius.

.M6   Mo, Ti.

.W3   Wang, Shou-jen.

.W8   Wu Ming Fu.

The philosopher Mencius is chosen to illustrate the problem in using this schedule and its tables. For example, the two or three Cutter number tables cannot be applied to the Chines philosopher Mencius. Mencius is given the Cutter number ".M32" in the schedule. In order to use this number the classifier must make a search of his own shelf list or both the Library of Congress printed author and subject catalogs. In this search the classifier will discern the following. The works of Mencius in the original language are classed "B128 .M32" with the second Cutter number for editor. For instance, an edition of the works of Mencius in Chinese edited by Chang is classed by the Library of Congress as "B 128 . M32 C5. " A similar edition edited by Miao is classed "B 128 . M32 M5. " An edition of Mencius translated into German by Richard Wilhelm is classed "B 128 . M33 G58. " An edition of Mencius translated into English by L. A. Lyall in 1932 is classed "B 128 . M33 E6. " Other English editions of Mencius are classed "B 128 . M33 E7, " Thomas Merton's edition; "B 128 . M33 E 8, " James R. Ware's translations; and "B 128 . M33 E54, " W. A. C. H. Dobson's translation. Biographical and critical works on Mencius are classed "B 128 . M35 C5, " Ch'eng's study of Mencius; "B 128 . M35 T3, " T'ai's study; "B 128 . M35 F3, " Faber's The Mind of Mencius; and "B 128 . M35 R5, " Richard's Mencius on the Mind. The following tabular analysis may be derived.

  B 128   Mencius

   .M32   Complete works in original language.
         By editor, A-Z.

.M33   Complete works in translation. By language, A-Z. Subarranged by translator.

.M35   Biography and criticism.

         By author.

It would seem to be a safe assumption that .M34 would be used for separate works of Mencius.

The Works of Mencius in Chinese, edited by Chang.

B------ The single letter for the subclass, Philosophy (General).

128 ---- The integral number for individual Chinese philosophers.

.M32 -- The first Cutter number for the individual philosopher, Mencius.

C5----- The second Cutter number for the editor, Chang.

The Works of Mencius in Chinese, edited by Miao.

B------ The single letter for the subclass, Philosophy (General).

128 ---- The integral number for individual Chinese philosophers.

.M32 -- The first Cutter number for the individual philosopher, Mencius.

M5 ---- The second Cutter number for the editor, Miao.

"The Works of Mencius" translated into German by Richard Wilhelm.

B------ The single letter for the subclass, Philosophy (General).

128 ---- The integral number for individual Chinese philosophers.

.M33 -- The first Cutter number for the individual philosopher, Mencius; with the successive element meaning translations.

G58---- The second Cutter number for the language of the translation, German.

The Works of Mencius translated into English by L. A. Lyall.

B------ The single letter for the subclass, Philosophy
        (General).

128 ---- The integral number for individual Chinese
        philosophers.

. M33 -- The first Cutter number for the individual
        philosopher, Mencius; with the successive
        element meaning translations.

E6----- The second Cutter number for the language of
        the translation, English.

Thomas Merton's edition of Mencius in English.

B------ The single letter for the subclass, Philosophy
        (General).

128 ---- The integral number for individual Chinese
        philosophers.

. M33 -- The first Cutter number for the individual
        philosopher, Mencius; with the successive
        element meaning translations.

E7----- The second Cutter number for the language of
        the translation, English.

James R. Ware's translation of Mencius in English.

B------ The single letter for the subclass, Philosophy
        (General).

128 ---- The integral number for individual Chinese
        philosophers.

. M33 -- The first Cutter number for the individual
        philosopher, Mencius; with the successive
        element meaning translations.

E8----- The second Cutter number for the language of
        the translation, English.

W. A. C. H. Dobson's translation of Mencius in English.

B------ The single letter for the subclass, Philosophy
(General).

128 ---- The integral number for individual Chinese
philosophers.

. M33 -- The first Cutter number for the individual
philosopher, Mencius; with the successive
element meaning translations.

E54---- The second Cutter number for the language of
the translation, English.

Ch'eng's biographical and critical study of Mencius.

B------ The single letter for the subclass, Philosophy
(General).

128 ---- The integral number for individual Chinese
philosophers.

. M35 -- The first Cutter number for the individual
philosopher, Mencius; with the successive
element meaning biography and criticism.

C5----- The second Cutter number for the author of the
criticism, Ch'eng.

T'ai's biographical and critical study of Mencius.

B------ The single letter for the subclass, Philosophy
(General).

128 ---- The integral number for individual Chinese
philosophers.

. M35 -- The first Cutter number for the individual
philosopher, Mencius; with the successive
element meaning biography and criticism.

T3----- The second Cutter number for the author of
the criticism, T'ai.

Faber's The Mind of Mencius.

B------ The single letter for the subclass, Philosophy (General).

128 ---- The integral number for individual Chinese philosophers.

. M35 -- The first Cutter number for the individual philosopher, Mencius; with the successive element meaning biography and criticism.

F3----- The second Cutter number for the author of the criticism, Faber.

Richard's Mencius on the Mind.

B------ The single letter for the subclass, Philosophy (General).

128 ---- The integral number for individual Chinese philosophers.

. M35 -- The first Cutter number for the individual philosopher, Mencius; with the successive element meaning biography and criticism.

R5----- The second Cutter number for the author, Richard.

After having determined this pattern a translation of Mencius' works into English by Lionel Giles which is not classed by the Library of Congress may be easily classed: "B 128 . M33 E56." This choice will place Giles' translation in its natural alphabetical sequence on the shelf.

Dobson	"B 128 . M33 E54"
Giles	"B 128 . M33 E56"
Lyall	"B 128 . M33 E6"
Merton	"B128 . M33 E7"
Ware	"B 128 . M33 E8"

Obviously the tables for three number or two number philosophers do not apply in the case of Mencius. In order to class Giles' translation of Mencius a full search must be made.

The philosopher Han Fei may be used as another example. In the schedules this Chinese philosopher is simply identified as ".H3."

In order to determine the range of his successive Cutter numbers a search of Library of Congress practice must be made. Original editions of Han Fei's works are classed "B 128 . H3. " Partial editions and edited texts are classed "B128 . H31. " An English translation of his works by W. K. Liao is classed "B 128 . H32 E55. " A biographical and critical study by Chung-ling Chou is classed "B128 . H34 C5. "

The Works of Han Fei in Chinese compiled by Hsien-shen Wang.

B------ The single letter for the subclass, Philosophy (General).

128 ---- The integral number for individual Chinese philosophers.

.H3---- The first Cutter number for the individual philosopher, Han Fei.

1896 --- The date of publication.

The Works of Han Fei with commentary by Ch'i-hsiung Liang.

B------ The single letter for the subclass, Philosophy (General).

128 ---- The integral number for individual Chinese philosophers.

.H31--- The first Cutter number for the individual philosopher, Han Fei; with the successive element for original language works with commentary.

L5----- The second Cutter number for the commentator, Laing.

An English translation of Han Fei by W. K. Liao.

B------ The single letter for the subclass, Philosophy (General).

128 ---- The integral number for individual Chinese philosophers.

.H32 ---The first Cutter number for the individual
philosopher, Han Fei; with the successive
element for translations.

E55 ----The second Cutter number for the language of
the translation with the decimal extension used
to interpolate for the alphabetizing of the translator's name, Liao.

A biographical and critical study by Chung-ling Chou of
Han Fei.

B------ The single letter for the subclass, Philosophy
(General).

128 ---- The integral number for individual Chinese
philosophers.

.H34--- The first Cutter number for the individual
philosopher, Han Fei; with the successive
element meaning biography and criticism.

C5----- The second Cutter number for the author of the
criticism, Chou.

From this set of four examples it may be discerned that the proper
table for Han Fei is not either of the tables provided for oriental
philosophers but rather Table V for Philosophers with Cutter numbers. (See also Figure 48.)

"For example, the Cutter number .B4 would be developed
thus:

Collected works.

(1)	. B4	Original texts. By date.
(2)	. B41	Partial editions, selections, etc.
		By editor.
(3)	. B42	Translations. By language, A-Z.
(4)	. B43	Separate works, A-Z.
(5)	. B44	General works.
		Biography, criticism, etc.

From these two examples it is apparent that the two tables for use
with oriental philosophers should be applied with extreme care in
original classification. However, it should be repeated that the
process used to determine the ranges of numbers for these two
philosophers is the correct process to use whenever assigning an
original call number in L. C. classification. The schedules are to
be used as a guide to classification but the schedule directions may
not always be followed. Library of Congress practice is far more
important than directions in the schedules.

BIBLIOGRAPHY

General Works Consulted for this Chapter

Grout, Catherine W. Explanation of the Tables Used in the Schedules of the Library of Congress Classification, Accompanied
by an Historical and Explanatory Introduction. New York:
Columbia University, School of Library Service, 1940.

LaMontagne, Leo E. American Library Classification with Special
Reference to the Library of Congress. Hamden, Conn.: Shoe
String Press, 1961.

Schedules Used for this Chapter

U. S. Library of Congress. Subject Cataloging Division. Classification. Class A. General Works, Polygraphy. 3d ed. Washington: 1947, reprinted with supplementary pages, 1963.

_____. Classification. Class B, Part 1, B-BJ. Philosophy.
2d ed. Washington: 1950, reprinted with supplementary pages,
1960.

_____. Classification. Class H. Social Sciences. 3d ed.
Washington: 1950, reprinted with supplementary pages, 1965.

_____. Classification. Class P. Subclasses PN, PR, PS,
PZ. Literature (general), English and American Literatures,
Fiction in English, Juvenile Literature. Washington: 1915,
reprinted with supplementary pages, 1964.

Figure 31

MUSEUMS

MUSEOGRAPHY AND MUSÉOLOGY

Cf. N400–490; QH61–71; T391–999.

AM

1   Periodicals, societies, collections, etc.

         Only publications devoted to the interests of museums, methodology, description, etc.

         Serials or collections of scientific contributions, memoirs, etc., on other subjects, in AC, AS, B–Z.

4   Early works (to 1800).

5   General treatises.

7   General special.

         Educational aspects, relations, etc.

8   Children's museums.

9   Minor. Pamphlets, etc.

     Museography.

10–99   By country.

         Under each country (Three numbers):

             (1)   General.

             (2)   States, provinces, etc.

             (3)   Cities, towns, etc.

         Under each country (Two numbers):

             (1)   .A1   Periodicals. Societies.

                    .A2   General.

                    .A3–Z   Provinces, etc.

             (2)   Cities, towns, etc.

         Under each country (One number):

             (1)   .A2   General.

             (2)   .A3–Z   Local.

10   America.

11–13   United States.

21–22   British America. Canada.

23–24   Mexico.

25–27   Central America.

29–31   West Indies.

33–35   South America.

40   Europe.

41–43   Great Britain.

44–45   Austria-Hungary.

46–48   France.

49–51   Germany.

Figure 31a

Museography.
  By country.
    Europe—Continued.

52–53	Greece.
54–55	Italy.
	Netherlands.
56	Belgium.
57–59	Holland.
60–61	Russia.
	Scandinavia.
62	Denmark.
63	Norway.
64	Sweden.
65–66	Spain and Portugal.
67–68	Switzerland.
69	Turkey and the Balkan states.
70	Other European countries, A–Z.
71	Asia.
72	China.
73	India.
74	Indochina.
75–76	Indonesia.
77–78	Japan.
79	Other Asiatic countries, A–Z.
80	Africa.
85–86	British Africa.
87–88	Egypt.
89	French Africa.
90	German Africa.
91	Other African countries, A–Z.
93–95	Australia.
99–100	Pacific Islands.
101	**Individual museums, A–Z.**

        Alphabetically by name.
        Under each (using successive Cutter numbers):

(0)	Collections, etc.
(1)	Acts of incorporation, statutes, by-laws, rules, and regulations. By date.
(2)	Administration. List of officers, etc.
(2.5)	Examinations.
(3)	Annual reports.
(4)	Other serials: Periodicals, collections, memoirs, etc.
(4.5)	Other minor official reports. By date.
(5)	Guidebooks, catalogs. By date.
(5.2)	Special minor exhibits. By date.

Figure 32

TABLES OF SUBDIVISIONS UNDER COUNTRIES (AY410–1725)

I (Ten numbers)

		Early (to 1800).
(0)		Collections, by date of first volume.
(1)	.A–Z5	Serial, by title or editor.
	.Z7	Other, by date.
(2)		Yearbooks (without almanacs).

Prefer classification by subject in Classes B–Z.

1800–

(3)		Collections.
(4)		General, by title or editor.
(5)		Newspaper, etc., by name of place, subarranged by title.
(6)		Other.
	.A3–Z3	Literary and magazine almanacs, etc., by title or editor.
	.Z5	Miscellaneous. Occasional issues. By date.
(7)		Almanacs in foreign languages, by language, A–Z.
(8)		Special, by subject, A–Z.

Cf. AY81.

Prefer classification by subject in Classes B–Z.

e. g.   Prophetic almanacs, *see* BF1651.

(9)		Local, by place, A–Z.

II (Two numbers)

(1)	Collections and general.
(2)	Local, by place, A–Z.

III (One number or Cutter number)

(1)	.A2	Collections.
(2)	.A3	Serial.
(3)	.A4–Z	Local, by place,

Figure 33

19th century, 1770/1800–1890/1900.
Individual authors—Continued.

4161.B2	Boucicault, Dion.
.B3	Bourdillon, Francis William.
.B4	Bowles, William Lisle.
.B42	Bowring, Sir John.
.B45	Boyd, Andrew Kennedy Hutchison.
	Braddon, Mary E., see Maxwell, Mrs. Mary Elizabeth (Braddon).
	Bradley, Katherine Harris, see Field, Michael, *pseud.*
.B57	Bray, Anna Eliza (Kempe).
.B6	Bridges, Robert.
.B7	Bristed, Charles Astor.
4162–4163	Brontë, Anne (XII).
4165–4169	**Brontë, Charlotte (VII).**
	(Including works on the Brontë family.)
4172–4173	Brontë, Emily (XII).
4174.B4	Brooks, Charles Shirley.
.B55	Broughton, John Cam Hobhouse, 1st baron.
.B6	Brown, George Douglas.
4175.B2	Brown, Dr. John.
.B5	Brown, Thomas Edward.
.B7	Browne, Thomas Alexander ("Rolf Boldrewood").
4180–4198	**Browning, Elizabeth Barrett (III^a).**
	Separate works.
4185	Aurora Leigh.
4186	Casa Guidi windows.
4187	Lady Geraldine's courtship.
4188	Poems before Congress.
4189	Sonnets from the Portuguese.
4190	Other, A–Z.
4205–4248	**Browning, Robert (II).**
	Separate works.
4205	The blot on the 'scutcheon.
4206	Dramatic idyls.
4207	Dramatic lyrics.
4208	Dramatic romances.
4209	Dramatic personae.
4210	In a balcony.
4211	Jocoseria.
4212	King Victor and Prince Charles.
4213	Luria.
4214	Men and women.
4215	Paracelsus.
4216	Parleyings.
4217	Pauline.
4218	Pippa passes.
4219	Ring and the book.
4220	Sordello.
4221	Strafford.
4222	Other, A–Z.
4250.B5	Browning, Samuel.

Figure 34

TABLE OF SUBDIVISIONS UNDER INDIVIDUAL AUTHORS.

May be modified in application to specific cases whenever it seems desirable.

I (98 nos.)	II (48 nos.)		Authors with forty-eight or ninety-eight numbers.
			Collected works.
0	0 or	50	Original editions, and reprints. By date.
			To 1500: A00–A99.
			1500–1599: B00–B99.
			1600–1699: C00–C99.
			1700–1799: D00–D99.
			1800–1899: E00–E99.
			1900–1999: F00–F99.
1	1	51	Editions with commentary etc. By editor, A–Z.
2	2	52	Selected works. Minor works. Inedited works, fragments, etc.
3	3	53	Selections. Anthologies. Extracts.
4	4	54	Translaiions. By language; subarranged by translator.
			.F5, French.
			.G5, German.
			.I5, Italian.
			.S5, Spanish.
			.Z5, Other.
5–40	5–22	55–72	Separate works, alphabetically by title.
			(Only the more important have a special number or numbers assigned to them, the lesser works are to have Cutter numbers.)
			For subdivisions where one number is assigned to a work use Table X. For Cutter numbers, use Table XI.
			Under each:
			0 │ Texts.
			0 │ 0 By date.
			1 │ 1 By editor.
			2 │ 2 Selections.

Figure 35

SUBDIVISIONS UNDER INDIVIDUAL AUTHORS

I (98 nos.)	II (48 nos.)		Authors with forty-eight or ninety-eight numbers.
			Biography, Criticism, etc.—Continued.
52	30	80	Dictionaries, Indexes, etc.
			General encyclopedic dictionaries only.
			Special dictionaries with subject.
			e. g. Characters, see 78 (Table I); 39, 89 (Table II).
			Concordances and dictionaries, see 91-92 (Table I); 45, 95 (Table II).
			General works.
53	31.A2	81.A2	Autobiography.
54	.A3	.A3	Journals; Letters; Memoirs.
55	.A5–Z	.A5–Z	General works.
56			Early life. Education.
57	32	82	Love and marriage. Relation to women.
58			Later life.
59	33	83	Relations to contemporaries. Times, etc.
			Cf. 73 (Table I); 36, 86 (Table II).
60	34	84	Homes and haunts. Local associations.
			Landmarks.
			Cf. DA.
61			Anniversaries. Celebrations.
62			Memorial addresses. Treatment in literature.
63			Poetry.
64	35	85	Fiction.
65			Iconography.
			Portraits.
66			Monuments.
67			Relics.
68	36	86	Authorship.
69			Manuscripts. Authorship.
			For textual criticism, see 89 (Table I); 43, 93 (Table II).
70			Forgeries, etc.
			Cf. 42, 43, 45 (Table I); 23–4, 73–4 (Table II).
71			Sources.
72			Forerunners.
73			Associates. Followers. Circle. School.
			Cf. 59 (Table I); 33, 83 (Table II).

Figure 36

SUBDIVISIONS UNDER INDIVIDUAL AUTHORS

I (98 nos.)	II (48 nos.)		Authors with forty-eight or ninety-eight numbers.
			Authorship—Continued.
74			Allusions.
75	37	87	Chronology of works.
			Criticism and interpretation.
76	38	88	General works. Genius, etc.
			Prefer 55 (Table I); 31, 81 (Table II).
77			Philosophy.
			Prefer 76 or 82 (Table I), and corresponding numbers of Table II.
			Characters.
78	39	89	General.
			Special.
79			Groups, Classes.
			e. g. Women.
80	40	90	Individual.
81	41	91	Plots, Scenes, Time, etc.
	42.A–Z	92.A–Z	Treatment and knowledge of special subjects.
82			Philosophy. Religion. Ethics.
83			Law, Politics, etc.
84			History.
85			Art.
86			Nature.
87			Science.
88			Other, A–Z.
89	43	93	Textual criticism, commentaries, etc.
			To include discussion of manuscripts of classical or medieval authors and works.
90	44	94	Language, Style, etc.
			Prefer 76 (Table I); 38, 88 (Table II).
91	45	95	Dictionaries. Concordances.
92			Dictionaries.
			Concordances.
	46	96	Grammar.
93			General.
			Special.
94			Use of words.
95			Syntax.
96	47	97	Versification, meter, rhythm, etc.
97	48	98	Dialect, etc.

Figure 37

19th century, 1770/1800–1890/1900.
Individual authors.
Scott, Sir Walter.
Criticism—Continued.

5343	Special subjects, A–Z.
	5343.C7, Criticism.
	(Sir Walter Scott as a critic.)
5344	Textual criticism. Commentaries.
5345	Language. Style.
5346	Grammar.
5347	Versification.
5348	Dialect.
5349.S2	Scott, William Bell.
.S25	Seabridge, Charles.
.S4	Selby, Charles.
.S5	Sewell, Elizabeth M.
.S55	Sewell, Mrs. Mary (of Chertsey).
.S6	Sewell, Mrs. Mary (Wright).
.S8	Shairp, John Campbell.
5350–5358	Sharp, William (Fiona McLeod) (1Vᵃ).
5360–5368	Shaw, George Bernard (IVᵃ).
5360	Complete works (also collected dramas).
5361	Selections.
5362	Translations.
5363	Separate dramas, A–Z.
.A2,	The doctor's dilemma, etc.
.A25,	Misalliance, the dark lady of the sonnets, and Fanny's first play.
.A3,	Plays pleasant and unpleasant.
.A5,	Three plays for Puritans.
.A8–Z,	Separate dramas, A–Z.
	Other works.
5364	Collected.
5365	Separate, A–Z.
5376	Shee, Sir Martin Archer.
5377.S5	Sheehan, Patrick Augustine.
5379.S2	Sheil, Richard Lalor.
5397–5398	Shelley, Mary Wollstonecraft.
5400–5448	**Shelley, Percy Bysshe (II).**
	Collected works.
5400	Original editions, and reprints. By date.
5401	Editions with commentary, by editor, A–Z.
5402	Poems.
5403	Selections. Anthologies.
5404	Translations. By language, subarranged by translator.
5405	Prose works.
	Separate works. Table X.
5406	Adonais.
5407	Alastor.
5408	Cenci.
5409	Epipsychidion.

Figure 38

SUBDIVISIONS UNDER INDIVIDUAL AUTHORS

III	IV	Authors with eight or eighteen numbers.
		Collected works.
0	0	By date.
1	1	By editor.
2	2	Selections.
		Separate parts, see Separate works.
	3	Translations.
3	.A2A–Z	Modern English. By translator.
4	.A3–Z	Other, by language, subarranged by translator.
5–10	4.A–Z	Separate works.
		Under each:
		III, see Table X, or XI.
		IV, see Table XI.
11	5	Apocryphal, spurious works, etc.
12.A1–5	6.A1–19	Periodicals. Societies. Collections.
.A6–Z	.A2–3	Dictionaries, indexes, etc.
13	.A5–Z	Biography and criticism.
		Criticism.
14	7	General.
15		Textual. Manuscripts, etc.
		Special.
16		Sources.
17	8	Other, A–Z.
		e. g. Language, grammar, style, etc.
18		Language. Grammar. Style.
III*	IV*	Same as III and IV, using the following date letters:
		To 1500: A00–A99.
		1500–1599: B00–B99.
		1600–1699: C00–C99.
		1700–1799: D00–D99.
		1800–1899: E00–E99.
		1900–1999: F00–F99.
V (8 nos.)	VI (5 nos.)	**Single works with five or eight numbers.**
0	0 or 5	Texts (including texts with commentaries.)
		.A1, To 1800.
		.A2, 1801–1900, by date, when no editor is given.
		.A5–Z, 1801+, by editor.

Figure 39

SUBDIVISIONS UNDER INDIVIDUAL AUTHORS

VIII (1 no.)	IX (Cutter no.)	Authors with one number or Cutter number.* Use Tables VIII^a and IX^a when possible.
		Collected works.
.A1	.x	By date.
.A11–19	.xA11–19	By editor (alphabetically).
		Translations.
.A2–29	.xA2–29	English. By translator.
.A3–39	.xA3–39	French. By translator.
.A4–49	.xA4–49	German. By translator.
.A5–59	.xA5–59	Other. By language.
.A6–69	.xA6–69	Separate works. By title.
.A8–Z	.xA8–Z	Biography and criticism.
		Collected works.

* In Table IX and modifications, x= Cutter number.

VIII^a (1 no.)	IX^a (Cutter no.)	Authors with one number or Cutter number.
		Collected works.
.A1	.x	By date.
.A11–14	.xA11–14	By editor.
.A15	.xA15	Collected novels.
.A16	.xA16	Essays, Miscellanies, etc.
.A17	.xA17	Collected poems.
.A19	.xA19	Collected plays.
		Translations.
.A2–29	.xA2–29	English. By translator.
.A3–39	.xA3–39	French. By translator.
.A4–49	.xA4–49	German. By translator.
.A5–59	.xA5–59	Other. By language.
.A6–Z4	.xA6–Z4	Separate works.
.Z5A–Z	.xZ5–99	Biography and criticism.

150

Figure 40

ADDITIONS AND CHANGES TO MARCH 1963

PS

3535	R—Continued.
.I224	Rice, Elmer L.
.I429	Richter, Conrad.
.I436	Ridge, Lola.
.I43627	Riding, Laura.
.I46	Riesenberg, Felix.
.I645	Riggs, Lynn.
.I73	Rinehart, Mary (Roberts).
.I866	Ritchie, Ward.
.I88	Rittenhouse, Jessie Belle.
.O172	Roberts, Elizabeth Madox.
.O176	Roberts, Kenneth Lewis.
.O25	Robinson, Edwin Arlington.
.O758	Rosten, Norman.
.U4	Rukeyser, Muriel.
.U52	Runyon, Damon.
3537	S.
.A618	Sandburg, Carl.
.A667	Sandoz, Mari.
.A795	Sarett, Lew R.
.A826	Saroyan, William.
.C16	Scarborough, Dorothy.
.C164	Scarborough, Robert Lee.
.C26	Schauffler, Robert Haven.
.C54	Schneider, Isidor.
.C79	Schwartz, Delmore.
.C89	Scott, Evelyn.
.E22	Sedgwick, Anne Douglas.
.E26	Seeger, Alan.
.H27	Shapiro, Karl Jay.
.H3	Sharp, Dallas Lore.
.H384	Shaw, Irwin.
.H524	Sheean, Vincent.
.H693	Shepard, Odell.
.H775	Sherman, Stuart Pratt.
.H825	Sherwood, Robert Emmet.
.K53	Skinner, Constance Lindsay.
.K533	Skinner, Cornelia Otis.
.M2895	Smith, Betty.
.M327	Smith, Chard Powers.
.M835	Smith, Thorne.
.M89	Smith, Winchell.
.P54	Spewack, Bella (Cohen).
.P543	Spewack, Samuel.
.P56	Speyer, Leonora (von Stosch).
.T246	Starrett, Vincent.
.T252	Stead, Christina.
.T2787	Steele, Wilbur Daniel.
.T316	Stegner, Wallace Earle.
.T323	Stein, Gertrude.
.T3234	Steinbeck, John.

Figure 41

Labor. By country.
United States—Continued.
Labor in politics.
8076   General works.
8079   Local, A–Z.
(8080)   Negro labor, *see* E 185.8.
8081   Immigrant labor, by race, A–Z.
    .A1–5 General.
    .A5   Nonofficial works.
    Under each (using successive Cutter numbers):
    .A1–5 General.
          Documents.
    .A15   Serial.
    .A2   Other. By date.
    .A6–Z Nonofficial works.
8083   By state or region, A–W.
8085   By city, A–Z.
    Under each:
      (1) Associations (General).
      (2) Directories.
      (3) Other.
8101–8942 **Other countries.** Table VIII,[1] modified.
    In connection with HD 8455, compare HD 7887–7889 and
      HX 279.
    Under each:

20 nos.	10 nos.	5 nos.	
			Documents.
(1)	(1)	(1)	General.
			Department of labor.
			e. g. "Ministère du travail."
.A1–3			Serial publications, in order of priority of first issue.
.A4–9			Special bureaus.
			Legislative documents.
.B1–4			House.
			Serial.
			Special.
.B5–8			Senate.
			Serial.
			Special.
.C			Commissions. By date.
(2)			State.
(3)	(2)	(2)	Associations and periodicals.

    To include non-technical reports of
      mechanics institutes, Gewerbever-
      eine, etc. Technical publications,
      in T.

[1] For Table VIII, *see* p. 527–532. Add country number in Table to 8100.

Figure 42

Labor. By country.

8101–8942 Other countries. Table VIII. [1]

Under each—Continued.

20 nos.	10 nos.	5 nos.	
(4)			Conferences.
(5)	(3)		Annuals.
(6)			Directories.
(7)			Statistics.
(8)	(4)	(3)	History (General).
			General works and history.
			By period.
(9)	(5)		Early to 1848.
(10)	(6)		Later, 1849–
(13)	(7)		Biography, A–Z.
			.A1 Collective.
	(8)		Labor in politics.
(15)			General works.
(16)			Chartist movement (Great Britain).
(17)			Local, A–Z.
(18)	(8.5)		Immigrant labor, by race, A–Z.
			e. g. .A2 General works.
			.N5 Negro.
(19)	(9)	(4)	By state, A–Z.
			Under each:
			(1) Collections. (Documents in subdivisions (1)–(2) above).
			(2) General works. History.
			(3) Other.
(20)	(10)	(5)	By city, A–Z.
			Under each:
			(1) Early to 1848.
			(2) 1848–

NOTE. For Pacific islands use:

8931	General.	
8933	American possessions.	
8934	Hawaii.	
8935	Other.	
8936–8937	British possessions.	Under each:
8938–8939	French possessions.	(1) General.
8940–8941	German possessions (Former).	(2) Local, A–Z.
8942	Other.	

[1] For Table VIII, *see* p. 527–532. Add country number in Table to 8100.

Figure 43

TABLES OF GEOGRAPHICAL DIVISIONS

I	II	III	IV		V	VI	VII	VIII	IX	X
24	45	65	85	West Indies	20	16	101	91	51	241
24.5	47	68	89	Bahamas	20.5	------	106	96	53	246
25	49	71	93	Cuba	21	------	111	101	56	251
26	51	74	97	Haiti	22	------	121	111	61	261
26.5	52	76	99	Santo Domingo	22.5	------	126	116	64	266
27	53	77	101	Jamaica	23	------	131	121	66	271
28	55	80	105	Puerto Rico	24	------	141	131	71	281
28.5	56.5	83	109	Virgin Islands of the United States (Danish West Indies).	24.5	------	150.5	141-3 [1]	75.5	286
29	57	85	112	Other	25	------	------	------	75.7	-----
----	----	----		British West Indies..	-------	------	151	144	------	291
				Barbadoes.						
				Bermudas.						
				Falkland Islands.						
				Leeward Islands.						
				Trinidad.						
				Windward Islands.						
----	----	----		Dutch West Indies...	-------	------	157	147	------	297
				Curaçao.						
----	----	----		French West Indies and other island possessions.[2]	-------	------	159	149	------	299
				Guadeloupe.						
				Martinique.						
				Miquelon.						
				St. Pierre.						
30	58	86	113	South America	26	18	161	151	76	301
31	59	89	117	Argentine Republic	27-30	20	171	161	81	311
32	61	92	121	Bolivia	31	25	181	171	86	321
33	63	95	125	Brazil	32-35	28	191	181	91	331
34	65	98	129	Chile	36	33	201	191	96	341
35	67	101	133	Colombia	37	38	211	201	101	351
36	69	104	137	Ecuador	38	40	221	211	106	361
37	71	107	141	Guiana	39	42	231	221	111	371
----	----	----		British	---------	------	------	------	------	-----
----	----	----		Dutch	---------	------	------	------	------	-----
----	----	----		French	---------	------	------	------	------	-----
38	73	110	145	Paraguay	40	44	241	231	116	381
39	75	113	149	Peru	41	46	251	241	121	391
40	77	116	153	Uruguay	42	48	261	251	126	401
41	79	119	157	Venezuela	43	50	271	261	131	411
42	81	122	161	Europe	44	52	281	271	136	421
43	83	125	165	Great Britain [3]	45-48	54	291	281	141	431
44	85	128	169	England and Wales	--------	60	301	------	------	441
45	87	131	173	Scotland	---------	62	311	------	------	451
46	89	133	177	Ireland	---------	64	321	------	------	461
----	----	----		Colonial possessions in general.	---------	------	------	------	------	-----
I	II	III	IV		V	VI	VII	VIII	IX	X

[1] Cf. HG 2701–3540.
[2] May be used for all French possessions in America or combinations of several of them.
[3] May be used for British Empire, "Greater Britain," etc.

Figure 44

TABLES OF GEOGRAPHICAL DIVISIONS

I	II	III	IV		V	VI	VII	VIII	IX	X
				Europe—Continued.						
47	91	136	181	Austria................	49–52	66	331	301	151	471
				States and Provinces A-Z	------	-----	-----	-----	-----	----
				Austria, Lower. Görz and Gradiska.						
				Austria, Upper. Istria.						
				Bohemia. Moravia.						
				Bosnia and Herze- Salzburg.						
				govina. Silesia.						
				Buckowina. Styria.						
				Carinthia. Trieste.						
				Carniola. Tyrol.						
				Dalmatia. Vorarlberg.						
				Galicia.						
				Czechoslovak Republic[1]	------	-----	-----	-----	-----	----
	----	----	----	Hungary[1]...............	------	-----	-----	-----	-----	----
	----	----	----	Croatia and Slavonia[1]	------	-----	-----	-----	-----	----
	----	----	----	Transylvania[1].........	------	-----	-----	-----	-----	----
	----	----	----	Liechtenstein[1]........	------	-----	-----	-----	-----	----
48	93	139	185	France..................	53–56	70	341	321	161	481
	----	----	----	Colonial possessions in general.	------	-----	-----	-----	-----	----
	----	----	----	Andorra.................	------	-----	-----	-----	-----	----
	----	----	----	Monaco..................	------	-----	-----	-----	-----	----
49	95	142	189	Germany.................	57–60	75	351	341	171	491
				Alsace-Lorraine. Oldenburg.						
				Anhalt. PRUSSIA.						
				BADEN. Reuss, Elder branch.						
				BAVARIA. Reuss, Younger branch.						
				Bremen. Saxe-Altenburg.						
				Brunswick. Saxe-Coburg-Gotha.						
				Hamburg. Saxe-Meiningen.						
				Hanover. Saxe-Weimar.						
				Hesse. SAXONY.						
				Lippe. Schaumburg-Lippe.						
				Lübeck. Schwarzburg-Rudolstadt.						
				Mecklenburg- Schwarzburg-Sondershausen.						
				Schwerin. Thuringia.						
				Mecklenburg- Waldeck.						
				Strelitz. WÜRTTEMBERG.						
	----	----	----	Colonial possessions in general.	------	-----	-----	-----	-----	----
50	97	145	193	Greece..................	61	80	361	361	181	501
51	99	148	197	Italy...................	62–65	85	371	371	186	511
	----	----	----	San Marino..............	------	-----	-----	-----	-----	----
52	101	151	201	Netherlands (Low Countries)	--------	90	381	391	196	521
53	103	154	205	Belgium.................	66–69	95	391	401	201	531
54	105	157	209	Netherlands (Holland)...	70–73	100	401	411	206	541
54.5	106.5	159.5	212.5	Luxemburg...............	73.5	104.5	410.5	420.5	210.5	550.5
55	107	160	213	Russia..................	74–77	105	411	421	211	551
55.2	108.2	162.2	216.2	Estonia.................	77.2	109.2	420.5	430.2	215.3	560.5
55.3	108.3	162.3	217	Finland.................	77.3	110	421	431	215.5	561
55.5	108.5	162.5	217.5	Latvia..................	77.5	110.5	425.5	435.5	215.6	565.5
55.6	108.6	162.6	217.6	Lithuania	77.6	110.6	425.7	435.7	215.65	565.6
55.7	108.7	162.7	218	Poland..................	77.7	111	426	436	215.7	566
56	109	163	219	Scandinavia.............	78	112	430	440	216	570
57	111	166	221	Denmark.................	79	115	431	441	221	571
58	113	169	225	Iceland.................		120	441	451	226	581
59	115	172	229	Norway..................	80	125	451	461	231	591
60	117	175	233	Sweden..................	81–84	130	461	471	236	601
I	II	III	IV		V	VI	VII	VIII	IX	X

[1] May be arranged with "States and Provinces."

Figure 45

TABLES OF GEOGRAPHICAL DIVISIONS

I	II	III	IV	Asia—Continued.	V	VI	VII	VIII	IX	X
74	145	217	289	Indonesia	103	------	------	------	------	741
75	147	220	293	Dutch East Indies¹	104	------	591	601	301	751
76	149	223	297	Philippine Islands	105	------	601	611	306	761
77	151	226	301	Japan	107	165	611	621	311	771
....	....	....		Korea	--------	------	------	------	------	-----
78	153	229	305	Persia. Iran	109	168	621	631	316	781
79	155	232	309	Russia in Asia	111	170	631	641	321	791
----	----	----		Central Asia	--------	------	------	------	------	-----
----	----	----		Siberia	--------	------	------	------	------	-----
----	----	----		Siam	--------	------	------	------	------	-----
80	157	235	313	Turkey in Asia	113	173	641	651	326	801
81	159	238	317	Other divisions of Asia²	115	175	651	661	331	811
82	161	241	321	Africa	117	180	661	671	336	821
83	163	244	325	Egypt	119	182	671	681	341	831
84	165	247	329	British possessions³	121	184⁴	681	691	346	841

UNION OF SOUTH AFRICA:
Cape of Good Hope.
Basutoland.
Natal.
Zululand
(Orange Free State; to 1900).
(Orange River Colony, 1900-1910).
Orange Free State, 1910-
(South African Republic to 1900).
Transvaal, 1900-
Swaziland.
SOUTH CENTRAL AFRICA:
Bechuanaland.
Nyasaland.
Rhodesia.
Northeastern.
Northwestern.
Southern.
Mashonaland.
Matabeleland.

EAST AFRICA:
British East Africa.
East Africa Protectorate.
Uganda.
Zanzibar.
Somaliland.
WEST AFRICA:
Gambia.
Gold Coast.
Ashanti.
Lagos.
Nigeria.
Northern.
Southern.
Sierra Leone.
ISLANDS:
Atlantic Ocean:
Ascension.
St. Helena.
Tristan da Cunha.
Indian Ocean.
Mauritius.
Seychelles.

| 85 | 167 | 250 | 333 | French possessions | 122 | ------ | 691 | 701 | 351 | 851 |

Algeria.
Tunis.
WEST AFRICA:
Dahomey.
Guinea.
Ivory Coast.
Mauritania.
Senegal. Upper Senegal and Niger.

Kongo.
Somali Coast.
ISLANDS:
Madagascar.
Comoro Islands.
Mayotte.
Réunion.

| I | II | III | IV | | V | VI | VII | VIII | IX | X |

¹ United States of Indonesia.

² By division, A-Z, unless otherwise provided for; e. g. .K8, Korea; .P3, Palestine. Cf. HF 3221-4040, Table VII, Note 4: HF 3865, Korea; HF 3868, Siam. Cf. HE 6651-7500, Table X, Modifications: HE 7315, Korea; HE 7317, Siam.

³ The general number or numbers may be used for the Union of South Africa as a whole, unless otherwise provided for. Cf. HE 6651-7500, Table X, Modifications: HE 7343, South Africa, Union of South Africa.

⁴ Cf. HG 8724-8725, British Africa.

Figure 45a

TABLES OF GEOGRAPHICAL DIVISIONS

I	II	III	IV		V	VI	VII	VIII	IX	X
				Africa—Continued.						
86	169	253	337	German possessions....	123	------	701	711	356	861
				(Former).						
				Cameroons.	Southwest Africa.					
				East Africa.	Togoland.					
86.5	170	255	340	Italian possessions......	124	------	706-7	716-17	358-9	866-7
				Kongo Free State.[1]						
----	----	----		Congo Belge.......	---------	------	709	719	------	-----
87	171	256	341	Portuguese possessions.[2]	125	------	711	721	361	871
				Angola, West Africa.	Guinea.					
				Cape Verde Islands.	Principe and S. Thomé					
				East Africa.	Islands.					
87.5	172.5	258.5	344.5	Spanish possessions....	125.5	186.5	720.5	730.5	365.5	880.5
88	173	259	345	Other divisions, native	126	187	721	731	366	881
				states, etc.[3]						
----	----	----		Ethiopia.............	---------	------	------	------	------	-----
----	----	----		Liberia.............	---------	------	------	------	------	-----
----	----	----		Morocco.............	---------	------	------	------	------	-----
89	175	262	349	Australia and New Zealand[4]	130[5]	190	731	741	371	891
90	177	265	353	New South Wales......	---------	------	741	751	376	901
91	179	268	357	New Zealand...........	---------	------	751	761	381	911
92	181	271	361	North Australia........	---------	------	761	771	386	921
93	183	274	365	Queensland.............	---------	------	771	781	391	931
94	185	277	369	South Australia........	---------	------	781	791	396	941
95	187	280	373	Tasmania...............	---------	------	791	801	401	951
96	189	283	377	Victoria...............	---------	------	801	811	406	961
97	191	286	381	Western Australia......	---------	------	811	821	411	971
98	193	289	385	Pacific islands[6]...........	(7)	195[8]	821	831	416	981
				UNITED STATES POSSESSIONS:	GERMAN (Former):					
				Guam.	Bismarck Archipelago.					
				Hawaii.	Caroline Islands.					
				Samoa.	Kaiser Wilhelm's					
				BRITISH:	Land (New					
				Fiji.	Guinea).					
				Papua (New Guinea).	Marianne Islands.					
				Tonga (Friendly Islands).	Marshall Islands.					
				FRENCH:	Palau or Pelew Islands.					
				New Caledonia and	Solomon Islands.					
				dependencies.						
				Oceania (Tahiti, etc.).	Samoan Islands.					
99	195	292	389	Arctic regions.............	---------	200	------	------	------	991
100	197	295	393	Antarctic regions..........	---------	-----	-----	------	------	996
I	II	III	IV		V	VI	VII	VIII	IX	X

[1] Cf. HF 271.
[2] Cf. HE 7371-7380.
[3] By division, native state, etc., A-Z, unless otherwise provided for.
[4] May be used for Commonwealth of Australia.
[5] May be given 127-128. Cf. HD 2927-2928, 7957-7958, etc.
[6] By island or group of islands, A-Z, unless otherwise provided for. Cf. HD 2196-2206.
[7] May be given 130 or 130.5. Cf. Note 5; HD 2929-2930; HF 1400. etc.
[8] Cf. HG 8735-8739.

Figure 46

General works—Continued.

99   Other, by language, A–Z.

          Each subdivided like B 71–74, using successive Cutter numbers.

          e. g.   Dutch and Flemish.

             .D8   Early to 1800.

             .D82   1801–

                   Polish.

             .P6   Early to 1800.

             .P62   1801–

103   Compends for Catholic students.

105   Special topics, A–Z.

          e. g. .C5   Continuity.

             .H8   Humanism.

             .M6   Monism.

             .P6   Positivism.

             .W6 Women as philosophers.

General history of individual countries, *see* B 790–4628.

Ancient (600 B. C.–430 A. D.).

108   Collections.

        General works.

110   Latin.

111   English.

112   French.

113   German.

115   Other, by language, A–Z.

            e. g. .I7   Italian.

        Special topics.

118   Nature philosophy of the ancients.

Orient.

121   General works.

123   Special aspects of the subject as a whole.

          e. g. Buddhist philosophy.

By country.

       Under each:

         0 5   Collections.

         1 6   History, etc.

         2 7   Special topics, A–Z.

         3 8   Individual philosophers, A–Z.

              Under each (using successive Cutter numbers):

              Three Cutter-number table.

              (1)   Complete works.

              (2)   Separate works. By title.

              (3)   Biography, criticism, etc.

                  By author.

             Two Cutter-number table, *see* page 4.

Figure 47

B   PHILOSOPHY (GENERAL)   **B**

Orient.
  By country.
    Under each.
      Individual philosophers, A–Z.
        Under each—Continued.
          Two Cutter-number table.
            (1) .A1–3 Complete works.
                  .A4–Z Separate works.
                        By title.
            (2) .A–Z Biography, criticism,
                        etc. By author.

125–128	**China.**	
128	Individual philosophers, A–Z.	
	Confucius.	
	Cf. BL 1830–1870, Religion.	
	PL 2948, 3277–3278, The Confucian canon.	
.C6	Collections by two or more authors.	
	Translations.	
.C7	English.	
.C72	Latin.	
.C75	Other, by language, A–Z.	
.C8	Biography and criticism.	
.H3	Han, Fei.	
	Hsün-tze.	
.H65	Complete works.	
.H66	Translations. By language, A–Z.	
	Subarranged by translator.	
.H67–69	Separate works (alphabetically).	
.H7	Biography and criticism.	
.K25	Kaibara, Ekken.	
.K3	K'ang-hsi, emperor of China.	
	Lao-tzŭ, see BL 1900.	
.M32	Mencius.	
.M6	Mo, Ti.	
.W3	Wang, Shou-jên.	
.W8	Wu Ming Fu.	
130–133	**India.**	
132	Special topics, A–Z.	
	e. g. .I3	Idealism.
	.J3	Jainism.
		Cf. BL 1300–1365.
	.K6	Knowledge.
	.L6	Lokāyata.
	.M27	Man.
		Materialism, see Lokāyata, .L6.
	.M5	Mīmāṃsā.
	.N8	Nyaya.
	.R4	Realism.
	.S3	Sankhya.
	.V2	Vaiśeṣika.
	.V3	Vedanta.
	.Y6	Yoga.

Figure 48

TABLES OF SUBDIVISIONS

Table 4 (Philosophers with 1 number)

		Collected works.
(1)	.A3	Original texts. By date.
(2)	.A35	Partial editions, selections, etc. By editor.
(3)	.A4	Translations. By language, A–Z.
(4)	.A5–Z6	Separate works.
		Subarranged:
		(1) Original texts. By date.
		(2) Translations.
		Subarranged either by language, A–Z or by the following scheme:
		.1 Greek.
		.2 Latin.
		.3 English.
		.4 French.
		.5 German.
		.6 Italian.
		.7 Spanish and Portuguese.
		.8 Dutch.
		.9 Other, A–Z.
		(3) Criticism and interpretation.
(5)	.Z7	General works.
		Biography, criticism, etc.

Table 5 (Philosophers with Cutter number)

The subarrangement as presented in Table 4 is followed, using successive Cutter numbers in place of .A3, .A35, .A4, .A5–Z6, and .Z7. For example, the Cutter number .B4 would be developed thus:

		Collected works.
(1)	.B4	Original texts. By date.
(2)	.B41	Partial editions, selections, etc. By editor.
(3)	.B42	Translations. By language, A–Z.
(4)	.B43	Separate works, A–Z.
		Subarranged like item (4), Table 4.
(5)	.B44	General works.
		Biography, criticism, etc.

CHAPTER 5

INDIVIDUAL CLASSES OF
LIBRARY OF CONGRESS CLASSIFICATION

INTRODUCTION

This chapter introduces the reader to the individual classes
of Library of Congress classification. Each unit of this chapter
begins with a synopsis of the class as found in the official Outline
of the Library of Congress Classification. Its inclusion is intended
to orient the reader to the scope of the individual class. Next a
brief history traces the development of the schedule or schedules
making up each class. The names of classifiers responsible for
the planning and editing of each class or subclass are given in most
cases. Additional tables or extensions of important schedules
found only in supplements to the class schedule or in Additions and
Changes are mentioned. Significant problems in the use of each
class schedule are discussed: inclusiveness and exclusiveness of
the scope, and problems of terminology and typography. Typical
problems in the use of auxiliary and/or internal tables are presented and explained with examples of Library of Congress class
numbers in the same fashion as used in Chapter 4. Any unusual
elements that may occur in the notation of each class are explained,
e. g. the use of triple letters in subclass KF, or the use of special
workmarks in class L, etc. At the end of the chapter is a complete
bibliography of editions of the individual schedules and material
written about them followed by tables and schedules referred to in
the chapter. Some tables and schedules reproduced for use in previous chapters are cited by chapter number as well as figure number; the reader is asked to refer to the appropriate chapter for this
material.

It is hoped that this chapter may serve to orient classifiers
to individual schedules which may be unfamiliar to them. Each
unit is designed to provide an introductory rather than a definitive
treatment of the problems involved in using each class schedule.
In each unit examples illustrate typical tables or tables that were
not previously analyzed, an important or confusing variation in the
use of notation, or clarify directions provided within the schedule
or tables. Only parts of schedules or tables posing new or some
special kind of difficulty to the classifier are discussed, consequently

many subclasses are not analyzed. It is restated here that the reader will benefit by studying the class schedule as a whole in conjunction with the examples and tables presented in the individual units of this chapter. In addition the reader may wish to check his library's shelf list for additional examples of each problem. The most effective use of this chapter can be achieved by the following steps.

1) Careful reading of introductory and explanatory material in each unit.

2) Studying of examples provided in the text.

3) Consulting L. C. classification schedules for each class.

CLASS A

Class A: General Works, Polygraphy is the generalia class
in Library of Congress classification. The outline of the class was
developed in 1906 and first published in 1911. Charles Martel was
the editor of the first edition. The second edition was published in
1915 with Clarence W. Perley as the editor. The third edition issued in 1947 was prepared for publication by Miss L. Belle Voegelein.

Class A is designed for multitopical works. It should not be
used for works that can possibly be classed in a special subject in
classes B-Z. The individual subclasses are arbitrarily arranged
in an alphabetical order: AC, Collections; AE, Encyclopedias;
AG, General reference works; AM, Museums, etc. The letters
forming the subclasses demonstrate the use of mnemonics. This
is one of the few instances in Library of Congress classification
where mnemonics are used in the subclasses. Subclass AZ is the
only subclass in Class A that does not use this mnemonic device.

This schedule presents no major problems in use. There
is only one auxiliary table and a few internal ones. The use of
some of these tables has already been discussed in Chapter 4. The
following examples are designed to demonstrate two of the typical
uses of auxiliary tables in Class A.

Ten Number Countries

In subclass AY, Yearbooks, Almanacs, Directories, Great
Britain is a ten number country. Within the schedule the numbers
"AY 750-759" are assigned to Great Britain for yearbooks, almanacs, and directories. A part of the schedule "AY" is reproduced
below:

AY   Yearbooks, Almanacs, Directories.

       Foreign countries. *

       Europe.

   750-759   Great Britain.

   *For subdivision under each country, see Tables.

As Great Britain is assigned a range of ten numbers, "AY 750-759, "
it is called a ten number country. The "Tables of Subdivisions under Countries (AY 410-1725)" are designed to be used for "I (Ten
numbers), " "II (Two numbers) " and "III (One number or Cutter

A

GENERAL WORKS—POLYGRAPHY

AC   Collections. Series. Collected works

         1- 95   Collections of monographs, essays, etc.

               Classified by language

     901–995   Pamphlet collections

        999   Scrapbooks

AE   Encyclopedias (General)

AG   General reference works (other than encyclopedias)

         5- 91   Minor encyclopedias. Popular and juvenile

    103–191   General works, pocketbooks, receipts, etc.

        195   Questions and answers

    305–313   Notes and queries

    500–571   Information bureaus. Literary agents

AI   Indexes (General)

AM   Museums

     11–101   Museography

        101   Individual museums, A–Z

    111–157   Museology. Museum methods, technique, etc.

    200–501   Collectors and collecting. Private collections

AN   Newspapers

AP   Periodicals (General)

       Classified by language; subarrangement, geographical

     91- 93   Periodicals for Jewish readers

    101–115   Humorous periodicals

    200–230   Juvenile periodicals

AS   Societies. Academies

       Learned societies of a general character, arranged by country

      3–4   International associations, congresses, conferences, etc.

AY   Yearbooks (General)

    30–1725   Almanacs (General)

          Classified by country

     2001   Directories

         General works on compilation, etc.

         Directories are classified by subject in B–Z.

AZ   General history of knowledge and learning

     999   Popular errors, delusions and superstitions

number)." Refer to Figure 32 in Chapter 4 for these tables. As was previously explained in Chapter 4, the use of the table for ten number countries is simply a matter of matching the sequence of numbers in the table with the integral numbers assigned to the geographic divisions. The range of ten numbers of Great Britain must be matched with the range of ten numbers in Table I (see below).

AY 750-759   Table I

Early (to 1800).

750	(0)	Collections, by date of first volume.
751	(1).A-Z5	Serial, by title or editor.
	.Z7	Other, by date.
752	(2)	Yearbooks (without almanacs).

1800—

753	(3)	Collections.
754	(4)	General, by title or editor.
755	(5)	Newspaper, etc., by name of place, subarranged by title.
756	(6)	Other.
	.A3-Z3	Literary and magazine almanacs, etc., by title or editor.
	.Z5	Miscellaneous. Occasional issues. By date.
757	(7)	Almanacs in foreign languages, by language, A-Z.
758	(8)	Special, by subject, A-Z.
759	(9)	Local, by place, A-Z.

A general British Almanac, <u>Old Moore's Almanack,</u> is classed
"AY 754 . Ø58. " "AY 754" means a general British almanac;
".Ø58" is the Cutter number for the main entry, which in this case
is the title, <u>Old Moore's Almanack.</u>

<u>Old Moore's Almanack,</u> a general British almanac.

AY ----- The double letters for the subclass, Yearbooks.

754 ---- The integral number meaning a general British
almanac.

.Ø58 --- The first Cutter number for the main entry,
<u>Old</u>...

Miles Hadfield's <u>An English Almanac,</u> an introduction to the English year: its calendar, traditions, anniversaries, and events,
published in 1950 is classed as "AY 756 . Z5 1950. " "AY 756"
means a 19th or 20th century almanac which does not fit any particular type as given in the table. ". Z5" is the reserved Cutter
number for miscellaneous almanacs under the "Other" category;
"1950" is the date for an occasional issue as specified in the table
directions. It should be noted that in this case the date is the only
distinguishing element.

Miles Hadfield's <u>An English Almanac,</u> 1950.

AY ----- The double letters for the subclass, Yearbooks.

756 ---- The integral number meaning "other" 19th/20th
century British almanacs.

. Z5 ---- The reserved Cutter number for miscellaneous
almanacs.

1950 --- The date of publication as required by Table I.

Another example is <u>Europa-Journal,</u> a German yearbook which is
not an almanac. Germany's range of numbers is "AY 850-860"
with "AY 859" for states and "AY 860" for places. Except for
these last two numbers, as was noted in Chapter 4, Germany may
use the table for ten number countries even though it is really an
eleven number country. This yearbook is classed in the third
number in the table which is "2. " The complete call number is
"AY 852 . E8. " "AY 852" means a German yearbook without

almanacs; ". E8" is the Cutter number for the main entry, Europa-Journal.

Europa-Journal.

AY----- The double letters for the subclass, Yearbooks.

852 ---- The integral number meaning a German year-book without almanacs.

. E8 ---- The first Cutter number for the main entry, Europa-Journal.

The Geographic Table in Subclass AZ

The internal tables for geographic subdivisions in sub-class AZ, History of Sciences in General, create a special prob-lem of interpretation. These tables are designated for ten num-ber countries, five number countries, three number countries, and one number countries. (See also Figure 49.)

I	II	III	IV	
10 nos.	5 nos.	3 nos.	1 no.	
(0)	(1)	(1). A1-A3	. A1-A2	Collections.
(1)	(2)	. A5-Z3	. A5-Z3	General works. History.
(2)				Early. Origins.
(3)				Middle Ages.
(4)				Modern.
(6)				General special. Relations, aspects, etc.
(7)	(3)	. Z5	. Z5	Addresses, essays, lectures. Pamphlets.

(8)	(4)	(2)	. Z7A-Z	States, provinces, etc.

Under each:

(1) Collections.

(2) History.

(3) Other: Minor.

[9]	[5]	[3]	[. Z8A-Z]	Cities, see DA-DU, E, F.

There is no problem in assigning numbers to ten number countries. Either an area has its full allotment of ten numbers such as Germany, "AZ 660-669, " or it is assigned eight numbers with special numbers for its regions such as Great Britain, "AZ 610-617, " and England--Local, "AZ 620-623"; Scotland, "AZ 625-628"; Ireland, "AZ 630-633"; Wales, "AZ 635-638. " For example, Robert Weiss' Humanism in England during the Fifteenth Century is classed "AZ 613 .W4. " "AZ 613" means a general work on scholarship and learning in Great Britain during the Middle Ages. "613" is the fourth number assigned to Great Britain and is represented in the table by the number "3" with "0" for collections, "1" for general works, "2" for early history, "3" for history of the Middle Ages, "4" for modern history, etc. ".W4" is the Cutter number for the main entry, Weiss.

Robert Weiss' Humanism in England during the Fifteenth Century.

AZ----- The double letters for the subclass AZ, History of the sciences in general.

613 ---- The integral number meaning a general work on scholarship and learning in Great Britain during the Middle Ages.

.W4---- The first Cutter number for the main entry, Weiss.

Tables II and III for five number and three number countries do create a special problem of interpretation. The following note is given in the schedule.

> "Countries to which 2 numbers are assigned in the schedule use subdivisions (1) and (2) of Table III; countries with four numbers use subdivisions (1)-(4) of Table II. "

For example, Canada is assigned "AZ 515-516" which makes Canada a two number country. In order to class works on Canadian learning and scholarship, Table III for three number countries must be used. Only the first two numbers of Table III are used; however, this creates no problem as the third number in Table III is an optional number. The 1949-1951 Report of the Canadian Royal Commission on National Development in the Arts, Letters and Sciences is classed "AZ 515 .A53. " This book is classed in the first number for Canada "AZ 515" as it is a general work and not a regional or local one. ". A53" is one of the first possible Cutter numbers within the assigned range of ". A5-Z3" for general works. It is placed at the beginning of this range as this is an official publication.

> The 1949-1951 Report of the Canadian Royal Commission on National Development in the Arts, Letters and Sciences.
>
> AZ----- The double letter for the subclass AZ, History of the sciences in general.
>
> 515 ---- The integral number meaning a general work on learning and scholarship in Canada.
>
> . A53 --- The first Cutter number from the range of . A5-Z3 meaning general works with this number chosen from the beginning of the range as this is an official publication.

A regional or provincal work on learning and scholarship in Canada would use the second number "AZ 516. "

In addition to the use of this table in subclass AZ, the subclass itself may create problems of interpretation. This subclass, as the foregoing examples indicate, is used for those interdisciplinary works which do not naturally fit into any of the individual schedules. Two additional examples are presented here to clarify further the types of books that are classed in subclass, AZ.

William Jones' The Romantic Syndrome toward a New
Method in Cultural Anthropology: A History of Ideas.

AZ----- The double letters for the subclass AZ, History
   of the sciences in general.

101 ---- The integral number meaning general philosophies
   and theories of scholarship and learning.

.J6 ---- The first Cutter number for the main entry, Jones.

Sir Charles Snow's Two Cultures.

AZ----- The double letters for the subclass AZ, History
   of the sciences in general.

361 ---- The integral number meaning history of 20th
   century scholarship and learning.

.S56 --- The first Cutter number for the main entry,
   Snow.

CLASS B

Class B: Philosophy and Religion consists of two separately published schedules — Part 1, B-BJ Philosophy and Part 2, BL-BX Religion. Edwin Wiley edited the first edition of Part 1, under the direction of Charles Martel, in 1910. Part 2 edited by Clarence W. Perley, did not appear until 1927. Miss Voegelein edited the second edition of Part 1 which was published in 1950. The second edition of Part 2, largely the work of Theodore A. Mueller, was published in 1962.

The principle sources for the philosophy schedules were Cutter's Expansive Classification, Dewey's Decimal Classification and its revision the Universal Decimal Classification. Other sources which are acknowledged are Otto Harwig's Halle Schema, the works of Schleiermacher, Benjamin Rand's Bibliography of Philosophy, Psychology and Cognate Subjects, the Psychological Index, and the index to Zeitschrift für Psychologie und Physiologie der Sinnesorgane. The inclusion of subclass BF, Psychology within the philosophy class demonstrates the influence of the nineteenth century point of view in the development of this schedule.

The treatment of individual philosophers in subclass B is similar to the treatment of individual authors in literature. Subclass B is used for works by and about philosophers as well as general philosophical works. Subclasses BC, Logic; BD, Metaphysics; BF, Psychology; BH, Esthetics; and BJ, Ethics, contain added entries in the shelf list, i. e. shelf list numbers, for the particular subject or subjects of an individual philosopher's works. The general form or pattern for individual philosophers who are classed in subclass B is:

1) Collected works.

2) Separate works.

3) Biography, criticism, etc.

However, all individual philosophers are not classed entirely in subclass B. This is especially true of modern philosophers. For example, although Lord Bertrand Russell is given a specific number in subclass B, many of his works of a philosophic nature are not classed there. His number is "B 1649 . R9, " but his work Human Knowledge; its Scope and Limits is classed "BD 161 . R78, " its appropriate subject number in epistemology. This problem is even more apparent when the philosopher is also a theologian. The works of theologians, particularly modern theologians, are usually

B

PHILOSOPHY—RELIGION

	Philosophy
B	Collections. History. Systems
BC	Logic
BD	Metaphysics

	10– 41	Introductions to philosophy
	100–131	General works
	150–241	Epistemology. Theory of knowledge
	300–444	Ontology
	493–708	Cosmology. Teleology

BF	Psychology
	1001–1999 Metapsychology. Psychic research. Occult sciences

BH	Esthetics
BJ	Ethics

	1–1531	General works, history, systems, etc.
	1545–1725	Practical and applied ethics. Conduct of life, etc.
	1801–2193	Manners. Etiquette. Social usages

	Religion. Theology
BL	Religions. Mythology. Free thought
BM	Judaism
BP	Mohammedanism. Bahaism. Theosophy
	Christianity
BR	Generalities. Church history
BS	Bible and Exegesis
BT	Doctrinal theology. Apologetics
BV	Practical theology

	5– 525	Worship (public and private)
	590–3799	Ecclesiastical theology. The church
	1460–1615	Religious education
	2000–3705	Missions
	4000–4470	Pastoral theology
	4490–5099	Practical religion. The Christian life

BX	Special sects
	1–9 Church unity. Interdenominational cooperation

scattered throughout the entire Class B.

The philosophers that are classed in subclass B must each be carefully verified with Library of Congress Practice. This, of course, can be done by checking the philosopher under his entries in the Library of Congress printed catalogs and cards. Subclass B has tables for individual philosophers that are very similar to the tables for individual authors in literature. There are tables for philosophers with fifty numbers, nine numbers, five numbers, four numbers, one number and Cutter numbers. There is also a special table for oriental philosophers (discussed in Chapter 4).

Bertrand Russell's works may be used as an example of the classing of a philosopher's works in subclass B. As already pointed out not all of Russell's philosophical works are classed together; however, those works that are classed together present a clear example. As Russell is a Cutter number philosopher, "B 1649 . R9, " his works are classed using Table 5 for philosophers with Cutter numbers. (See also Figure 48 in Chapter 4.)

Table 5 (Philosophers with Cutter number)

The arrangement as presented in Table 4 is followed, using successive Cutter numbers in place of . A3, . A35, . A4, . A5-Z6, and . Z7. For example, the Cutter number . B4 would be developed thus:

		Collected works.
(1)	. B4	Original texts. By date.
(2)	. B41	Partial editions, selections, etc. By editor.
(3)	. B42	Translations. By language, A-Z.
(4)	. B43	Separate works, A-Z.
		Subarranged like item (4), Table 4.
(5)	. B44	General works.
		Biography, criticism, etc.

Development of successive Cutter numbers for Russell will be:

Collected works.

(1) . R9	Original texts. By date.	
(2) . R91	Partial editions, selections, etc. By editor.	
(3) . R92	Translations. By language, A-Z.	
(4) . R93	Separate works, A-Z.	
(5) . R94	General works. Biography, criticism, etc.	

For instance, Russell's Basic Writing, 1903-1959, edited by Robert Egner, is classed as a selection or partial edition of Russell's collected works, "B 1649 . R91E58. "

Russell's Basic Writing, 1903-1959, edited by Robert Egner.

B------ The single letter for the subclass B, Philosophy (general).

1649 --- The integral number meaning an individual British philosopher of the later 19th and 20th centuries.

. R91--- The first Cutter number meaning the individual philosopher, Bertrand Russell (. R9), and the successive element (1) meaning a partial edition or selection of his works.

E58---- The second Cutter number for the editor of the selection, Egner.

Another selection of Russell's works edited by Egner is Bertrand Russell's Best which is classed "B 1649 . R91E4. "

Bertrand Russell's Best, edited by Egner.

B------ The single letter for the subclass B, Philosophy (general).

1649 --- The integral number meaning an individual British philosopher of the later 19th and 20th centuries.

.R91----The first Cutter number meaning the individual
philosopher, Bertrand Russell (.R9), and the
successive element (1) meaning a partial edition
or selection of his works.

E4------The second Cutter number for the editor of the
selection, Egner.

Both of these examples are selections or partial editions of the
philosopher's work and thus use the first extension of Russell's
Cutter number ".R9." The second expansion of Russell's Cutter
number is ".R92." According to Table 5 this is reserved for translations of collected works or selections. The following is a selection
of Russell's works translated into Spanish.

La Filosofía en el Siglo XX y Otros Ensayos, Seguidos
de Cuatro Estudios sobre la Obra de Bertrand Russell.

B------ The single letter for the subclass B, Philosophy
(general).

1649 --- The integral number meaning an individual
British philosopher of the later 19th and 20th
centuries.

.R92--- The first Cutter number meaning the individual
philosopher, Bertrand Russell (.R9), and the
successive element (2) meaning a translation
of his collected or selected works.

S66 ---- The second Cutter number for the language of the
translation, Spanish.

Following translations of collected works or selections, the next
successive Cutter number is ".R93" to be used for separate works
of the philosopher. The following are examples of the use of this
number.

Bertrand Russell Speaks his Mind.

B------ The single letter for the subclass B, Philosophy
(general).

1649 --- The integral number meaning an individual
British philosopher of the later 19th and 20th
centuries.

. R93----The first Cutter number meaning the individual philosopher, Bertrand Russell (. R9), and the successive element (3) meaning a separate work of Russell.

B4------The second Cutter number used for the title of the separate work, Bertrand...

Logic and Knowledge; Essays, 1901-1950, by Russell.

B------ The single letter for the subclass B, Philosophy (general).

1649 --- The integral number meaning an individual British philosopher of the later 19th and 20th centuries.

. R93--- The first Cutter number meaning the individual philosopher, Bertrand Russell (. R9), and the successive element (3) meaning a separate work of Russell.

L6----- The second Cutter number used for the title of the separate work, Logic...

Russell's An Outline of Philosophy, 1961.

B------ The single letter for the subclass B, Philosophy (general).

1649 --- The integral number meaning an individual British philosopher of the later 19th and 20th centuries.

. R93--- The first Cutter number meaning the individual philosopher, Bertrand Russell (. R9), and the successive element (3) meaning a separate work of Russell.

O9 ------The second Cutter number used for the title of the separate work, Outline...

1961 ----The date of publication.

Mysticism and Logic, and Other Essays, 1932.
[originally published as Philosophical Essays.]

B------ The single letter for the subclass B, Philosophy
(general).

1649 --- The integral number meaning an individual
British philosopher of the later 19th and 20th
centuries.

.R93--- The first Cutter number meaning the individual
philosopher, Bertrand Russell (.R9), and the
successive element (3) meaning a separate work
of Russell.

P5----- The second Cutter number used for the original
title of the separate work, Philosophical. . .

1932 --- The date of publication.

Frihet og Fornuft, a Norwegian translation of Russell's
Philosophical Essays.

B------ The single letter for the subclass B, Philosophy
(general).

1649 --- The integral number meaning an individual
British philosopher of the later 19th and 20th
centuries.

.R93--- The first Cutter number meaning the individual
philosopher, Bertrand Russell (.R9), and the
successive element (3) meaning a separate
work of Russell.

P516--- The second Cutter number used for the original
title of the separate work, Philosophical Essays
(P5), and a successive element (16) in this case
meaning a translation into Norwegian.

It should be noted that the translations of a separate work are cuttered immediately following the original separate work.

Portraits from Memory, and Other Essays, by Russell.
London, 1956.

B------ The single letter for the subclass B, Philosophy
(general).

1649----The integral number meaning an individual British
philosopher of the later 19th and 20th centuries.

. R93 ---The first Cutter number meaning the individual
philosopher, Bertrand Russell (. R9), and the
successive element (3) meaning a separate
work of Russell.

P6----- The second Cutter number used for the title of
the separate work, Portraits. . .

1956----The date of publication.

The New York edition of this book has a most interesting classification.

Portraits from Memory, and Other Essays, by Russell.
New York, 1956.

B------ The single letter for the subclass B, Philosophy
(general).

1649 --- The integral number meaning an individual British
philosopher of the later 19th and 20th centuries.

. R94--- The first Cutter number meaning the individual
philosopher, Bertrand Russell (. R9), and the
successive element (4) meaning a general work
about Russell.

A3----- The second Cutter number used to place this
autobiographical work at the beginning of the
group of works about Russell.

This work, naturally of an autobiographical nature, is classed
both as a separate work of Russell and as a general work about
Russell. The last expansion of Russell's successive Cutter numbers is ". R94" for biography, criticism, etc. about Russell. The
first works under this number are the autobiographical ones.

Russell's My Philosophical Development.

B------ The single letter for the subclass B, Philosophy
(general).

1649 --- The integral number meaning an individual British
philosopher of the later 19th and 20th centuries.

. R94--- The first Cutter number meaning the individual
philosopher, Bertrand Russell (. R9), and the
successive element (4) meaning a general work
about Russell.

A28---- The second Cutter number used to place this autobiographical work at the beginning of the group of works about Russell.

The Autobiography of Bertrand Russell.

B------ The single letter for the subclass B, Philosophy (general).

1649 --- The integral number meaning an individual British philosopher of the later 19th and 20th centuries.

. R94--- The first Cutter number meaning the individual philosopher, Bertrand Russell (. R9), and the successive element (4) meaning a general work about Russell.

A32---- The second Cutter number used to place this autobiographical work at the beginning of the group of works about Russell.

After these autobiographical works, are the general works about Russell written by other authors. The following are two examples of these.

Lillian Woodworth Aiken's Bertrand Russell's Philosophy of Morals.

B------ The single letter for the subclass B, Philosophy (general).

1649 --- The integral number meaning an individual British philosopher of the later 19th and 20th centuries.

. R94--- The first Cutter number meaning the individual philosopher, Bertrand Russell (. R9), and the successive element (4) meaning a general work about Russell.

A47---- The second Cutter number for the author of the general work about Russell, Aiken.

Paul Arthur Schilpp's The Philosophy of Bertrand Russell, 1963.

B------ The single letter meaning the subclass, philosophy (general).

1649 --- The integral number meaning an individual British philosopher of the later 19th and 20th centuries.

.R94--- The first Cutter number meaning the individual philosopher, Bertrand Russell (.R9), and the successive element (4) meaning a general work about Russell.

S35 ---- The second Cutter number for the author of the general work, Schilpp.

1963----The date of publication.

These examples readily demonstrate the general pattern for the works of an individual philosopher. The other tables in Class B present no major problems and are basically simple tables which require only the matching of final digits.

Part 2 Religion presents certain problems in usage. This was one of the last schedules to be developed, and as a result, much material related to religion was classed in other schedules, e. g. Church and social problems in subclass HN; Education and the church in subclass LC; Church music in class M; Art and architecture in class N; Biblical languages in subclasses PA and PJ; and Bibliography in class Z. The other major problem deals with subclass BX, Denominations and sects. Before the appearance of the second edition in 1962, many libraries found this section to be incomplete. This was especially true of theological libraries. As a result there were several expansions made for individual denominations. Some of these expansions are listed in the bibliography following this unit. In the second edition this subclass was expanded to over two hundred pages, yet it remains insufficiently developed for special theological libraries. The expanded second edition reflects the nature of Library of Congress classification which is intentionally devised for the collections in the Library of Congress not for other general libraries or special libraries. Nevertheless, one great advantage of Class B for other libraries is the detailed treatment of subclass BS, Bible and Exegesis. Special tables for Bible classification are clearly defined within the schedules and need no further explanation.

In addition Class B has certain features which may be useful in reference work: the list of philosophers by nationality, the list of denominations in subclass BX, and the lists of various editions of the Bible in subclass BS. The possible reference functions of L. C. schedules in other classes and subclasses will be cited as the individual class is discussed.

CLASS C

Class C, The Auxiliary Sciences of History, was first published in 1915. Clarence Perley served as editor for the schedule as well as being personally responsible for subclasses CC, Antiquities (General), Archeology; and, CT, Biography. J. D. Wolcott prepared subclasses CB, History of civilization; CJ, Numismatics, Coins; and, CR, Heraldry. Julian Leavitt also worked on subclass CB. Subclasses CD, Archives, Diplomatics; and, CE, Chronology, were prepared by Alfred Schmidt. Chief Classifier Charles Martel and Malma A. Gilkey constructed subclass CS, Genealogy. Subclass CN, Epigraphy, was not contained in the first edition in 1915. This subclass was delayed until the completion of subclass PA to avoid any possible duplication. Clarence Perley began the work on this subclass which was completed for publication by Miss L. Belle Voegelein in 1942. The second edition of Class C was published in 1948 also under Miss Voegelein's editorship. This publication was the first time that Class C was issued in its complete form including subclass CN.

Class C may be considered to be the generalia and miscellania class for history. Each of the subclasses represent very precisely defined fields of study. There is little relationship among the subclasses: each subclass is a complete development within itself.

The tables in Class C present little difficulty in use. The only possible problem in the tables is the use of Table III for individual biography in subclass CT. This table was not included in the second edition of Class C and can only be found in the quarterly Additions and Changes. This table is reproduced below.

Table III (CT National Biography)

Individual biography.

. x	Cutter number for the individual.
. xA2	Collected works.
. xA3	Autobiography, diary, etc.
. xA4	Letters.
. xA41-49	Letters to particular individuals, A-Z by correspondent.
. xA5	Speeches, etc.
. xA6-Z	Works by other persons about the individual.

C

HISTORY—AUXILIARY SCIENCES

CB   History of civilization (General)
           Special countries in DA–DU, E, F
           Cf. AZ, GT

CC   Antiquities (General). Archeology
           200–260 Bells. Campanology
           300–350 Crosses

CD   Archives. Diplomatics
           Cf. Paleography, Z 105–115
           5001–6471 Sphragistics. Seals. Sigillography

CE   Chronology
           71–85 Technical chronology. The calendar

CJ   Numismatics. Coins
           4801–5450 Tokens
           5501–6651 Medals and medallions

CN   Epigraphy. Inscriptions

CR   Heraldry
           101– 115 Flags, banners, and standards
           191–1020 Public and official heraldry
           1101–1131 Ecclesiastical and sacred heraldry
           1179–3400 Family heraldry
           3499–4420 Honor, rank, precedence, etc.
           4501–6305 Chivalry and knighthood
                  Tournaments, dueling, orders, decorations, etc.

CS   Genealogy
           2300–3090 Personal and family names

CT   Biography
           Biography, collective and individual, illustrative of any subject provided
             for in B–Z, is classified with that subject, as far as practicable.
           93– 205 Collections (General. Universal)
                  Classified by language
           210–3150 National biography
           3200–3830 Biography of women
           9960–9998 Miscellaneous groups: Impostors, cripples, etc.

The following three examples of individual American biography demonstrate the use of this table.

Forest W. McNair's Forest McNair of Texas.

CT----- The double letters for the subclass, Biography.

275 ---- The integral number meaning individual American biography.

. M4444- The first Cutter number for the subject of the biography, McNair.

A3 ----- The second Cutter number from Table III meaning an autobiographical work.

Catherine Gabrielson's The Story of Gabrielle.

CT----- The double letters for the subclass, Biography.

275 ---- The integral number meaning individual American biography.

. G223 -- The first Cutter number for the subject of the biography, Gabrielle.

G3 ----- The second Cutter number for the author of the biography, Gabrielson.

Miriam Allen DeFord's Up-hill All the Way, The Life of Maynard Shipley.

CT----- The double letters for the subclass, Biography.

275 ---- The integral number meaning individual American biography.

. S48814- The first Cutter number for the subject of the biography, Shipley.

D4 ----- The second Cutter number for the author of the biography, DeFord.

Tables I and II for National Biography represent simply the problem of matching the final digits of the specific geographic area's range of numbers with the table. Both Table I and II are contained in Figure 50. Great Britain is a nineteen number country, "CT 770-788" for national biography of Great Britain, using Table I. Its range of numbers may be matched to Table I in the following fashion:

CT 770-788   Table I

770	0	Serials. Yearbooks.
771	1	Collections.
772	2	Early works to 1800.
773	3	Dictionaries, 1801—
774	4	General works, 1801—
775	5	General special. Special aspects.
776	6	Miscellaneous and minor.
777	7	Juvenile.
		By period.
(778)	(8)	Ancient, see D.
(779)	(9)	Medieval, see D.
		Modern.
780	10	15th-16th centuries.
781	11	17th-18th centuries.
782	12	19th-20th centuries.
783	13	20th century.
784	14	Colonies (General).
785	15	Local division, A-Z.
(786)	(16)	Cities, see D.
(787)	(17)	Rulers, see D-F.
788	18	Individual biography, A-Z.
	.Z9	Persons not known by name.

Leonard Alfred George Strong's Sixteen Portraits of People Whose Houses Have Been Preserved by the National Trust is classed as a collection of British national biography, "CT 771 . S7. "

Strong's Sixteen Portraits of People...

CT----- The double letters for the subclass, Biography.

771 ---- The integral number meaning a collection of British national biography.

. S7 ---- The first Cutter number for the author of the biography.

A. L. Rowse's The English Past is classed as a general work of British national biography in the fifth number in Great Britain's range "CT 774. "

Rowse's The English Past.

CT----- The double letters for the subclass, Biography

774-----The integral number meaning a general work of
British national biography.

. R6 ----The first Cutter number for the author of the
biography.

A work classed as general special is Sir James Marchant's If I
Had my Time Again, an Anthology Contributed by Twenty Distin-
quished Men and Women, "CT 775 . M3. " The sixth number in
Table I and hence the sixth number in Great Britain's range of
numbers is for general special works.

Marchant's If I Had my Time Again.

CT----- The double letters for the subclass, Biography.

775 ---- The integral number meaning a general special
work of British national biography.

. M3---- The first Cutter number for the main entry,
Marchant.

Vivian de Sola Pinto's English Biography in the Seventeenth Century
is classed in the chronological subdivision "17th-18th centuries" as
"CT 781 . P5. "

Pinto's English Biography in the Seventeenth Century.

CT----- The double letters for the subclass, Biography.

781 ---- The integral number meaning a work on 17th-18th
century British national biography.

. P5---- The first Cutter number for the main entry,
Pinto.

Some Victorian Portraits and Others by Hilda Martindale is another
example of a chronologically subdivided work. It is classed in the
"19th-20th centuries" in number "12" as "CT 782 . M3. "

Martindale's Some Victorian Portraits. . .

CT----- The double letters for the subclass, Biography.

782 ---- The integral number meaning a work on 19th-20th
century British national biography.

. M3---- The first Cutter number for the main entry,
Martindale.

Lucie Simpson's autobiographical <u>Contacts, Literary and Political</u> is classed as individual British national biography using Table III. The call number is "CT 788 . S536A3. "

<u>Contacts, Literary and Political</u>, by Lucie Simpson.

CT----- The double letters for the subclass, Biography.

788 ---- The integral number meaning an individual British national biography.

. S536 -- The first Cutter number for the subject of the biography, Simpson.

A3 ----- The second Cutter number from Table III meaning an autobiographical work.

As L. C. classification prefers to class biography by subject, subclass CT is used only for a biography for which a subject may not be readily discernible. This is true of both collective and individual biography as the foregoing examples show. Previous examples showed biographies of literary writers and philosophers classed with the work of the individual author or philosopher. Another example showed both collective and individual biographies of editors and journalists being classed with the subject, journalism. This characteristic of classing biography by subject rather than by form is generally followed throughout the classification. The many pages of shelf list numbers in subclass CT are a witness to this fact. (See Figure 28 in Chapter 3.) These numbers could be used by any library wishing to assume the responsibility for consistently reclassifying L. C. printed cards for all material to be classed in CT. The following examples illustrate the subject approach used by the Library of Congress in classing major biographical dictionaries, and demonstrates the alternative of reclassifying in subclass "CT. "

<u>Dictionary of National Biography</u>.

DA----- The double letters for the subclass, British history.

28 ----- The integral number meaning general collective biography of England.

. D4 ---- The first Cutter number for the main entry, <u>Dictionary</u>...

Dictionary of Canadian Biography, 1945.

 F------ The single letter for the class, U.S. local history
    and general history of other American countries.

 1005 --- The integral number meaning collective Canadian
    biography.

 .D5---- The first Cutter number for the main entry,
    Dictionary...

 1945 --- The date of publication

Dictionary of American Biography.

 E------ The single letter for the class, United States
    history.

 176 ---- The integral number meaning general collective
    U.S. biography.

 .D563-- The first Cutter number for the main entry,
    Dictionary...

National Cyclopedia of American Biography.

 E------ The single letter for the class, United States
    history.

 176 ---- The integral number meaning general collective
    U.S. biography.

 .N28 -- The first Cutter number for the main entry,
    National...

Who's Who in America.

 E------The single letter for the class, United States
    history.

 663 ---- The integral number meaning collective U.S.
    biography of the late 19th and 20th century.

 .W56---- The first Cutter number for the main entry,
    Who's...

The appropriate number for United States national biography in subclass CT is "CT 213"; the appropriate number for Great Britain's national biography is "CT 773." Some libraries prefer to reclassify all national biographies in the appropriate numbers in subclass CT, Biography. This would move the Dictionary of American Biography from "E 176" to "CT 213" and the Dictionary of National Biography from "DA 28" to "CT 773." Whether such collocations are desirable is debatable. Some reference librarians prefer to have the national biography of each country side by side with the history of that country; others prefer to have all national biography together in subclass CT.

Dictionary of American Biography, reclassified.

CT------ The double letters for the subclass, Biography.

213 ----- The integral number meaning an American biographical dictionary.

. D5 ----- The first Cutter number for the main entry, Dictionary...

Dictionary of National Biography, in CT.

CT------ The double letters for the subclass, Biography.

773 ----- The integral number meaning a British biographical dictionary.

. D5 ----- The first Cutter for the main entry, Dictionary...

CLASS D

Class D, History and Topography (except America), was initially drafted by Charles Martel in 1901 and 1902. The first edition was published in 1916 with Alfred Schmidt serving as editor. As in the case of Class C, the subclasses of Class D were developed by a group of experts: W. Dawson Johnston planned subclass DA, Great Britain; DK, Russia, and DR, Turkey and the Balkan States, were the responsibility of Alexis V. Babine; DP, Spain and Portugal, and DT, Africa, were developed by Cecil K. Jones. Schmidt was primarily responsible for the remaining subclasses: D, General history; DB, Austria-Hungary; DC, France; DD, Germany; DE, Classical antiquity; DF, Greece; DG, Italy; DH-DJ, Netherlands; and DQ, Switzerland. The second edition was published in 1959 with Miss Voegelein as editor. Prior to the publication of the second edition there were two separately published supplements for World War I and World War II. The first supplement for World War I was published in 1921 with Schmidt as the editor. A second edition of this supplement was published in 1933. The supplement for World War II was published in 1946. The second edition of Class D incorporated these two supplements into the text.

Class D was the first class to use the second letter in the notation for the subclasses. This device was designed to allow individual classifiers a whole subclass to develop instead of the restriction of a specified range of numbers. The preface to the first edition of Class D is extremely helpful not only as a guide to this class but as a sound general statement on the theory of classification for history. This preface was not retained in the second edition.

The general pattern of arrangement in history subclasses and individual countries is:

1) General works.

2) Description and travel.

3) Antiquities. Social life and customs, etc.

4) History.

5) Local history and description.

The main exception to this pattern is subclass DA, Great Britain, in which the order is 1) General works, 2) History, including antiquities, etc., 3) Description and travel, 4) Local history and description.

The local history numbers for individual countries make use

D

HISTORY and TOPOGRAPHY (except America)

D	General history		
DA	Great Britain		
	20–690	England	
	700–745	Wales	
	750–890	Scotland	
	900–995	Ireland	
DB	Austria-Hungary		
DC	France		
DD	Germany		
DE	Classical antiquity		
DF	Greece		
DG	Italy		
DH–DJ	Netherlands		
	DH 1–207	Belgium and Holland	
	DH 401–811	Belgium	
	DH 901–925	Luxemburg (Grand duchy)	
	DJ	Holland	
DK	Russia		
	1–272	Russia (General)	
	401–441	Poland	
	445–465	Finland	
	750–891	Russia in Asia	
DL	Scandinavia		
	1– 85	Scandinavia (General)	
	101–291	Denmark	
	301–398	Iceland	
	401–596	Norway	
	601–991	Sweden	
DP	Spain and Portugal		
	1–402	Spain	
	501–900	Portugal	
DQ	Switzerland		
DR	Turkey and the Balkan States		
DS	Asia		
DT	Africa		
DU	Australia and Oceania		
DX	Gipsies		

of extensive special tables within the schedules accompanied by complete directions for their use. In most cases a careful analysis of the Library of Congress practice with an individual number should show how to fit original call numbers into the previously classed material. (Cf. Analysis of numbers used for oriental philosophers. Chapter 4, pp 130 - 139.)

French local history and description in subclass DC, French history, may be used as an example of special tables within the schedules. The local history and description of the individual regions, provinces, departments, etc. of France is classed under the number "DC 611." The following table and instructions are given in the schedule under this one number. (See also Figures 51 and 51a.)

> Under each:
> | | |
> |---|---|
> | (1) | Periodicals. Societies. |
> | (2) | Sources and documents. Collections. |
> | (23) | Gazetteers. Directories. Dictionaries, etc. |
> | (25) | Biography (Collective). |
> | (3) | General works. Description and travel. Guidebooks. |
> | (4) | Antiquities. |
> | (5) | History (General). |
> | | By period (History and description). |
> | (6) | Early. |
> | (7) | Medieval and early modern. |
> | (8) | Modern. |
> | (9) | Special topics. |

> The table shows the sequence of topics when nine basic numerals are available. If eleven are indicated, the numerals (23), (25), (3), etc., become (3), (4), (5), etc. If fewer than nine numerals are available, longer decimal or Cutter numbers may be introduced, as for example (23) and (25) above; or a number may cover more than one topic, e.g. (1) may cover (1) and (2), or (5) may cover (5) through (8). When one numeral only is indicated, .A1-9 or .A1A-Z may be used for serials.

Many of the better known localities, e.g. Alpes, and Alquitaine, are fully developed in the schedules (cf. Figure 51a). Brittany is given a range of successive Cutter numbers, ".B841-915." The successions are then clearly assigned in the schedule. The following is the first part of this assignment. (See also Figure 52.)

DC   FRANCE

611   Regions, provinces, departments, etc., A-Z.

.B841-915 Brittany (Bretagne).

           .B841 Periodicals. Societies.

           .B842 Sources and documents. Collections.

           .B843 Collected works.

           .B844 Minor works. Pamphlets, etc.

           .B845 Biography (Collective).

           .B846 Gazetteers. Directories, etc.

           .B847 General works.

           .B848 Description and travel.

                  Including the picturesque.

           .B85   Antiquities.

           .B851 Social life and customs. Civilization.

           .B852 Ethnography.

                  History.

           .B854 General works.

           .B855 General special.

For example René Pleven's general work on Brittany entitled <u>Avenin de la Bretagne</u> is classed "DC 611 .B847P56." This book uses the assigned successive Cutter number for general works on Brittany, ".B847."

      Rene Pleven's <u>Avenin de la Bretagne.</u>

        DC----- The double letters for the subclass, French history.

        611 ---- The integral number meaning local history and description of an individual region, etc. of France.

        .B847 -- The first Cutter number meaning a general work on Brittany.

P56---- The second Cutter number used for the main
       entry, Pleven.

A book on description and travel in Brittany is Roger Vercel's
Bretagne aux Cent Visages. This uses the assigned successive
Cutter number, ".B848." Its complete call number is "DC 611
.B848V33."

    Roger Vercel's Bretagne aux Cent Visages.

    DC----- The double letters for the subclass, French
        history.

    611 ---- The integral number meaning local history and
        description of an individual region, etc. of
        France.

    .B848-- The first Cutter number meaning a work on des-
        cription and travel in Brittany.

    V33 ---- The second Cutter number used for the main
        entry, Vercel.

A final example of the use of these assigned successive Cutter numbers is Henri Queffélec's La Bretagne des Pardons, a work on the
religious life and customs of Brittany. This is classed under ".B851"
for social life and customs.

    Henri Queffélec's La Bretagne des Pardons.

    DC----- The double letters for the subclass, French
        history.

    611 ---- The integral number meaning local history and
        description of an individual region, etc. of
        France.

    .B851-- The first Cutter number meaning social life and
        customs in Brittany.

    Q4----- The second Cutter number for the main entry,
        Queffélec.

Similar patterns of assigned successive Cutter numbers must be
verified for those localities that are not developed in the schedules.
Bourbonnais is an example of this. This locality is assigned a
range of five successive Cutter numbers ".B764-768." (See also
Figure 52.) In this case the table of nine basic subdivisions given
previously (see also Figure 51) must be reduced to five subdivisions.

The directions following this table may be directly applied. (See also Figure 51a.) The first two numbers may be combined and the four history numbers may be combined.

	(1)	Periodicals, Societies.
	(2)	Sources and documents. Collections.
(1)	(23)	Gazetteers. Directories. Dictionaries, etc.
	(25)	Biography (Collective).
(2)	(3)	General works. Description and travel. Guidebooks.
(3)	(4)	Antiquities.
	(5)	History (General).
		By period (History and description).
	(6)	Early.
(4)	(7)	Medieval and early modern.
	(8)	Modern.
(5)	(9)	Special topics.

Bourbonnais' numbers may be then tentatively assigned as:

.B764	(1)	Periodicals. Societies. Sources and documents. Collections. etc.
.B765	(2)	General works. Description and travel. Guidebooks.
.B766	(3)	Antiquities.
.B767	(4)	History.
.B768	(5)	Special topics.

The following examples of classification by the Library of Congress may be used to verify this development. A work on description and travel of Bourbonnais by Camille Gagnon entitled Visages du Bourbonnais is classed "DC 611 . B765V5. " ". B765" is the second successive Cutter number assigned to Bourbonnais and fits into the table development already worked out. The third number in the original table is now the second number and this number includes both general works and description and travel.

Visages du Bourbonnais.

DC----- The double letters for the subclass, French
   history.

611 ---- The integral number meaning local history and
   description of an individual region, etc. of
   France.

. B765 -- The first Cutter number meaning a general work
   including description and travel of Bourbonnais.

V5 ----- The second Cutter number for the main entry,
   Visages. . .

André Leguai's Histoire du Bourbonnais is classed as a history in
". B767. " This, again, is the proper number according to the previous tentative assignment.

André Leguai's Histoire du Bourbonnais.

DC----- The double letters for the subclass, French
   history.

611 ---- The integral number meaning local history and
   description of an individual region, etc. of
   France.

. B767 -- The first Cutter number meaning a history of
   Bourbonnais.

L4 ----- The second Cutter number for the main entry,
   Leguai.

Another work dealing with the history of Bourbonnais, although in
a more specialized sense, is Marcel Genermont's Chateaux en
Bourbonnais. It is also classed as history, "DC 611 . B767G4. "

Marcel Genermont's Chateaux en Bourbonnais.

DC----- The double letters for the subclass, French
   history.

611 ---- The integral number meaning local history and
   description of an individual region, etc. of
   France.

. B767 -- The first Cutter number meaning a history of
   Bourbonnais.

G4 ----- The second Cutter number for the main entry,
   Genermont.

A specialized work dealing with the peasant life and customs of Bourbonnais is Claude Joly's Croquis Bourbonnais. This is classed in the number ". B768" for special topics.

Claude Joly's Croquis Bourbonnais.

DC----- The double letters for the subclass, French history.

611 ---- The integral number meaning local history and description of an individual region, etc. of France.

. B768 -- The first Cutter number meaning a special topic dealing with local history of Bourbonnais.

J6 ----- The second Cutter number for the main entry, Joly.

These examples all verify the tentative assignment of successive Cutter numbers for Bourbonnais. This same process of tentative reduction of the table, and then verification from Library of Congress practice, should be done in all instances using unspecified successive Cutter numbers.

Class D has often been criticized for being a far better classification of Western European history than any other area. Obviously the single subclasses for Africa and Asia do not contain as many numbers as the ten subclasses for Western Europe. Another problem is the use in Class D of geographic areas rather than the ever changing political areas. Usually the geographic name of an area is chosen rather than the political name.

Class D is another of the schedules which has potential reference uses. The local history numbers for the European countries contain comprehensive lists of counties, regions and some cities. The list of English counties in subclass DA is particularly useful. The index to Class D is a satisfactory reference aid.

CLASS E-F

Class E-F, American History, was the first schedule to be published in 1901 and was prepared by the Chief Classifier at the Library of Congress, Charles Martel. The second edition appeared in 1913 and was edited by Charles A. Flagg under the supervision of Martel. The third edition was published in 1958 and represented the work of Willard O. Waters, Irma I. Blake, Florence B. Currie, and Kathleen F. Clifford. Miss Voegelein served as the editor of this edition and Miss Dorothy Norberg prepared the index and the list of counties, departments, etc., in local history.

As Class E-F does not use double letters for subclasses, one major problem in using this schedule involves expansions. Many expansions are created by the use of decimal extensions which tend to make the notation somewhat cumbersome. Basically this schedule presents no major problems to the classifier; a complete outline as well as a detailed index are provided.

There are four tables to be used with Class F which precede F instead of following it as auxiliary tables usually do. Tables I, II and III are for states and IV is for metropolitan areas. Table I is used primarily for states with a long historical background. However, as all the individual states are fully worked out in the schedules, these tables serve as summaries and guides to interpretation and not as auxiliary tables. Table IV may be used for original classing of extensive local history material in a particular collection.

An example of the use of Tables I-III may be readily observed in the following comparison of the numbers assigned to the state of Wisconsin and its designated table, Table II. (Figures 53 and 53a.) Figures 54, 54a, and 54b show the assignment of numbers to Wisconsin. For example, the first of Wisconsin's fifteen numbers is "F 576." This number is for "Periodicals, Societies, Collections." The first number in Table II is also for "Periodicals, Societies, Collections." The following comparison of the two tables demonstrates this point throughout.

E-F

AMERICA

Table II	F576-590 Wisconsin.
(1) Periodicals. Societies. Collections.	576 Periodicals. Societies. Collections.
(3) Museums. Exhibitions, exhibits.	578 Museums. Exhibitions, exhibits.
(4) Gazetteers. Dictionaries. Geographic names.	579 Gazetteers. Dictionaries. Geographic names.
(4.3) Guidebooks.	.3 Guidebooks.
Directories.	
(4.5) General.	
(4.6) Elite.	₍State directories are no longer classified at the Library of Congress. ₎
(4.7) Business.	
(5) Biography (Collective). Genealogy (Collective).	580 Biography (Collective). Genealogy (Collective).
(5.2) Historiography.	.2 Historiography.
Historians, see E 175.5	Historians, see E 175.5.
(5.5) Study and teaching.	.5 Study and teaching.
(6) General works. Histories.	581 General works. Histories.
(6.3) Juvenile works.	.3 Juvenile works.
(6.5) Minor works. Pamphlets, addresses, essays etc.	.5 Minor works. Pamphlets, addresses, essays, etc.
(6.6) Anecdotes, legends, pageants, etc.	.6 Anecdotes, legends, pageants, etc.
(7) Historic monuments. Illustrative material.	582 Historic monuments (General). Illustrative material.
(8) Antiquities (Non-Indian).	583 Antiquities (Non-Indian).
(9)-(11) By period.	By period.
	584 Early to 1848.
	585 1836-1848. Wisconsin Territory.
	586 1848-1950.
(11.2) 1951-	.2 1951-

(12)   Regions, counties, etc.   587   Regions, counties, etc.
         A-Z.   A-Z.

(13)   Metropolis, Chief city.
         ₁Thus far, subdivision (13) has been used only for
         Chicago at the Library of Congress. ₁

(14)   Cities, towns, etc., A-Z.   589   Cities, towns, etc., A-Z.

(15)   Elements in the population. 590   Elements in the population.

    The extensive list of American Indians under the number
"E 99" is a noteworthy reference feature of Class E.
    The classifier should remember that subject is paramount
when classing in history. Although the complete works of a literary
author or a philosopher may be carefully classed together, the works
of a historian are usually not classed together. The works of a
historian are classed by the subject content of the individual works.
For example Thomas Carlyle's French Revolution is classed in
subclass DC for French history; Carlyle's Chartism is classed in
subclass DA for English history; and his Early Kings of Norway is
classed in subclass DL for Scandinavian history. Only if a historian
wrote solely on one subject could his works be classed together.

CLASS G

INTRODUCTION

The first edition of Class G, Geography, Anthropology, Sports and Games, was published in 1910 under the editorship of Clarence Perley. The preliminary work on the schedule was handled by W. Dawson Johnston, C. K. Jones and J. Christian Bay under the direction of Martel in 1904 and 1905. They were responsible for subclasses G, Geography (General); GA Mathematical and astronomical geography; GB, Physical geography; GC, Oceanology and oceanography; GF, Anthropogeography; and, GN, Anthropology. S. C. Stuntz prepared subclass GV, Sports and games. Subclasses GR, Folk-lore; and, GT, Manners and customs, were omitted in the first edition. These two subclasses were first published separately in 1915. The second edition of Class G appeared in 1928 and included a provisional scheme for atlases (G 1001-3035). In 1945 C. W. Buffum of the Map Division of the Library of Congress prepared a preliminary draft for a classification of maps using the numbers G 3160-9999 from subclass G. This material was incorporated into the third edition of Class G issued in 1954 under the editorship of Miss Voegelein.

Class G may be seen as a connective schedule between the history classes on one side, and the remaining social sciences on the other. Five of Class G's subclasses are related directly to geography, nevertheless much geographical material, especially works related to travel, is classed in history. This schedule, as most of the schedules in the social sciences, may be criticized for being outdated. This is certainly true in the schedule for anthropology: subclass GN reflects the structure and terminology used in anthropology at the beginning of the twentieth century.

TABLES FOR MAPS AND ATLASES

The main problem to be discussed in this section is the use of the detailed tables for atlases and maps at the end of subclass G. The other tables in this schedule create no major problems in use and are similar to previously discussed tables. The tables for atlases and maps (Figures 55-55j) include both directions and examples. These eleven pages of tables are to be examined and studied in conjunction with the following explanation. This unit is intended to supplement, not replace, the tables and directions provided by the Library of Congress.

G

GEOGRAPHY—ANTHROPOLOGY

G   Geography (General)
- 149– 570   Voyages and travels (General)
  - Discoveries, tours, mountaineering, adventures, etc.
  - Travel in special continents or countries is classified in D–F.
- 575– 890   Arctic and Antarctic regions
- 725– 765   Greenland
- 1001–3035   Atlases

GA   Mathematical and astronomical geography
- 101–1999   Cartography. Map drawing. Maps

GB   Physical geography
- 401– 638   Geomorphology
  - Shore lines, reefs, islands, mountains, deserts, etc.
- 651–2397   Water. Hydrology and hydrography
  - Springs, rivers, waterfalls, lakes, ponds, etc.

GC   Oceanology and oceanography
- 201–399   Dynamics of the sea: Waves, currents, tides, deposits

Biogeography. *See* QH–QL

GF   Anthropogeography

GN   Anthropology. Somatology. Ethnology. Ethnography (General)
- Ethnography of special continents or countries is classified in D–F.
- 51–161   Anthropometry. Skeleton. Craniometry
- 400–499   Customs and institutions (Primitive)
- 537–686   Special races
- 700–875   Prehistoric archeology

GR   Folk-lore
- 440–975   Folk-lore relating to special subjects

GT   Manners and customs (General)
- Manners and customs of special countries are classified in D–F.
- 170– 485   Houses. Dwellings
- 500–2370   Dress. Costume
- 2400–5090   Customs of private and social life
- 5320–6750   Customs of special classes, by birth, occupation, etc.

GV   Sports and amusements. Games
- 201– 547   Physical training
- 1580–1799   Dancing

In order to class maps and atlases Table I must be used.
(See Figures 55-55b). Table I is designed for major areas and sub-
areas. A major area is the general geographic area to which a
specific range of integral numbers is assigned in the schedule.
For instance, the range of numbers "G3800-3804" is assigned in
the schedule for maps of New York State. The major area, in
this case is New York State. A sub-area is a specific geographic
area within the major area. A sub-area may be a region or natural
feature of the major area, a major political division of the major
area (e. g. a county), or a city or town in the major area. There
are five subdivisions in Table I. (See also Figures 55-55b).

Table I (abridged)

(1) 0 or 5   General.

(2) 1 or 6   By subject.

(3) 2 or 7   By region, natural feature, etc.,
                       when not assigned individual num-
                       bers, A-Z.

(4) 3 or 8   By major political division (counties,
                       states, provinces, etc.) when not
                       assigned individual number, A-Z.

(5) 4 or 9   By city or town, A-Z.

Major Areas

The first two numbers in Table I are used for major areas
only. The first number "0 or 5" is used for general maps and atlases of the major area which have no special subject interest.
The second number "1 or 6" is used for maps and atlases of the
major area which have special subject interest. This second number is further subarranged by Table II. A general New York State
map which has no special subject interest will be classed in the
first number of the range of numbers for New York State "G3800."
New York State is in this case a major area. A New York State map
of special subject interest, such as a railroad map of New York
State, will be classed in the second number of the range of numbers
for New York State, "G 3801." This number would then be further
subdivided using Table II. Table II will be discussed in the following
section entitled "Subject Letter-numbers." New York State has a
specific range of numbers assigned for maps "G 3800-3804," which
makes New York State a major area. The first number of this

range, "G 3800, " is used for general maps of the major area which have no special subject interest. The second number of this range, "G 3801, " is used for maps of the major area which have special subject interest. Figure 55 demonstrates the use of these numbers for both maps and atlases.

Sub-areas

The other three numbers of Table I are used for sub-areas. The three types of sub-areas are: regions or natural features of the major area, major political divisions of the major area, and cities or towns in the major area. The third number of Table I, "2 or 7, " is used for maps and atlases covering only a region or natural feature of the major area. A map of the Adirondack Mountains or New York State will be classed in the third number of the range of numbers for New York State, "G 3802 . A2" --not "G 3801, " as the example in Figure 55 shows. ". A2" is the Cutter number for the specific region, Adirondack Mountains, in the major area, New York State. The Adirondack Mountains are, in this case, a sub-area of New York State.

The fourth number of Table I, "3 or 7, " is used for maps and atlases covering only a major political division (such as a county) of the major area. A map of Monroe County, New York, will be classes in the fourth number of the range of numbers for New York State, G 3803 . M6. " ". M6" is the Cutter number for the specific major political division, in this case, Monroe County. Monroe County is thus a sub-area of New York State.

The fifth number of Table I, "4 or 9, " is used for maps and atlases covering only a city or town of the major area. A map of Rochester, New York, will be classed in the fifth number of the range of numbers for New York State, "G 3804 . R6. " ". R6" is the Cutter number for the specific city or town, in this case, Rochester. Rochester is thus a sub-area of New York State. All sub-areas use Cutter numbers for specific subarrangement.

Subject Letter-numbers

The directions for the use of Table II explain that Table II is used for maps and atlases with specific subject interest. (See Figure 55c.) General maps and atlases as well as maps and atlases covering several subjects or topics do not use Table II. This table consists of seventeen main subject areas which are represented by capital letters; subtopics are designated by numbers. These symbols are called "subject letter-numbers" but do not have any alphabetical significance. These subject letter-numbers are treated as decimals. They may be applied to any major area map or atlas using the second number of Table I. They may also be applied to any sub-area map but not to sub-area atlases. This variation may well result from the fact that Table II was developed primarily to class maps. The summary of the seventeen main subject groups in Table II is shown below. (See also Figure 55d.)

Table II

Summary of Subject Subdivisions

A	Special category atlases and maps.
B	Mathematical geography. Cartography and surveying.
C	Physical sciences.
D	Biogeography.
E	Human and cultural geography.
F	Political geography.
G	Economic geography.
H	Mines and mineral resources.
J	Agriculture.
K	Forests and forestry.
L	Fisheries.
M	Manufacturing and processing.
N	Technology. Engineering. Public works.
P	Transportation and communication.
Q	Commerce and trade. Finance.
R	Military and naval geography.
S	Historical geography.

A typical development of subject letter-numbers is seen under the initial letter B for mathematical geography. It should be noted again that these letters and numbers have no alphabetical significance.

B   Mathematical geography.

Atlases and maps illustrating subjects of cartography, surveying, mapping.

1   Astronomical observatories and observations.

2   Movements of the earth.
Including time, time zones, date line.

3   Geodetic surveys.
         Triangulation and triangulation nets, precise
         levelling nets, including prime meridians, base
         lines, meridians.

5   Surveying. Extent of areas surveyed.

7   Cartography.
         Including projections.

8   Comparative area maps.

The use of these tables results in unusual elements in the notation.
A subject letter-number may appear to be a Cutter number, and it
is certainly treated as one within the call number.

Examples of the Use of Tables I and II

The following examples supplement those shown in Tables I
and II for maps and atlases. The numbers "G3800-3804, " assigned
in the schedules for maps of New York State, are used in the problems. [1] The Superior Map of New York produced by the George F.
Cram Company in 1954 is classed as a general map of the major
area in the first number, "G3800. " The next element of the call
number is the date of the map, "1954. " The final element is the
Cutter number for the source of the map in the main entry form,
Cram, ". C7. "

Superior Map of New York, 1954, by George F. Cram Co.

    G------ The single letter for the subclass, Geography
            (general).

    3800 --- The integral number meaning a general map of
            New York State.

    1954 --- The date of the map.

    . C7---- The first Cutter number for the source of the map,
            Cram.

---

[1]Note the difference in writing the parts of the call number
for an atlas versus a map as illustrated in Figure 55c.

The U. S. Geological Survey's Geologic Map Index of New York is classed as a subject map of the major area in the second number "G 3801"; its subject subdivision is that of an index map ". A2" in Table II, part A; the third element is the date "1952"; and the final element is the Cutter number for the source of the map in main entry from ". U5." It should be observed that both the subject letter-number and the Cutter number are prefaced with decimal points.

U. S. Geological Survey, Geologic Map Index of New York, 1952.

G------- The single letter for the subclass, Geography (general).

3801---- The integral number meaning a subject map of New York State.

. A2----- The subject letter-number meaning an index map.

1952---- The date of the map.

. U5----- The first Cutter number for the source of the map, U. S. ...

The fourth number under New York, "G 3803, " is used for county maps of New York State. For instance, the Department of Highways Map of Livingston County, New York, issued by Livingston County, New York, Superintendent of Highways in 1954 is classed "G 3803 . L5 1954 . L5. "

Department of Highways Map of Livingston County, New York, 1954.

G------- The single letter for the subclass, Geography (general).

3803---- The integral number meaning a sub-area map of New York State, in this case a county map.

. L5----- The first Cutter number for the county that is the subject of the map, Livingston.

1954---- The date of the map.

. L5----- The second Cutter number for the source of the map, Livingston County...

The fifth number for New York State, "G 3804, " is used for cities.
The Visitors Map of New York City issued by the New York City
Department of Commerce and Public Events is classed "G 3804
. N4 year . N4. "

Visitors Map of New York City

G------- The single letter for the subclass, Geography
(general).

3804 ---- The integral number meaning a city or town map
of New York State.

. N4----- The first Cutter number for the city that is the
subject of the map, New York City.

year ---- The date of map.

. N4----- The second Cutter number for the source of the
map, New York City Department of Commerce
and Public Events.

In some instances a sub-area map, such as a region, county, or a
city, may also have subject subdivisions. For instance, the Port
of New York Authority's New York Harbor Terminals is classed
"G 3804 . N4 P55 year . P6. "

New York Harbor Terminals.

G------- The single letter for the subclass, Geography
(general).

3804 ---- The integral number meaning a city or town map
of New York State.

. N4----- The first Cutter number for the city that is the
subject of the map, New York City.

P55----- The subject letter-number for the subject of the
port facilities.

year ---- The date of the map.

. P6----- The Cutter number for the source of the map,
Port of...

It should be noted that although the date for maps occurs before the Cutter number for source in main entry form, this does not happen with atlases. The following are two examples of atlases using the number for atlases of New York State, "G 1250-1254" (See also Figure 55c).

Richards' Atlas of New York State, 1959.

G------- The single letter for the subclass, Geography (general).

1250---- The integral number for a general atlas of New York State.

.R5----- The first Cutter number for the source of the atlas, Richards....

1959---- The date of the atlas.

American Map Co. Colorprint Atlas of New York City, Five Boroughs, 1960.

G------- The single letter for the subclass, Geography (general).

1254---- The integral number meaning an atlas of a city or town in New York State.

.N4----- The first Cutter number for the area of the atlas, New York City.

A6------ The second Cutter number for the source of the atlas, American Map Co.

1960---- The date of the atlas.

OTHER AUXILIARY TABLES IN CLASS G

There are three tables of geographical subdivisions at the end of the schedule. These present no serious problems in use. The first of these tables provides a list of decimal extensions to be added to any subject number in order to further subdivide geographically. The following is a part of this table (see also Figure 56).

.3	South America
.31	Argentina
.32	Bolivia

.33   Brazil
.34   Chile

This type of decimal extension may be seen as a development from Charles Ammi Cutter's "Local List" in his <u>Expansive Classification</u> rather than from Melvil Dewey's <u>Decimal Classification</u>.

    The schedule GR, Folklore, is not difficult to use, but it does demonstrate a typical situation which confronts the classifier. Provision is made for folklore to be classed in GR, but numbers in PN 905-1008, folk tales and folk literature, may be the better choice in some circumstances. Normally any work of literary interest should be classed in literature, even if the work is one of folklore. Another similar problem deals with works about manners and etiquette. These subjects are not classed together: GT is the subclass for manners; BJ, a part of philosophy, is used for etiquette. Thus, Maureen Daly's <u>Twelve Around the World</u> is classed "GT 75 .D3" whereas Betty Allen's <u>Mind Your Manners</u> is classed as etiquette in "BJ 1857 .C5 A42."

CLASS H

Class H, Social Sciences, includes only the generalia class
for the social sciences and two individual social science disciplines,
economics and sociology. The remaining individual disciplines may
be found in classes C, D, E-F for history, G for geography and
anthropology, and the following classes J for political science, K
for law, and L for education.

Dr. Roland R. Falkner and Charles Martel worked together
in developing the original pattern of schedules H-J-L. They were
assisted by W. Dawson Johnston, Luis Perez, and Edwin Wiley.
George M. Churchill prepared subclasses HS, Associations; and
HT, Communities. The first edition of Class H was published in
1910 without subclass HT which was published separately in 1915.
A second edition of Class H including subclass HT was issued in
1920. The third edition of Class H appeared in 1950 under the
editorship of Miss Voegelein. Classifiers in charge of Class H
from 1920 to 1950 were C. K. Jones, Leo La Montagne, and Philip
Krichbaum.

Examples of the use of tables in Class H are provided in
Chapter 4. Although Class H contains more tables than any other
schedule, few of these present any unusual or complicated features.
The exceptions are the auxiliary "Tables of Geographical Divisions."
Ten tables make use of a single column of geographic locations.
(See Figure 17 in Chapter 3.) The use of these tables is further
complicated because the subject subdivisions are represented by
tables within the schedules. For example, general works dealing
with theory of communism in geographic areas including the United
States are classed within the range of "HX 651-780" using Table V.
Following the statement of the range of numbers in the schedule is
the table for subject subdivisions for four number countries and one
number countries. (See also Figure 57.)

4 nos.	1 no.	
(1)	. A3	History.
(2)		General works.
(4)	. A4-Z	Particular communities, A-Z.

Before using this subject table, the classifier must determine the
range of geographic numbers available to the geographic area in
question.

H

SOCIAL SCIENCES

H	Social sciences (General)
HA	Statistics

ECONOMICS

HB		Economic theory
		Value, price, capital, interest, profit, etc.
	881–3700	Demography. Vital statistics
	3711–3840	Crises
HC		Economic history and conditions. National production, by country
HD		Economic history: Agriculture and industries
	101–2206	Land. Agriculture
	2321–3570	Industry. Corporations. Cooperation
	3611–4730	State and industrial organization
	4801–8942	Labor
		Wages, hours, strikes, trade unions, etc.
	9000–9999	Special industries and trades
HE		Transportation and communication
		Roads, waterways, railways, postal service, telegraph, etc.
HF		Commerce (General)
	1701–2701	Tariff policy
	5001–5780	Business. Accounting
	5801–6201	Advertising
HG		Finance
	201–1490	Money
	1501–3540	Banking
	3701–4000	Credit. Exchange
	4001–4497	Corporation finance. Trust companies
	4501–7933	Investment, speculation, etc.
	8011–9970	Insurance
HJ		Public finance
	2005–2199	Income and expenditure. The budget
	2240–7395	Revenue. Taxation. Customs. Tariff
	8003–8963	Public credit. Debts. Loans. Claims
	9000–9697	Local finance
	9701–9995	Public accounting

H

SOCIOLOGY

HM   Sociology (General and theoretical)

          101–121 Civilization. Culture. Progress
                  Cf. CB

          201–219 Social elements, forces, laws

          251–299 Social psychology

HN   Social history. Social reform

          30–39 The church and social problems
                  Cf. BR 115.S6

      Social groups

HQ   Family. Marriage. Home

            16– 471 Sex relations

           750– 799 Eugenics. Child culture, study, etc.

          1101–1870 Woman. Feminism

          1871–2030 Women's clubs

HS   Associations: Secret societies, clubs, etc.

HT   Communities. Classes. Races

          101– 381 Urban groups: The city

          401– 485 Rural groups: The country

          851–1445 Slavery
                  Works on slavery in the United States of America are
                  classified in E441–453.

HV   Social pathology. Philanthropy. Charities and corrections

          530– 696 Social welfare

          697–4630 Protection, assistance and relief of special classes
                        according to age, defects, race, occupation, etc.

          4701–4959 Protection of animals

          4961–4998 Degeneration

          5001–5720 Alcoholism. Intemperance. Temperance reform

          5725–5840 Tobacco and drug habits

          6001–6249 Criminology (General)

          6251–7220 Crimes and offenses

          7231–9920 Penology

          7551–8280 Police. Detectives. Constabulary

          8301–9920 Prisons. Penitentiaries. Punishment and reform

HX   Socialism. Communism. Anarchism. Bolshevism

          806–811 Utopias

Four Number Countries

For instance in Table V, the United States has a range of numbers "3-6." (See Figure 17 in Chapter 3.) The United States is thus a four number country in Table V. These four numbers, "3-6," are to be applied to the subject subdivisions for a four number country in the above subject table. Robert V. Hine's Cali- fornia's Utopian Colonies is classed by the Library of Congress as an historical work on the theories of communism in the United States. As the United States is a four number country in Table V, the four number column of the table for "HX 651-780" is used. An historical work will use the first number in the United States' range of 3 through 6. The first number in that range is "3". This number is then added to the base number as indicated in the foot- note to the range of numbers "HX 651-780." This footnote instructs the classifier to add the country number directly to "650." This gives the number "HX 653." The Cutter number for the main entry is ".H65." The complete call number is thus "HX 653 .H65."

Robert V. Hine's California's Utopian Colonies.

HX------ The double letters for the subclass, Socialism,
               communism, etc.

        650--- the base number for theories of communism
             by geographic area as given in the footnote.
          3--- the adjusted country number meaning a
        653   history of theories of communism in the
              United States.

653 ----- The integral number meaning a history of theories
             of communism in the United States.

.H65 ---- The first Cutter number for the main entry, Hine.

Another example is the classification of Arthur Eugene Bestor's Backwoods Utopias, which is classed "HX 654 .B4." This work is classed by the Library of Congress as a general work on theoretical communism in the United States, which uses the second number in the subject table. The second number in the United States' range is "4." When "4" is added to "650," as instructed by the footnote, the result is "654." The correct class number for this work is "HX 654." The classing is completed by cuttering for the main entry, Bestor, ".B4."

Bestor's Backwoods Utopias.

HX------ The double letters for the subclass, Socialism,
communism, etc.

650--- the base number for theories of communism
by geographic area as given in the footnote.

4--- the adjusted country number meaning a
general work on theories of communism
in the United States.

654

654 ----- The integral number meaning a general work on
theories of communism in the United States.

.B4 ----- The first Cutter number for the main entry, Bestor.

One Number Countries

Europe may be used as an example of a one number geographic
area. In Table V Europe has a range of numbers of "44 to 45."
As "45" is the first number of Great Britain's range, Europe has
only one number, "44," in Table V. (See Figure 43 in Chapter 4.)
A history of the theories of communism in Europe by Mario Einaudi
entitled Communism in Western Europe is classed "HX 694 . A3E5."
When Europe's country number "44" is added to "650," "694" is
the result. ". A3" is the reserved Cutter number for histories for
one number countries in the subject subdivision table. The second
Cutter number "E5" is the Cutter number for the main entry,
Einaudi.

Mario Einaudi's Communism in Western Europe.

HX------ The double letters for the subclass, Socialism,
communism, etc.

650--- the base number for theories of communism
by geographic area as given in the footnote.

44--- the country for Europe in Table V.

694

694 ----- The integral number meaning a work on theories of
communism in Europe.

. A3------The first Cutter number meaning a history of the
theories of communism.

E5-------The second Cutter number for the main entry,
Einaudi.

A detailed discussion of similar problems in Class H is provided
in Chapter 4, pp. 126-130, "Complex Tables of Geographical
Division."
Perhaps the greatest single problem in the use of Class H
and the other social science classes is where to class material
dealing with more than one of the disciplines in the social sciences.
The safest solution to this problem is to establish a precedent within
Library of Congress practice for a particular type of material.

CLASS J

Class J, Political science, was first published in 1910 under the editorship of Edwin Wiley. Subclasses JA, General works; JC, Political science, Theory of the state; and JK, United States Constitutional history and administration, were constructed by W. Dawson Johnston. Subclass JX, International law was prepared by Philip D. Phair. The second edition which was issued in 1924 was prepared by George M. Churchill and C. K. Jones. No new edition of this class has yet been published although one is currently in preparation. In 1961 the second edition was reprinted with supplementary pages of additions and changes to the class as of April, 1960.

W. C. Berwick Sayers described this class as the most revolutionary notion used in the entire system: "It is no less than the application of the 'national' method of grouping (familiar in the treatment of literature), conjoined with a chronological development, in complete contrast to the 'topical' method so familiar to users of the Decimal scheme."[2] This method of inserting the geographical divisions between the topical or subject divisions of a subject may be seen in the scheme for Constitutional history and administration. Subclass JF is for General works, but subclasses JK, JL, JN, and JQ are all for geographic areas: the United States; British America, Latin America; Europe; and Asia, Africa, Australia, and the Pacific Islands. This device allows the further subdivisions under geographic areas to be designed directly in relation to an individual area's constitutional history. Obviously the United States has a different pattern of development for its constitutional history than France or Germany. For example, there are eleven numbers allotted to suffrage for women in the United States, JK 1880-1911 while the similar topic in French constitutional history has only one number JN 2954 for woman's suffrage; similarly Germany has only one number for this topic JN 3825. Another example is political parties; over a hundred numbers are assigned for political parties in the United States, JK 2251-2391. France has only three numbers, JN 2997, JN 2999, and JN 3007, and Germany has six numbers, JN 3925, JN 3931, JN 3933, JN 3934, JN 3941, and JN 3946. In each case the appropriate range of numbers was assigned in relation to the amount of material at the Library of Congress.

---

[2] W. C. Berwick Sayers, A Manual of Classification for Librarians and Bibliographers. Rev. 3d ed. London: Grafton, 1955, p. 160.

J

POLITICAL SCIENCE

J   Documents
       1– 9   Official gazettes
               General serial documents not classified by subject
      10– 99   United States
      100–981   Foreign

JA   General works

JC   Political science.   Theory of the state
        Origin, nature, symbolism, functions, relations, etc. of the state
      311–323   Nationalism.   Minorities.   Geopolitics
      348–481   Forms of the state
           Imperialism, the world state, monarchy, aristocracy, democracy, fascism, corporate state, etc.
      571–628   The state and the individual.   Individual rights.   Liberty

CONSTITUTIONAL HISTORY AND ADMINISTRATION

JF   General works

JK   United States

JL   British America.   Latin America

JN   Europe

JQ   Asia, Africa, Australia, and Pacific Islands

JS   Local government

JV   Colonies and colonization.   Emigration and immigration

JX   International law
      1305–1598   International relations.   Diplomatic history
      1621–1896   Diplomacy.   The diplomatic service
      1901–1995   International arbitration.   World peace
      6001–6650   Private international law

There are several tables in Class J which are similar to the tables already discussed in Chapter 4. There are five auxiliary tables to be used for local government in subclass JS. (See Figures 58-58c.) Table 1 is for states or cities with 99 numbers; Table 2 is for states or cities with 20 numbers; Table 3 is for states or cities with 9 numbers; Table 4 is for states or cities with 1 number; and, Table 5 is for cities with a Cutter number.

Twenty Number States or Cities

Chicago is a city which is assigned twenty numbers in the schedule, "JS 701-720." Chicago thus uses Table 2 for its subdivisions. The following is an abridgment of Table 2. (See also Figures 58-58b.)

1	Periodicals, societies, etc.
	Manuals, registers, etc., by date.
2. A1-2	Administrative, judicial, etc., districts.
. A3	Registers, etc.
3	Separate documents, charters, etc., by date.
4	Laws, ordinances, codes, digests, etc.
	History and description.
5. A2	Collections: statistics, etc.
. A5-Z	General.
6	Early history (Medieval, etc.)
7	19th century to 1880.
8	Recent history.
10	Reform literature, etc.
	Special.
11	Local government and the state.
12	Other special, A-Z.
13	Local government other than municipal.
	Executive: Mayor, etc. Administration.
14. A1	General.
. A13	Special offices, departments, commissions, etc., A-Z.
. A15	Special subjects, A-Z.
	Civil service.
. A2	Report.
. A3	Rules.
. A4	Other, by date.
15	Legislative: Alderman, Council, etc.
16	Judiciary: Municipal courts.

17   Citizenship.
        Suffrage.
.A3   General.
.A4   Board of election commissioners. Annual report,
         etc.
.A5   Lists of voters, etc., by date.
        Election practice and systems.
18   Election law.
 .A2   Codes, manuals, by date.
 .A5   Separate, by date.
 .A7-Z Other, A-Z.
19   Political corruption.
20   Local, by city, borough, parish, district, ward, etc.,
       A-Z.

For example the 1867 Charter of Chicago is classed "JS 703 1867."
"3" is the appropriate number in Table 2 for "separate, documents,
charters, etc." which are subdivided by date. As Chicago's range
of numbers begins with "701" and as Table 2 begins with "1," all
of Chicago's numbers may be gained by direct numerical transfer
from Table 2 plus "700." This type of direct numerical transfer
may be applied any time the final digit of the first number of a
range of numbers is the same as the first number in the auxiliary
table.

The 1867 Charter of Chicago.

JS------The double letters for the subclass, Local govern-
         ment.

703-----The integral number for separate documents,
         charters, etc. of Chicago.

1867----The date of the charter as called for by the table.

The 1856 Charter and Ordinances of the City of Chicago is classed
under laws, ordinances, etc. in the fourth number in the table as
"JS 704 .A3 1856."

The 1856 Charter and Ordinances of the City of Chicago.

JS------The double letters for the subclass, Local govern-
         ment.

704-----The integral number for laws, ordinances, etc. of
         Chicago.

.A3------The first Cutter number meaning an official publication.

1856 -----The date of publication.

A recent history of Chicago contained in the Chicago Home Rule
Commission's report entitled Modernizing a City Government is
classed using the eighth number in Chicago's range of numbers
"708. "

Modernizing a City Government.

JS------- The double letters for the subclass, Local government.

708------ The integral number for a recent history of Chicago.

.A53 ---- The first Cutter number meaning an official publication.

A nonofficial recent history of Chicago by Harvey M. Karlen entitled The Governments of Chicago is classed "JS 708 . K3. "

Karlen's The Governments of Chicago.

JS------- The double letters for the subclass, Local government.

708------ The integral number for a recent history of Chicago.

.K3 ----- The first Cutter number for the main entry, Karlen.

The Annual Report of the Chicago Civil Service Commission is
classed under the executive branch of the local government using
the number "14. " This number is subdivided with reserved Cutter
numbers, one of which is ".A2" for Civil Service reports. The
appropriate classification within Chicago's range of numbers is
"JS 714 . A2. "

Chicago Civil Service Commission. Annual Report.

JS------- The double letters for the subclass, Local government.

714------ The integral number for the Chicago executive
government.

.A2 ----- The reserved official Cutter number meaning a
report of the Civil Service Commission.

Another similar example is the Chicago Board of Election Commissioners' Instructions on Election Laws and Election Procedure issued in 1940. This work uses the number "18" in Table 2 for "Election practice and systems." The subdivisions for this number include the reserved Cutter number ".A5" for separate election laws by date. The complete number is "JS 718 .A5 1940."

Instructions on Election Laws and Election Procedure, 1940.

JS------The double letters for the subclass, Local government.

718-----The integral number meaning election practice and systems in Chicago.

.A5 ----The reserved Cutter number meaning separate laws.

1940----The date as required by the table.

In general Class "J" does not create any unusual problems. However, it should be noted that political and diplomatic history is usually classed in the appropriate history class in "D," or "E-F," and not in "J."

CLASS K

In May of 1967 subclass KF, Law of the United States, the first
part of Class K Law, was made available in an electrostatic copy by
the Photoduplication Services of the Library of Congress. This
subclass was prepared by Werner B. Ellinger with the assistance
of John Fischer and the consultations of Miles O. Price and Carleton
W. Kenyon. The actual publication date is projected for later 1967
or early 1968.

This section represents the first subclass in the development
of the entire Class K for law. Although Class K was included in
the original outline for the classification, little work was done on
developing a classification schedule for law at the Library of Congress. There are several reasons for this. First much of the
material to be classed in this schedule was already assigned by
subject in Martel's seven points: school law in Class L for education, library law in Class Z for library science, etc. Second as
the Library of Congress maintains a separate Law Library which
utilizes the traditional form arrangement of law libraries, a subject classification was not vital.

In 1948 a scheme constructed by Miss Elizabeth Benyon for
the Law Library of the University of Chicago was published by the
Library of Congress but not adopted by the Library. Other nonofficial Class K schemes were developed by other libraries. One
of the most important of these Class K variants was the scheme
developed by the Los Angeles County Law Library.

In 1949 a joint meeting of the Library of Congress Committee
on a Classification for Law and the Committee on Cooperation with
the Library of Congress of the American Association of Law Libraries
began work on developing Class K. The content of Class K was projected and a tentative outline and notation was developed. Between
1953 and 1960 nine working papers were prepared at the Library
and distributed to librarians and scholars covering the following
topics: (1) German law; (2) Roman law; (3) History of German
law; (4) Canon law; (5) Chinese law; (6) English law; (7) Law of
Japan; (8) Classification of American law (A Survey); and (9) Law
of the United States. Subclass KF is the result of working paper (9).
As the notation planned for the tentative outline of Class K is not
being followed and some shifting of letters occurred, the tentative
outline of Class K is omitted in this chapter.

Subclass KF, law of the United States, encompasses federal
law and state law. An outline of federal law, summarized on p. 223,
is a detailed schedule but contains no new or unusual notation. The
subclass for state law introduces a new device to Library of Congress
notation, triple capital letters. States are arranged alphabetically

SUBCLASS KF, LAW OF THE UNITED STATES
SUMMARY OUTLINE OF KF FEDERAL LAW

1-8	Bibliography.
16-49	Legislative documents.
50-90	Statutes and administrative regulations.
101-152	Law reports and related material.
154	Encyclopedias.
156	Law dictionaries. "Words and Phrases. "
159	Legal maxims. Quotations.
165	Uniform State Laws.
170	Form books.
(175)	Periodicals.
178	Yearbooks.
180-185	Judicial statistics.
190-195	Directories.
200	Society and bar association journals and yearbooks.
202	Congresses.
209-224	Collections.
228	Records and brief of individual civil suits.
240-246	Legal research. Legal bibliography.
250-251	Legal composition and draftsmanship.
255	Law reporting.
260	Cases and materials.
262-292	Legal education.
294	Law societies, A-Z.
297-334	The legal profession.
336-337	Legal aid. Legal aid societies.
338	Lawyer referral services.
350-375	History.
379-384	Jurisprudence and philosophy of American law.
385-391	General and comprehensive works.
394-395	Common law in the U.S.
398-400	Equity.
410-418	Conflict of laws.
420	Retroactive law. "Intertemporal law. "
425-435	General principles and concepts.
445-450	Concepts applying to several branches of law.
465-553	Persons.
560-720	Property.
726-745	Trusts and trustees.
746-750	Estate planning.
753-780	Succession upon death.
801-1241	Contracts.

1244	Restitution. Quasi contracts. Unjust enrichment.
1246-1327	Torts.
1341-1348	Agency.
1355-1480	Associations.
1501-1548	Insolvency and bankruptcy. Creditor's rights.
1600-2940	Regulation of industry, trade, and commerce. Occupational law.
2971-3192	Intellectual property.
3195-3198	Unfair competition
3300-3750	Social legislation.
3775-3813	Public health. Sanitation.
3821-3829	Medical legislation.
3832	Eugenics. Sterilization.
3835-3838	Veterinary laws. Veterinary hygiene.
3841-3845	Prevention of cruelty to animals.
3861-3894	Food. Drugs. Cosmetics.
3901-3925	Liquor control. Prohibition.
3941-3977	Public safety.
3985-3995	Control of social activities.
4101-4258	Education.
4270-4330	Science and arts. Research.
4501-5130	Constitutional law.
5150	National emblems. Flag. Seal. Seat of government. National anthem.
5152	Patriotic customs and observances.
5153-5154	Decorations of honor. Awards.
5155-5156	Commemorative medals.
5300-5332	Local government.
5336-5398	Civil service. Government officials and employees.
5399	Police and power of the police.
5401-5425	Administrative organization and procedure.
5500-5865	Public property. Public restraints on private property
5900-6075.5	Government measures in time of war, national emergency, or economic crisis. Emergency economic legislation.
6200-6795	Public finance.
7201-7755	National defense. Military law.
8201-8228	Indians.
8700-9075	Courts. Procedure.
9085	Arbitration and award. Commercial arbitration.
9201-9461	Criminal law.
9601-9760	Criminal procedure.

by initial letter: all states beginning with "C" are arranged in KFC; all states beginning with "N" are located in "KFN, " etc. Fully developed sections are complete for California law, "KFC, " and New York law, "KFN. " There is also a table of subject divisions for the law of other states and an example of the necessary modifications for Pennsylvania law. Tables for states and territories, for cities, and for form divisions are included in addition to complete instructions on the use of all tables. Although as yet not a large amount of material has been classed in KF, the schedule appears to be clear and easy to use. There are form division tables for 20 number subjects, Table I; 10 number subjects, Table II; 5 number subjects, Table III and IV; 2 number subjects, Table V; and 1 number subjects, Table VI. In addition there is a form division table for Cutter number topics, Table VII, as well as two other tables of special modifications. The following are three examples of recently assigned KF numbers.

U.S. Laws, statutes, etc. The Bankruptcy Act, Enacted July 2, 1898, as amended through December 31, 1966, with annotations, 1967, edited by John Hanna and James Angell Mac Lachen.

KF------ The double letters for the subclass, Law of the United States.

1511 ---- The integral number meaning a U.S. bankruptcy statute.

.53 ----- The decimal extension of the integral number using successive Cutter numbers as directed by Table I.

.H3 ----- The first Cutter number meaning an annotated edition of the statute annotated by Hanna.

1967 ---- The date of publication.

Commerce Clearing House. Tax Rewards in Personal and Business Life Insurance, 1964.

KF------ The double letters for the subclass, Law of the United States.

6428 ---- The integral number meaning a work on a particular source of tax income.

. L5------The first Cutter number for the particular source of tax income, life insurance proceeds.

C6-------The second Cutter number for the main entry, Commerce...

Commerce Clearing House. Federal Estate and Gift Taxes Explained, Including Estate Planning, 1967.

KF------ The double letters for the subclass, Law of the United States.

6572 ---- The integral number meaning a general work on estate, inheritance and gift taxes.

. Z9 ----- The reserved Cutter number for compends, outlines, minor works, etc. according to Table V.

C6 ------ The second Cutter number for the main entry, Commerce...

An example of a KFN number is the following:

New York (State) Laws, statutes, etc. The Tax Law of the State of New York, Including Law Provisions Imposing Admissions and Sales Tax as Amended to Date, as of August 1966.

KFN----- The triple letters for the subclass, Law of states of the United States beginning with "N."

5860----- The integral number meaning a general work on taxation in New York State.

. A3 ----- The reserved Cutter number meaning a collection.

Two examples of KFC numbers are:

California. Laws, statutes, etc. Evidence Code, Annotated, of the State of California, Adopted May 18, 1965, Effective January 1, 1967.

KFC------ The triple letters for the subclass, Law of states of the United States beginning with "C."

1030----- The integral number meaning a general work on
   evidence procedure in California.

.A33 ---- The reserved Cutter number meaning a collection
   of regulations.

1965----- The date of publication.

.D4 ----- The second Cutter number meaning an annotated
   edition cuttered by the annotator, Deering.

California. Laws, statutes, etc. Penal Code of California.
Peace Officers Abridged Edition. Prepared under the
direction of Thomas C. Lynch, 1965.

KFC----- The triple letters for the subclass, Law of states
   of the United States beginning with "C."

1100----- The integral number meaning general works on
   criminal law in California.

.Z9 ----- The reserved Cutter number meaning a minor work,
   in this case an abridged edition.

A5 ------ The second Cutter number indicating this is an
   official work.

CLASS L

Class L, Education, was first published in 1911. J. C. Bay
and W. D. Johnston developed subclasses L, General works; LA,
History of education; LB, Theory and practice of education; LC,
Special forms, relations and applications; LD, Universities and
colleges of the United States; LE, Other American universities and
colleges; and, LG, Universities and colleges of Europe. A. F.
Schmidt revised the work of Bay and Johnston and completed the
schedule with the exception of subclasses LC, Special forms; LJ,
College fraternities and their publications; and, LT, Textbooks:
These three subclasses were developed by J. D. Wolcott. In 1928
the second edition of Class L was issued. G. M. Churchill and
C. K. Jones were responsible for the revisions in the second edition.
The third edition, published in 1951, represented the successive
work of C. K. Jones, Leo LaMontagne, R. O. Sutter, Philip Krichbaum, and Leonard Ellinwood. Miss Voegelein served as the editor
of this edition of Class L.

This class presents no serious problems to the classifier.
There are several tables in this class, all relatively easy to use.
The most complex tables are for the subdivisions for individual
institutions in subclasses LD and LE. However these tables are
similar to the tables already discussed and should create no problem
in application. The only difference is in the use of Table I which
is used for all institutions without a particular designated table.
Table I is designed to establish a constant successive Cutter number sequence to use with a designated range of Cutter numbers.
Although such a device may appear confusing to the beginner, it is
clearly illustrated in two examples included in Table I (see Figures
60, 60a and 60b). The other tables in this class do not contain such
elements.

Trinity College, Hartford, Conn., is assigned a range of
Cutter numbers, ". T37-46" under the integral number "LD 5361. "
(See also Figure 59.) As Trinity College is not designated to use
Table II-V, it uses Table I. The directions to use Table I call for
substituting for "x1, x2" of Table I, the initial and first digit or
digits of the assigned Cutter numbers. In the case of Trinity Col-
lege, "T3" is substituted for "x1" and "T4" is substituted for "x2. "
The number in Table I for college statutes, by-laws, etc. is "x175. "
The Statutes of Trinity College of 1857 are classed "LD 5361 . T375
1857. " "x175" is replaced by the appropriate numbers in Trinity
College's range of Cutter numbers, ". T375"; i. e., ". T3" is substituted for "x1. "

L

EDUCATION

L	General works
LA	History of education
LB	Theory and practice of education. Teaching

Pre-school, kindergarten, primary, elementary, secondary, higher

1051–1140	Educational psychology and child study
1705–2285	Education and training of teachers
2503–3095	School administration, organization, discipline, etc.
3205–3325	School architecture and equipment
3401–3497	School hygiene
3525–3635	Special days, school life, etc.

LC	Special forms, relations and applications
8– 63	Special forms of education

Self culture; home, private, and public education

71– 245	Sociological aspects of education

Education and the state, secularization, etc.

129– 145	Compulsory education. Attendance
149– 160	Illiteracy
221– 235	Schools as social centers
251– 951	Character education. Religion and education. Education under church control
1001–1261	Types of education: Humanistic, vocational, professional, etc.
1390–5140	Education of special classes of persons

Women, Negroes, exceptional children, defectives, etc.

5201–6691	Education extension. Adult education

Universities and colleges

LD	United States
LE	Other American
LF	Europe
LG	Asia, Africa, Oceania
LH	University, college, and school magazines, etc.
LJ	College fraternities and their publications
LT	Textbooks

Only textbooks covering several subjects are classified here. Textbooks of particular subjects are classified with those subjects in B–Z.

Statutes of Trinity College, 1857.

LD------ The double letters for the subclass, Colleges and universities of the United States.

5361 ---- The integral number meaning an individual institution, whose initial letters are "Tri-. "

. T375 --- The first Cutter number meaning the statutes and by-laws of Trinity College, Hartford, Conn.

1857 ---- The date of publication.

The Catalogue of the Officers and Students is classed as an annual catalog using the number "x2" of Table I. "T4" is substituted for "x2" and the resulting number is "LD 5361 . T4. "

Catalogue of the Officers and Students of Trinity College.

LD------ The double letters for the subclass, Colleges and universities of the United States.

5361 ---- The integral number meaning an individual institution, whose initial letters are "Tri-. "

. T4 ----- The first Cutter number meaning an annual catalog of Trinity College, Hartford, Conn.

"x2j" in Table I represents "Degrees and honors. " A work by Trinity College entitled Prizes and Prizemen, 1849-1907, is classed "LD 5361 . T4j 1907. " This is an example of the use of workmarks on Cutter numbers that Table I uses extensively.

Prizes and Prizemen, 1849-1907, of Trinity College, 1907.

LD------ The double letters for the subclass, Colleges and universities of the United States.

5361 ---- The integral number meaning an individual institution, whose initial letters are "Tri-. "

. T4j ---- The first Cutter number meaning a work on degrees and honors at Trinity College, Hartford, Conn.

1907 ---- The date of publication.

Alumni directories use the number "21a" in Table I. The Trinity College Alumni Directory is classed "LD 5361 . T41a. " Again "T4" has been substituted for "x2" in the table number "x21a. "

Alumni Directory, Trinity College.

LD------ The double letters for the subclass, Colleges and
            universities of the United States.

5361 ---- The integral number meaning an individual insti-
            tution, whose initial letters are "Tri-. "

. T41a --- The first Cutter number meaning an alumni directory
            of Trinity College, Hartford, Conn.

"21c" is the number in Table I for an "Obituary record. " Necrology:
Trinity Men who Died during the Years is classed "LD 5361 . T41c. "
"T4" has been substituted for "2x" in the table number "x21c. "

Necrology: Trinity Men who Died during the Years.

LD------ The double letters for the subclass, Colleges and
            universities of the United States.

5361 ---- The integral number meaning an individual insti-
            tution, whose initial letters are "Tri-. "

. T41c" -- The first Cutter number meaning an obituary record
            of Trinity College, Hartford, Conn.

"x22" is the number in Table I for a general history. An official
publication of Trinity College, Trinity College, Historical and Descriptive, is classed "LD 5361 . T42. " "T4" has been substituted
for "x2" in the table number "x22. "

Trinity College, Historical and Descriptive.

LD------ The double letters for the subclass, Colleges and
            universities of the United States.

5361 ---- The integral number meaning an individual insti-
            tution, whose initial letters are "Tri-. "

. T42 ---- The first Cutter number meaning a general history
            of Trinity College, Hartford, Conn.

The interpretation of subclass LT for textbooks may raise
some problems. This subclass is designed only for textbooks
covering several subjects; textbooks on a particular subject are
classed with that subject. If one wishes to collect all textbooks, as
in a curriculum library, it is possible to affix a locational label
"LT" to the spine of the book in addition to its subject call number.
Without using such a device, however, it would be impossible to
collocate all textbooks in one place using Library of Congress classification.

CLASS M

Oscar G. Sonneck, Chief of the Division of Music of the Library of Congress developed Class M, Music, in 1902, and the first edition was published in 1904. A revised edition was issued in 1917.

In the prefatory note to the first edition Mr. Sonneck described the development of this class: "As a matter of course the scheme, at least so far as it concerns music proper, took a form leaning toward the classified catalogues of publishers, and somewhat different from the schemes adopted by the notable American and European libraries. But care was taken to profit by the experience of these. In its present form the scheme embodies many valuable suggestions of the Chief classifier of the Library, Mr. Charles Martel, besides such modifications as he considered necessary in conformity with the arrangement of other classes of books in the Library."

This schedule differs in several ways from the other schedules that were prepared entirely by classifiers. There are only three subclasses: M, Music; ML, Literature of Music; and, MT, Musical instruction and study. Each section has its own outline which is called a "synopsis." Subclass M has a section devoted to definitions of musical terms and special rules. In fact, the actual classification in this schedule tends to be a scheme based on physical form rather than subject classification. All of the works by and about a composer will not be found in one place. In subclass M separate numbers are given to different musical forms, i. e., M 452 for string quartets, M 1001 for symphonies, M 1500 for operas, etc. For example, Beethoven's Third Symphony is classed "M 1001 . B4 op. 55." In this case "M 1001" means the musical form the symphony; ". B4" is the Cutter number for the composer Beethoven; and, "op. 55" is the opus number for Beethoven's Third Symphony. It should be noted that opus numbers rather than symphony numbers are used.

Beethoven's Symphony no. 3.

M------ The single letter for the subclass, Music.

1001 --- The integral number meaning the musical form, a symphony.

. B4 ---- The first Cutter number for the main entry, Beethoven.

op. 55 -- The designation of the particular symphony, no. 3, by opus number.

M

MUSIC

Beethoven's First Symphony, opus 21, is classed "M 1001 . B4 op. 21. "

<u>Beethoven's Symphony no. 1.</u>

M------- The single letter for the subclass, Music.

1001 ---- The integral number meaning the musical form, the symphony.

. B4 ----- The first Cutter number for the main entry, Beethoven.

op. 21 --- The designation of the particular symphony, no. 1, by opus number.

The opus number is the distinctive element in the notation. The symphony number does not appear in the notation. A score of Beethoven's First Symphony containing a piano arrangement by Anis Fuleihan is classed "M 1001 . B4 op. 21 . F8. "

<u>Beethoven's Symphony no. 1</u>, with a piano arrangement by Anis Fuleihan.

M------- The single letter for the subclass, Music.

1001 ---- The integral number meaning the musical form, the symphony.

. B4 ----- The first Cutter number for the main entry, Beethoven.

op. 21 --- The designation of the particular symphony, no. 1, by opus number.

. F8 ----- The second Cutter number for the arranger, Fuleihan.

A Eulenburg miniature score edition of Beethoven's Second Symphony is classed "M 1001 . B4 op. 36 . E8. "

<u>Beethoven's Symphony no. 2</u>, Eulenburg miniature score.

M------- The single letter for the subclass, Music.

1001 ---- The integral number meaning the musical form, the symphony.

.B4 ----- The first Cutter number for the main entry,
Beethoven.

op. 36 --- The designation of the particular symphony, no. 2,
by opus number.

.E8 ----- The second Cutter number for the edition of the
score, Eulenburg.

There are other original additions to the notation that occur
in Class M. These are explained in the schedule and examples are
often provided. A special number in subclass ML is "ML 410" for
all biographies of musicians, including a complete expansion for
the German composer Richard Wagner. For instance Anton Felix
Schindler's Biographie von Ludwig van Beethoven published in 1949
is classed "ML 410 . B4S333 1949. "

Schindler's Biographie von Ludwig van Beethoven, 1949.

ML ------ The double letters for the subclass, Literature of
music.

410 ------ The integral number meaning biographies of
musicians.

.B4 ----- The first Cutter number for the subject of the
biography, Beethoven.

S333 ----- The second Cutter number for the author of the
biography, Schindler.

1949 ----- The date of publication.

It should also be noted that the range of numbers ML 111-158 is
provided for bibliography of music. This is one of the few instances
in L. C. classification that bibliography is classed with the subject
rather than separately in Class Z.

Another difference which may be found in this schedule is
the use of many divide-like notes instead of auxiliary tables. For
instance, instrumental music for the flute is classed in subclass
M in the following fashion.

Flute

60   Miscellaneous collections.

Original compositions.

61	Collections.
62	Separate works.
	Arrangements.
63	Collections.
64	Separate works.

However instrumental music for other instruments is simply given a range of five numbers to be subdivided like flute. Such devices are commonly used in Class M.

65-69	Oboe.
70-74	Clarinet.

Arrangement of Class M by physical form rather than by subject raises some criticism. However, it must be remembered that the author catalog will assemble all the works by a composer in one place, and in this case, the classification provides another access to the material. Such an arrangement of material is in all probability easier for the musician to use than the musiologist.

CLASS N

Class N, Fine Arts, was prepared under the direction and supervision of Charles Martel. The first edition was published in 1910 and a second edition appeared in 1917. The third and present edition was issued under the direction of Clarence W. Perley in 1922. This schedule was influenced by the fine arts' sections of both the Dewey Decimal Classification and Cutter's Expansive Classification. In addition the catalog of the Library of the Kunstgewerbe-Museum of Berlin was used for special features. Also the Library of the Art Institute of Chicago recommended ideas from its modifications of the Decimal Classification.

The close relationship of this schedule to the other two classification schemes may be observed in the use of subclasses for different artistic forms or media--NA Architecture; NB, Sculpture; NC, Graphic arts in general; ND, Painting; NE, Engraving. Because of this division, the pattern in the fine arts differs from the patterns in literature and philosophy. All of the works by and about an individual artist will not be classed in the same place.

There are six auxiliary tables at the end of Class N. The first four of these (I, II, III, and III-A) are relatively simple tables of geographic subdivisions. Table IV is a nine-page table of geographic subdivisions with special added elements such as collective and individual biography of artists.

The following is an excerpt from the first page of this table. (See also Figure 61.)

Table IV

01	America.
02	Spanish America.
03	North America.
05	United States.
07	Colonial period; 18th (and early 19th) century.
10	19th century.
12	20th century.
15	New England.
20	South.
25	West.
28	Pacific states.
30	States, A-Z.
35	Cities, A-Z.
36	Collective biography.
37	Special artists, A-Z.
	Canada.
40	General.

[etc.]

N

FINE ARTS

N   General
- 8700–9084   Art and the state.   Public art

NA   Architecture
- 4600–6113   Religious architecture
- 7100–7625   Domestic architecture
- 9000–9425   Esthetics of cities.   City and regional planning and beautifying

NB   Sculpture and related arts

NC   Graphic arts in general.   Drawing and design.   Illustration
- 1300–1765   Caricature.   Pictorial humor and satire

ND   Painting
- 1700–2399   Water-color painting
- 2890–3416   Illuminating of manuscripts and books

NE   Engraving.   Prints
- 1000–1325   Wood engraving.   Xylography.   Japanese prints
- 1400–1775   Metal engraving: Color prints
  - Copper, line, stipple, mezzotint, aquatint, etc.
- 1940–2225   Etching.   Dry point
- 2250–2529   Lithography

NK   Art applied to industry.   Decoration and Ornament
- 1700–3505   Interior decoration.   Home decoration
  - Furniture, rugs, tapestries, upholstery, etc.
- 3700–4695   Ceramics.   Pottery
  - Earthenware, porcelain, vases, tiles, etc.
- 5000–6050   Enamel.   Glass.   Stained glass.   Glyptic arts
- 6400–8450   Metal-work
  - Armor, plate, jewelry, bronzes, pewter, etc.
- 8800–9499   Textile arts and needlework
- 9600–9950   Woodwork
  - Wood-carving, lacquer, marquetry, fretwork, etc.

Landscape gardening.   *See* SB 469–479

Photography.   *See* TR

The range of numbers for Modern art "N 6501-7413" uses Table IV. This is indicated in the schedule by the Roman numeral "IV" which follows the listing of this range of numbers.

N Fine Art

    Modern Art.

6501-7413   Special countries (Table IV).

A work published by "Art in America" called <u>What is American in American Art</u> is treated as a general work on modern art in the United States. It is classed "N 6505 . A68. " The first two digits of Table IV and the first number in the subject range match. "N 6501" is for Modern Art in all the Americas as "01" is the table number for the geographic area "America. " Similarly in the above example the "05" from the table, meaning the geographic area of the United States, fits into the range of numbers "N 6501-7413" as the number "N 6505". In short the classifier finds that the table number, in this case, is added to a base number "N 6500".

  Art in America's <u>What is American in American Art</u>.

  N------ The single letter for the subclass, General fine arts.

  6505 --- The integral number meaning a work on modern art in the United States.

  . A68--- The first Cutter number for the main entry, Art in America.

Another example of a general work on modern art in the United States is Henri Dorra's <u>The American Muse</u>. This is similarly classed "N 6505 . D65. "

  Henri Dorra's <u>The American Muse</u>.

  N------- The single letter for the subclass, General fine arts.

  6505 ---- The integral number meaning a work on modern art in the United States.

  . D65---- The first Cutter number for the main entry, Dorra.

A typical semantic problem may be observed in both of these examples. The adjective "American" is used to mean the geographic area the United States. This usage also may be seen in Lloyd Goodrich's <u>Pioneers of Modern Art in America</u>. This work is classed as a work on modern art in the United States during the twentieth century. The appropriate table number for the twentieth century of the United States is "12". The appropriate subject number is then "N 6512" or "12" added to "N 6500." The complete call number is "N 6512 . G62."

Lloyd Goodrich's Pioneers of Modern Art in America.

N------ The single letter for the subclass, General fine arts.

6512 --- The integral number meaning twentieth century modern art in the United States.

. G62--- The first Cutter number for the main entry, Goodrich.

The Artist's Environment: West Coast issued by the Amon Carter Museum of Western Art, Fort Worth, Texas, is a more specialized example. This is a work dealing with modern art in the United States on the West Coast. The table number to be used here is "28" for "Pacific states." The resulting call number is "N 6528 . A4".

The Artist's Environment: West Coast, Amon Carter Museum of Western Art, Fort Worth, Texas.

N------ The single letter for the subclass, General fine arts.

6528 --- The integral number meaning modern art in the United States in the Pacific states region.

. A4---- The first Cutter number for the main entry, Amon...

A work on an individual state in the United States uses the table number "30". In the case of modern art this number is then used for the name of the individual state. A work issued by the Museum of Art of the University of Kansas entitled Kansiensiana is classed "N 6530 . K3K3."

Kansas. University. Museum of Art. Kansiensiana.

N------ The single letter for the subclass, General fine arts.

6530 --- The integral number meaning a work on modern art in the United States in an individual state.

. K3---- The first Cutter number for the individual state, Kansas.

K3----- The second Cutter number for the main entry, Kansas.

Similarly the number "35" is used in the table for an individual city in the United States. Bernard Harper Friedman's School of New York deals with modern art in New York City. This is classed "N 6535 . N5F7. " In this case the first Cutter number, ". N5, " is used for the name of the city, New York City.

> Friedman's School of New York.
>
> N------ The single letter for the subclass, General fine arts.
>
> 6535 --- The integral number meaning a work on modern art in the United States in an individual city.
>
> . N5---- The first Cutter number for the individual city, New York.
>
> F7----- The second Cutter number for the main entry, Friedman.

Works on individual artists in the United States use the table number "37". A work issued by the Solomon R. Guggenheim Museum entitled Frederick Kiesler: Environmental Sculpture is an example of the use of this number. This is classed "N 6537 . K5S6. " In this case the first Cutter number is used for the subject of the work, Kiesler.

> Solomon R. Guggenheim Museum, Frederick Kiesler: Environmental Sculpture.
>
> N------ The single letter for the subclass, General fine arts.
>
> 6537 --- The integral number meaning a work on modern art in the United States covering an individual artist.
>
> . K5---- The first Cutter number for the subject of the work, Kiesler.
>
> S6 ----- The second Cutter number for the main entry, Solomon...

Cedric Dover's American Negro Art poses a different problem. It is classed "N 6538 . N5D6. " Obviously the number taken from the table was "38"; however, "38" does not appear in the table. The table shows a gap from "37" to "40". In the "Additions and Changes" section at the back of Class N is the following addition to Table IV. (See also Figure 62.)

> "38   Special races and ethnic groups, A-Z.
>
>   e. g.   . N5 Negro. "

Cedric Dover's <u>American Negro Art</u>.

N------ The single letter for the subclass, General fine arts.

6538--- The integral number meaning a work on modern art in the United States covering a special race and/or ethnic group.

.N5---- The first Cutter number for the special race, Negro.

D6----- The second Cutter number for the main entry, Dover.

At the end of this table is a list of "art cities" which is used in conjunction with the range of numbers, "N6501-7413". For example Rome is an art city listed in this table as "N 6920. " (See Figure 22 in Chapter 3.) An exhibition catalog of modern art in Rome from 1930 to 1945 by Giorgio Castelfranco and Dario Durbé entitled <u>La Scuola Romana dal 1930 al 1945</u> is classed "N 6920 . C33. " This number may also be derived from Table IV as Italy has a range of numbers "411-423" with Rome given the specific number "420". (See also Figure 63.) When "420" is added to the base number "N 6500", the result is "N 6920".

<u>La Scuola Romana dal 1930 al 1945</u>, by Giorgio Castelfranco and Dario Durbé.

N------ The single letter for the subclass, General fine arts.

6920--- The integral number meaning modern art in Rome.

.C33--- The first Cutter number for the main entry, Castelfranco.

The sixth table is a list of English counties arranged by Cutter numbers. (See Figure 23 in Chapter 3.) There are other special tables within the schedules including some which use a prescribed range of successive numbers. "NA 4410-4510, " the architecture of government buildings is an example of this. (See also Figures 64 and 64a.)

NA   Architecture.

Special classes of buildings.

Classed by use.

4410-4510 Government buildings.

Under each:

0. General.

1. United States.

2.   States.

3.   Cities.

5. Foreign countries, A-Z.

      (1) General.

      (2) Local, A-Z.

            e. g. . G3, Germany--General.

                . G4, Germany--Local.

      Contracts and specifications.

6.   United States. By place only, A-Z.

7.   Foreign. By place only, A-Z.

4410-4417 Capitols.

4420-4427 Government offices and bureaus.

4430-4437 City halls. Town halls.

For example Walter Kiewert's <u>Deutsche Rathäuser</u>, a general work dealing with the architecture of German city halls, is classed "NA 4435 . G3K5. " The range of numbers for city halls is "NA 4430-4437. " "5" is the assigned number for foreign countries. The foreign countries are then to be subdivided alphabetically by country with two successive Cutter numbers, one for general works and the other for local works. As this is a general work the first of the successive Cutter numbers is used, ". G3".

Walter Kiewert's <u>Deutsche Rathäuser</u>.

NA----- The double letters for the subclass, Architecture.

4435 --- The integral number for architecture of city halls in foreign countries.

. G3 ---- The successive Cutter number meaning a general work on German city halls.

K5 ----- The second Cutter number for the main entry, Kiewert.

Examples illustrating the use of most of these tables are included in the subclass schedules. None of the tables in Class N creates any major difficulties. Problems arise more frequently in the selection of material to be assigned to Class N; a work may appear to fit into more than one category. Comparison of the work to be classed in "N" with similar books already cataloged will provide guidance to the best choice and will maintain consistency within established practice. For instance, material on esthetics may be classed in Class N or it may be classed in subclass BH. Works on photoengraving may be classed in subclass NE, Engraving, or in subclass TR, Photography. A work on alphabets such as E. Lebner's Alphabets and Ornaments is classed "NK 3600 . L36" while J. Bouuaert's Historie de l'alphabet is classed in "P 211 . B68." Both numbers are valid locations for material on alphabets--one from an artistic viewpoint and the other a philological one.

CLASS P

INTRODUCTION

Class P, Language and Literature, took over forty years to construct. Much of the work was done by Dr. Walter F. Koenig, who began the work in 1909. Class P was completed in 1948 with the publication of subclass PG, in part, Russian Literature. Class P contains over one-third of the pages of the entire classification. Class P is made up of eleven different schedules: (1) subclass P-PA, Philology, Linguistics, Classical Philology, Classical Literature; (2) a supplement to subclass PA for Byzantine and modern Greek literature, medieval and modern Latin literature; (3) subclasses PB-PH, Modern European languages; (4) subclass PG, in part, Russian literature; (5) subclasses PJ-PM, Languages and literatures of Asia, Africa, Oceania, America, Mixed languages, Artificial languages; (6) an Index to languages and dialects in P-PA, PB-PH, and PJ-PM; (7) subclasses PN, PR, PS, PZ, Literature (general), English and American literature, Fiction in English, Juvenile literature; (8) subclass PQ, part 1, French literature; (9) subclass PQ, part 2, Italian, Spanish and Portuguese literatures; (10) subclass PT, part 1, German literature; and subclass PT, part 2, Dutch and Scandinavian literatures. Of these eleven schedules only the Index to languages and dialects is in a second edition.

SUBCLASSES PN, PR, PS, PZ

Subclasses PN, PR, PS, and PZ represent the first of the Class P schedules issued. This schedule under the editorship of Edwin Wiley was published in 1915 and contains the four subclasses covering: world literature, English literature, American literature, fiction in English, and juvenile literature.

Within this schedule the recurring plan or pattern for each literature appears for the first time. This pattern is the following:

1) History and criticism;

2) Collections or anthologies of more than one author;

3) Individual authors; and

4) Non-national literature if appropriate.

The third element, individual authors, is a most important characteristic of Library of Congress classification. The complete literary

P

LANGUAGE AND LITERATURE

P		Philology and linguistics (General)
PA		CLASSICAL LANGUAGES AND LITERATURES
	201–1179	Greek language (Ancient, Medieval, and Modern)
	2001–2995	Latin language (Ancient, Medieval, and Modern)
	3050–5665	Greek literature (Ancient, Medieval, and Modern)
	6000–8595	Latin literature (Ancient, Medieval, and Modern)

MODERN EUROPEAN LANGUAGES

PB	201– 431	General works
		Celtic languages and literatures
	1201–1449	Irish
	1501–1709	Gaelic (Scotch)
	2101–2499	Welsh (Cymric)
	2501–3029	Breton. Cornish. Gallic
PC		Romance languages
	601– 872	Rumanian language and literature
	1001–1977	Italian
	2001–3761	French. Provençal
	3801–3975	Catalan language and literature
	4001–4977	Spanish
	5001–5498	Portuguese
		Germanic (Teutonic) languages
PD	1– 777	General works
	1501–1893	Scandinavian (General)
	2201–2392	Old Norse: Old Icelandic and Old Norwegian
	2401–2447	Icelandic (Modern)
	2501–2999	Norwegian. Landsmaal
	3001–3929	Danish
	5001–5929	Swedish
PE	1–3729	English. Anglo-Saxon. Middle English
PF	1–1184	Dutch. Flemish. Afrikaans
	1401–1558	Friesian language and literature
	3001–5999	German. Low German

P

LANGUAGE AND LITERATURE

P

LANGUAGE AND LITERATURE

work by and about an author is arranged in a single group as demonstrated in Chapter 4. Subdivision by literary form, common in the Decimal Classification, does not occur under individual authors in Library of Congress classification with the exception of Elizabethan drama in subclass PR, English literature, which is treated as a separate form.

Auxiliary Tables in PN, PR, PS, PZ

The use of auxiliary tables in this schedule is discussed in Chapter 4 in the section entitled "Complex Tables for Individual Authors in Literature, " pp. 114-126. As stated in that section, there are twenty-three form tables for use with all the individual authors and their separate works, in subclasses, PR, English literature, and PS, American literature. Only in a few cases are these tables worked out within the schedules--e. g. William Shakespeare, or Geoffrey Chaucer. Each author is assigned a certain range of numbers appropriate to the amount of material written by and about him. There are tables for authors assigned ninety-eight numbers (although none yet exist), forty-eight numbers, eighteen numbers, eight numbers, five numbers, four numbers, one number, or only a Cutter number. Separate works with eight, five, two, one and Cutter numbers have auxiliary tables as do anonymous literary works.

Thomas Carlyle is a nineteenth century English author with a range of eighteen numbers, "PR 4420-4438. " Carlyle's entry in the schedule includes the following elements. (See also Figures 65 and 65a.)

PR   English Literature.

4420-4438   Carlyle, Thomas (IIIa).

            Separate works.

                Chartism, see DA.

                Choice of books, see Z 1003.

                Cromwell's letters and speeches, see DA.

                Early kings of Norway (etc.), see DL 460.

4425   Essays.

                . A2,   Collected. By date.

                . A3,   Minor collections. By date.

.A5-Z, Separate essays and minor
collections. By title.

Frederick the Great, see DD.

French revolution, see DC.

4426   Heroes and hero worship.

Inaugural address, University of Edinburgh, 1866: Choice of books, see Z
1003.

4427   Latter day pamphlets.

4428   Past and present.

4429   Sartor resartus.

Schiller, Friedrich, see PT.

Sterling, John, Life of, see PR 5473. S8.

Translations from the German, see PT.

4430   Other works, A-Z.

Carlyle's more important literary works are assigned a whole
number, e. g. Heroes and Hero Worship "PR 4426". The lesser
literary works are assigned one number "PR 4430, A-Z". Carlyle's
non-literary works are classed by subject rather than in literature
as the above section demonstrates, e. g. Early Kings of Norway,
see "DL 460". However, to use Carlyle's entire range of eighteen
numbers, the appropriate auxiliary table must be identified. Following Carlyle's name in the schedule is "(III^a)". This means that
Table III^a for eighteen number authors is used to class Carlyle's
works. Following the schedule are auxiliary tables called "Table
of Subdivisions under Individual Authors." The first tables I and II
are for ninety-eight and forty-eight number authors, respectively.
The use of Table II is discussed in Chapter 4, pp. 114-120. Tables
III and IV are the next tables. Table III is to be used for eighteen
number authors. Date letters are to be used in Table III and Table
IV when the author is assigned III^a or IV^a. (See Figure 38 in Chapter
4.)

PR 4420-4438   Table III

                      Collected works.

4420   0   By date.

4421   1   By editor.

4422	2	Selections.
		Translations.
(4423)	3	Modern English. By translator.
4424	4	Other, by language, subarranged by translator.
4425-4430	5-10	Separate works.
		see Table X, or XI.
4431	11	Apocryphal, spurious works, etc.
4432. A1-5	12. A1-5	Periodicals. Societies. Collections.
. A6-Z	. A6-Z	Dictionaries, indexes, etc.
4433	13	Biography and criticism.
		Criticism.
4434	14	General.
4435	15	Textual. Manuscripts, etc.
		Special.
4436	16	Sources.
4437	17	Other, A-Z.
4438	18	Language. Grammar. Style.

Table III^a

Same as III using the following date letters:

To 1500:	A00-A99.
1500-1599:	B00-B99.
1600-1699:	C00-C99.
1700-1799:	D00-D99.
1800-1899:	E00-E99.
1900-1999:	F00-F99.

Carlyle's Complete Works published in 1885 is classed "PR 4420 . E85. " "PR 4420" means an edition without commentary of the collected works of Thomas Carlyle. ". E85" is the appropriate date letter from Table III^a meaning "1885".

Carlyle's Complete Works, 1885.

PR------ The double letters for the subclass, English literature.

4420 ---- The integral number meaning the collected works
without commentary of Thomas Carlyle.

. E85 ---- The date letter meaning the date of publication, 1885.

An edition with commentary of Carlyle's collected works would be
classed in the second number of his range according to Table III.
Selections from Carlyle with an introduction and notes by A. M. D.
Hughes is classed in the third number "PR 4422".

Selections, of Carlyle.

PR------ The double letters for the subclass, English literature.

4422 ---- The integral number meaning a selection of the works
of Thomas Carlyle.

. H8 ----- The first Cutter number for the editor of the selection,
Hughes.

The fourth number in Table III "3" for translations into modern
English is not used for Carlyle as Carlyle wrote in modern English.
A German edition of Carlyle's works translated by Friedrich Bremer
uses the fifth number in Table III. The call number for this work
is "PR 4424 . G4B7. " The first Cutter number is used for the
language of the translation, in this case German, and the second
for the name of the translator, Bremer.

Carlyle's Werke.

PR------ The double letters for the subclass, English literature.

4424 ---- The integral number meaning a translation of collected works of Thomas Carlyle.

. G4 ----- The first Cutter number for the language of the
translation, German.

B7 ------ The second Cutter number for the name of the
translator, Bremer.

Carlyle's separate works or individual titles are classed according to the assigned numbers in the schedule. For further subdivisions of these numbers use Table X^a, "Separate Works with One Number, " Chapter 4, pp. 117-119 and Table XI, "Separate Works with Cutter Numbers, " Chapter 3, pp. 80-82. Under Carlyle's separate works both his major literary and non-literary works are listed alphabetically. His first listed work is a non-literary work on English history, Chartism. An 1840 edition of this work is classed "DA 559. 7 . C3. "

Carlyle's Chartism, 1840.

DA------ The double letters for the subclass, British history.

559. 7 --- The integral number meaning Chartism during the Victorian period.

. C3 ----- The first Cutter number for the author, Carlyle.

1840 ---- The date of publication.

Early Kings of Norway is another of his historical works classed in history not literature.

Carlyle's Early Kings of Norway.

DL------ The double letters for the subclass, Scandinavian history.

460 ----- The integral number meaning general works on early and medieval Norway.

. C3 ----- The first Cutter number for the author, Carlyle.

In each of these examples the first Cutter number is for Carlyle. It would be incorrect to use a Cutter number for Carlyle within the range of literature numbers assigned to him as this range of numbers means Carlyle. The classifier must always take care not to be redundant when he is classing in literature.

The first listed of Carlyle's literary works, his essays, are assigned special subdivisions in the schedule.

PR

4425   Essays.

          . A2,   Collected. By date.

          . A3,   Minor collections. By date.

          . A5- Z,   Separate essays and minor collections. By title.

For instance his <u>Critical and Miscellaneous Essays: Collected and Republished</u>, 1847, is classed "PR 4425 . A2 1847. "

Critical and Miscellaneous Essays, 1847.

PR------ The double letters for the subclass, English literature.

4425 ---- The integral number meaning literary essays of
Thomas Carlyle.

. A2 ----- The reserved Cutter number meaning collected essays.

1847 ---- The date of publication as required by the schedule.

A Russian translation of selections from Carlyle's essays is classed, "PR 4425 . A4R8. " ". A4" is not a reserved Cutter number from the schedules, but its use in this case is a logical one for translations of collected essays of Carlyle. Obviously the second Cutter is for the language of the translation, Russian, "R8".

Istoricheskīe i Kriticheskīe Opyty.
ₗCarlyle's historical and critical essays. ₗ

PR------ The double letters for the subclass, English literature.

4425 ---- The integral number meaning literary essays of
Thomas Carlyle.

. A4 ----- The first Cutter number used for translations of
Carlyle's essays.

R8 ------ The second Cutter number for the language of the
translation, Russian.

"PR 4426" is the second number for Carlyle's separate literary works. This number is for <u>Heroes and Hero Worship</u>. As no subdivisions for this number are given in the schedule, Table X^a must be used. (See also Figure 16 in Chapter 3.)

Table X^a

Texts.

. A1	By date.
. A2A-Z.	By editor.
. A3	School texts.

Translations.

.A4-49   French.

.A5-59   German.

.A6-69   Other languages. By language.

.A7-Z. Criticism.

An edition of Heroes and Hero Worship published in 1841 is classed
"PR 4426 . A1 1841".   ". A1" means an edition without commentary
of the text of the work.

Heroes and Hero Worship, 1841.

PR------ The double letters for the subclass, English literature.

4426 ---- The integral number meaning Carlyle's Heroes and
Hero Worship.

. A1 ----- The reserved Cutter number for an edition without
commentary of the text of the work.

1841 ---- The date of publication as required by Table X^a.

A German translation of this work entitled Helden und Heldenverehrung
translated by Ernst Wicklein is classed "PR 4426 . A58".   ". A5-59"
is the range of reserved Cutter numbers for German translations
according to Table X^a.   ". A58" is a Cutter number within that
range with ". A5" meaning a German translation and "8" a translator
whose name is near the end of the alphabet such as Wicklein.

Helden und Heldenverehrung, translated by Ernst Wicklein.

PR------ The double letters for the subclass, English literature.

4426 ---- The integral number meaning Carlyle's Heroes and
Hero Worship.

. A58 ---- The reserved Cutter number meaning a German
translation of the above work translated by a person
whose last name is near the end of the alphabet.

A Russian translation of this same work translated by Valentin
Ivanovich Iakovenko is classed "PR 4426 . A64I3. " In this case
". A6-69" is reserved for languages other than French and German.
". A6" means a translation in a language other than the original

English or French or German; the decimal extension "4" in this case means Russian. The second Cutter number is used for the translator.

Geroi i Geroischeskoe v Istorii, translated by Valentin Ivanovich Iakovenko.

PR------ The double letters for the subclass, English literature.

4426 ---- The integral number meaning Carlyle's Heroes and
Hero Worship.

.A64---- The reserved Cutter number meaning a Russian
translation of the above work.

I3------- The second Cutter number for the translator,
Iakovenko.

A Spanish translation of Heroes and Hero Worship issued in 1932 is classed "PR 4426 .A65 1932". In this case the decimal extension "5" means Spanish.

Los Héroes.

PR------ The double letters for the subclass, English literature.

4426 ---- The integral number meaning Carlyle's Heroes and
Hero Worship.

.A65 ---- The reserved Cutter number meaning a Spanish
translation of the above work.

Carlyle's biographical works are classed with the subject of the biography and not with Carlyle's literary works. The following example demonstrates this.

Carlyle's Life of Friedrich Schiller, 1869.

PT------ The double letters for the subclass, Teutonic literatures.

2482 ---- The integral number meaning a general biography of
the individual author in German literature, Friedrich
Schiller.

.C3 ----- The first Cutter number for the author of the biography,
Carlyle.

1869 ---- The date of publication.

Carlyle's lesser works are classed under the one number, "PR 4430" and arranged alphabetically by Cutter number. For instance a text of Carlyle's Reminiscences issued in 1881 is classed "PR 4430 . R4 1881".

Carlyle's Reminiscences, 1881.

PR------ The double letters for the subclass, English litera-
    ture.

4430 ---- The integral number meaning a lesser work of
    Carlyle.

. R4 ----- The first Cutter number for the title of the lesser
    work, meaning that this is a text of the work.

1881 ---- The date of publication as required by Table XI.

To class biographical and critical material about Carlyle, Table III is used to locate the specific numbers "13-18" (PR 4433-4438.) Carlyle's Letters to His Wife is classed in the first of these num- bers as it is biographical. Its call number is "PR 4433 .A5C25". ".A5" is used to place all correspondence at the beginning of this number. "C25" is used for the second party of the correspondence, Jane Baillie Carlyle.

Thomas Carlyle: Letters to His Wife.

PR------ The double letters for the subclass, English litera-
    ture.

4433 ---- The integral number meaning a general biographical
    work about Thomas Carlyle.

. A5 ----- The first Cutter number used for all of Carlyle's
    correspondence.

C25 ----- The second Cutter number for the second party of
    the correspondence, Jane Baillie Carlyle.

Carlyle's correspondence with Ralph Waldo Emerson is classed "PR 4433 .A5E52".

Correspondence of Thomas Carlyle and Ralph Waldo Emerson.

PR------ The double letters for the subclass, English litera-
    ture.

4433 ---- The integral number meaning a general biographical
    work about Thomas Carlyle.

.A5------The first Cutter number used for all of Carlyle's
      correspondence.

E52------The second Cutter number for the second party of
      the correspondence, Ralph Waldo Emerson.

James Lorimer Halliday's Mr. Carlyle My Patient, a Psychoso-
matic Biography is also classed in this general biographical number, "PR 4433 . H27".

Halliday's Mr. Carlyle My Patient, a Psychsomatic Biography.

PR------ The double letters for the subclass, English litera-
      ture.

4433 ---- The integral number meaning a general biographical
      work about Thomas Carlyle.

. H27 ---- The first Cutter number for the author of the
      biography, Halliday.

Charles Frederick Harrold's general criticism, Carlyle and German Thought, published in 1963 is classed, "PR 4434 . H3 1963".

Harrold's Carlyle and German Thought, 1963.

PR------ The double letters for the subclass, English litera-
      ture.

4434 ---- The integral number meaning a general criticism
      of Carlyle.

. H3 ----- The first Cutter number for the author of the criti-
      cism, Harrold.

1963 ---- The date of publication.

Finally a specialized criticism on religion in Carlyle's works,
Teleogisches Geschichtshild und Theokratische Staatsauffassung
im Werke Thomas Carlyle, by Jürgen Kedenburg published in 1960
is classed "PR 4437 . R4K4 1960". "PR 4437" is a specialized
criticism of Thomas Carlyle. ". R4" is the Cutter number for the
special subject, religion.

Kedenburg's Teleogisches Geschichtshild und Theokratische
Staatsauffassung im Werke Thomas Carlyle, 1960.

PR------ The double letters for the subclass, English litera-
      ture.

4437----- The integral number meaning a specialized criticism of Carlyle.

. R4 ----- The first Cutter number for the special subject,
religion.

K4 ------ The second Cutter number for the author of the
criticism, Kedenburg.

A further discussion of other tables in this subclass, PN, PR, PS,
PZ may be found in Chapter 4, pp. 114-126.

Updating the schedule to include all additions and changes is
a necessity; no new edition which would incorporate all of the
changes has been published. Presently the section of additions
and changes represents nearly as many pages as the schedule itself. For the schedule to be useable it is necessary to annotate
within the schedule any variation that may appear in the additions
and changes sections. Color coded entries may be used: a blue
colored mark refers the classifier to the "Additions and Changes"
section at the back of the schedule; a red colored mark refers to
the "Additions and Changes" from the quarterly publication L. C.
Classification...Additions and Changes; and a black mark denotes
all local administrative decisions.

Another deterrent to use of this schedule is the lack of any
outline. On the following pages summary outlines for subclasses
PN, PR, PS and PZ are provided by the author. These summary
outlines are designed to aid the user of this schedule to discern
the internal organization and content of each subclass. These outlines are not official outlines prepared by the Library of Congress.

Outline of PN

LITERATURE: GENERAL AND UNIVERSAL

Literary History (and) Collections

<u>Literary History</u>

1-43	General.
45-72	Theory. Philosophy. Esthetics.
80-99	Criticism.
101-249	Authorship.
451-481	Biography.
451-466	General collections (by nationality).
471-481	Women authors.
500-519	Collections.
500-509	Various authors.
510-519	Collected essays of individual authors.
521-595	Comprehensive works. Universal histories, etc.
597-605	Special relations, movements, and currents of literature (general only).
611-779	By period.
801-820	Romance literatures.
821-840	Germanic literatures.
843-849	Literatures by area or country.
851-884	Comparative literature.
885-899	Translations.
905-1008	Folk literature.
1009	Juvenile literature (history and criticism).
1010-5639	(By special literary forms.)
1010-1551	Poetry.
1010-1279	(General)
1301-1333	Epic poetry.
1341	Folk poetry.
1351-1401	Lyric poetry.
1401-1551	(Others)
1600-3299	The Drama.
1600-1657	(General)
1660-1861	Technique of dramatic composition.
1870-1988	(Various special forms)
1991	Radio broadcasts.
1992	Television broadcasts.
1993-1999	Motion pictures.
2000-3300	Dramatic representation. The theater.
3311-3503	Prose. Prose fiction. The short story, etc.

4000-4321	Oratory, Elocution, etc.
4400	Letters (literary history).
4500	Essays (History, criticism, technique).
4700-5639	Journalism. The periodical press, etc.
4841-4900	By country. United States.
4901-5639	By country. Others (note use of special tables, p. 47).

Collections of General Literature

6010-6078	General collections.
6080-6095	Quotations.
6099-6110	Poetry.
6111-6120	Drama.
	Fiction, see PN 6010-6095.
6121-6129	Orations.
6130-6140	Letters.
6141-6146	Essays.
6147-6231	Wit and humor. Satire.
6233-6381	Miscellaneous minor.
6400-6525	Proverbs.

Outline of PR

ENGLISH LITERATURE

(Literary History)

1-55	Literary history and criticism.
57-78	Criticism.
81-976	History of English literature.
81-151	General works (etc.).
161-479	By period.
500-976	(By special form)
500-609	Poetry.
621-739	Drama.
751-889	Prose.
901-907	Oratory.
911-917	Letters.
921-927	Essays.
931-937	Wit and humor. Satire.
941-947	Miscellany. Curiosa. Eccentric literature.
951-976	Folk literature.

Collections (of English Literature)

1101-1116	General.

(1118)-1149	By period.
1171-1369	(By special form)
1171-1227	Poetry.
1241-1273	Drama.
1281-1309	Prose.
1321-1329	Oratory.
1341-1349	Letters.
1361-1369	Essays.
1490-1799	Anglo-Saxon literature.
1490-1508	Collections.

Individual authors and works.

1509-1799	Anglo-Saxon literature.
1804-2165	Anglo-Norman period. Early English. Middle English.
2199-3195	English renaissance (1500-1640).
2199-2405	Prose and poetry.
2411-3195	The drama.
3291-3784	17th and 18th centuries, 1640-1770.
3991-5990	19th century, 1770/1800-1890/1900.
6000-6049	1900-1960.
6050-6076	1961—
	Here are usually to be classified authors beginning to publish about 1950, flourishing after 1960.

English literature: Provincial, Local, etc. (Literary histories and collections, only; individual authors, see PR 1509-6076.)

8309-8489	Counties, regions, islands, etc.
8490-8499	Celtic literature (English).
8500-8697	Scotland.
8700-8897	Ireland.
8900-8997	Wales.
9080-9899	English literature outside of Great Britain. Including present and former British colonies and dependencies except the United States (PS).
9080-9089	General.
9090-9899	Special.
9090-9092	Europe.
9095-9380	America.
9395-9697	Oceania.
9698-9797	Asia.
9798-9898	Africa.
9899	Other, A-Z.

Outline of PS

AMERICAN LITERATURE

(Literary History)

1-49	(Literary history and criticism)
55-79	Criticism.
85-451	History of American literature.
85-173	General works.
185-228	By period.
241-285	Special regions, states, etc.
301-478	Special forms.
301-324	Poetry.
330-351	Drama.
362-379	Prose.
400-408	Oratory.
410-418	Letters.
420-428	Essays.
430-438	Wit and humor. Satire.
441	Miscellany. Curiosa. Eccentric literature.
451-478	Folk literature.

Collections (of American literature)

504-525	General.
530-536	By period.
538-572	By region.
581-690	(By special form)
581-619	Poetry.
623-635	Drama.
643-659	Prose (in general).
660-668	Oratory.
670-678	Letters.
680-688	Essays.
(690)	Wit and humor, see PN 6157-6161.

Individual authors.

700-892	Colonial period (17th and 18th centuries).
991-3390	19th century.
3500-3549	1900-1960.
3550-3576	1961—

Outline of PZ

FICTION AND JUVENILE LITERATURE

Fiction in English

1	Collections of novels, short stories, etc.
3-4	Individual authors.

Juvenile literature

5-10.7	American and English
11-18	Dutch Afrikaans
21-28	French
31-38	German
41-48	Italian
51-60.3	Scandinavian
61-68	Russian
69	Polish
70	Other Slavic, A-Z
71-78	Spanish
81-88	Portuguese
90	Other languages, A-Z.

Fiction in Subclass PZ

Subclass PZ often causes problems in usage. This subclass was first developed in 1906. At that time PZ consisted of two numbers only--PZ 1 and PZ 3. PZ 1 was used for collections of fiction in English--e.g. anthologies or short stories. PZ 3 was used for individual or separate works of individual authors. Recently PZ 3 has been qualified to include individual authors to 1950. PZ 4 has been developed for individual authors after 1950. Subdivision within each of these numbers is made alphabetically by modified three figure Cutter numbers.

The value of these three numbers is open to question. With the exception of these three PZ numbers, Library of Congress classification in literature keeps together all of an author's works and the works about the author. In 1918 Charles Martel cited this characteristic, "In some classifications individual authors in literature have been classified by form under Poetry, Drama, Fiction, Essays, etc. In the L. C. classification only collections are thus classified. A glance at the classification of individual American authors under Poetry, Drama, Fiction, etc., in the Dewey Decimal classification, for example, will quickly demonstrate the futility of such arrangements for the purpose of serious study. "[3]

Specific disadvantages of PZ 1, 3, and 4 may be cited in regard to the preceding statements. First, these numbers separate British and American fiction from the rest of British and American literature. Also critical works about an author's fiction are separated from the author's fiction. For instance, W. Somerset Maugham's novels will be classed in PZ 3 but all his plays, and biographical works as well as criticism of his fiction will be classed properly in PR.

Second, these PZ numbers separate English translations of foreign fiction from the original version and all other translations. The English translations of Thomas Mann's novels will be in PZ 3 but the original novels in German and all other literary works by and about Mann will be classed in PT in the section for German literature.

Third, the Library of Congress is not consistent in its use of these PZ numbers in regard to standard fiction in English. For example, some editions of the novels of Jane Austin are classed in PZ 3 while other editions of the same novels are classed in PR. This third disadvantage may be most disconcerting to a library patron. In PR he will find the works of English authors as well as criticisms and biographies of these authors. He will not, however, find all the library's holdings of an individual author's fiction.

In light of these three disadvantages, it is often found advisable to reclassify works falling into PZ 1, 3, and 4. If the author of a work of fiction in English has already been established in the appropriate literature schedules by the assignment of a number or Cutter number, it is an easy matter to place his fiction with his other literary work. If an author has not yet received a number or Cutter number in the literature schedules, it may be advisable to withhold the reclassification until there is an established number for him. Dr. Charles S. Bead, Principal Cataloger, Subject Cataloging Division at the Library of Congress, stated July 9, 1966 at an Institute on the Use of the Library of Congress Classification that printed L. C. cards with PZ 3 and 4 numbers may soon have the literature numbers (in PR, PS, PQ, PT, etc.) in brackets below the regular number on the card. This development when realized will be a great service for many libraries.

---

[3]Leo E. Montagne. American Library Classification with Special Reference to the Library of Congress. Hamden, Conn.: Shoe String Press, 1961. p. 326.

A final problem in the use of this schedule may be mentioned in regard to the classification of juvenile literature. The limited number of subdivisions in juvenile literature makes this section of the subclass very difficult to use. A library with a large collection of children's books may prefer to use the Decimal Classification instead of L. C. for this material.

SUBCLASS P-PA

Subclass P-PA, Philology, Linguistics, Classical Philology, Classical Literature, was prepared by Dr. Walter F. Koenig. The first edition was published in 1928. The supplement to this schedule for PA, Byzantine and Modern Greek literature and Medieval and Modern Latin Literature, was completed by Clarence Perley in 1933 and first published in 1942. This schedule represents one of the finest works of scholarship in all classification systems. Dr. Koenig provided a detailed introduction to the schedule with directions for the use of the schedule. In addition he provided many valuable footnotes throughout the schedule. The Appendix includes a list of subjects in other classes in Library of Congress classification that are related to classical philology, auxiliary tables with complete explanations and examples, and a list of authorities used in the preparation of this schedule. Further the sections of the schedules for Greek and Roman authors contain... "an extensive list of authors, designed to aid the classifier in distinguishing homonymous writers and in the occasionally difficult arrangement of names. The inclusion of many more or less obscure names may seem unnecessary; it is justified, nevertheless, because it enables the classifier to avoid cumbersome and injudicious notation. Inasmuch as the classical literature practically presents a closed fond, the extent of possibilities may be very nearly indicated, whereas with modern literature this is obviously impracticable," writes Dr. Koenig in his prefatory note. It should be pointed out that these lists of names of Greek and Latin authors are valuable reference sources. Both the Greek and Roman names are given in the traditional Latin form. In addition in the introduction Dr. Koenig observes a method for abridging this schedule. "The minute classification devised for some parts of the scheme may create the impression that it is intended for the use of large university libraries only; but an examination of the scheme will prove that any college library or any library desirous of owning a representative collection of classical literature may make use of this scheme by ignoring the minor subdivisions--in other words, by using the condensed schedules as represented in Synopsis III and IV. " Synopsis

III is the outline for Greek authors and Synopsis IV is the outline for Roman authors. The original Greek titles, with Latin translations, and the original Latin titles are provided for these authors' works although no English translations are given. The application of this schedule demands a certain amount of specialized knowledge, but the technical aspects of the schedule should create no unusual difficulty in classifying.

SUBCLASSES PB-PH

Subclasses PB-PH, Modern European Languages, were published in 1933. Dr. Koenig was chiefly responsible for the preparation of this schedule under the supervision of Charles Martel. Subclass PB includes general works on modern European languages and specifically Celtic languages and literatures. Romance languages are contained in subclass PC and Scandinavian languages in subclass PD. The English language is contained in subclass PE. German, Dutch and other Germanic languages are classed in PF. Subclass PG is designed for Slavic languages and literatures and PH is for Finno-Ugrian and Basque languages and literatures.

There are over thirty auxiliary tables in the schedule. These tables are similar to those discussed in Chapter 4 of this guide. The classifier should be aware when using these auxiliary tables that special modifications must be made, as directed, for each language. Tables I-V for language subdivisions are eight pages long. Middle English with a range of numbers "PE 501-685" is assigned to use Table III. This table consists of two hundred language subdivisions. Grammatical works on Middle English use the range of numbers for grammar in Table III. (See also Figure 66.)

Grammar—

Comparative (two or more languages)	29
Historical	31
Treatises	33
General special (Terminology, etc.)	34
Text-books	35
Readers	
Series	36
Primers. Primary grade readers.	37

           Intermediate and advanced.

Manuals for special classes of
    students, A-Z.   38

Karl Brunner's An Outline of Middle English Grammar is classed
as an historical grammar using the number "31" in Table III. The
31st number in the range of numbers "PE 501-685" is "PE 531".

    Brunner's An Outline of Middle English Grammar.

    PE------ The double letters for the subclass, English
              language.

    531 ----- The integral number meaning a historical Middle
              English grammar.

    .B713 --- The first Cutter number for the main entry,
              Brunner.

A Handbook of Middle English by Fernando Mossé is classed as a
textbook under grammar using the number "35" in Table III. The
35th number in the range of numbers "PE 501-685" is "PE 535".

    Mossé's A Handbook of Middle English.

    PE------ The double letters for the subclass, English
              language.

    535 ----- The integral number meaning a textbook on Middle
              English grammar.

    .M62---- The first Cutter number for the main entry, Mossé.

SUBCLASSES PJ-PM

    Subclasses PJ-PM, Languages and Literatures of Asia,
Africa, Oceania, America, Mixed Languages, Artificial Languages,
was first published in 1935, the work of Dr. Koenig. This schedule
contains the less common languages and literatures. It is especially
noteworthy that the sections for Chinese and Japanese literatures
were recently completely expanded and are represented by several
pages of additions and changes at the back of the schedule. There
are auxiliary tables similar to those in subclass PB-PH, Modern
European Languages. This schedule has been criticized as being
very dated.

    An index to the languages and dialects covered in subclasses

P-PM was published in 1936. This index was prepared by Miss Voegelein.

SUBCLASSES PQ AND PT

Subclass PQ, part 1, French literature, was developed and used at the Library of Congress as early as 1913. The schedule remained in manuscript form until the first publication in 1936. Dr. Koenig prepared the original scheme for this part as well as for part 2. Subclass PQ, part 2, Italian, Spanish and Portuguese Literature, was also used in manuscript form for some time. The first edition was published in 1937. C. K. Jones developed many of the details in these schedules, particularly the Spanish and Portuguese names. One deterrent in the use of these two schedules is the lack of an index. There is, however, a very detailed outline at the beginning of each schedule which may be used in place of an index. Both of these schedules contain valuable lists of names according to the correct main entry form including birth and death dates. Auxiliary tables similar to those used for English or American literature are used with these schedules.

Subclass PT, part 1, German Literature, also developed by Dr. Koenig, was not published until 1938. Clarence Perley revised and prepared this schedule for printing. Subclass PT, part 2, Dutch and Scandinavian Literatures, was not published until 1942. Clarence Perley prepared the sections on Dutch, Flemish and Afrikaans Literature, and he revised the section on Scandinavian literature which was originally prepared by Jules Dieserud in 1915-16. These schedules are similar to those making up subclass PQ. Neither part 1 nor 2 of PT has an index although long outlines do occur. The lists of names in both schedules are quite useful.

SUBCLASS PG, IN PART

Subclass PG, in part, Russian Literature, completes the eleven schedules making up Class P. Developed by Miss Voegelein and published in 1948, this schedule covers the range of numbers 2900-3560 in subclass PG. This scheme was begun by Clarence Perley in the 1930's to serve as a system to class translations of Russian literature. The prefatory note to the schedule states, "The discontinuance of the Slavic Division and incorporation of the Library's Russian collections, of which the Yudin Collection was the nucleus, into the general collections made it necessary to develop a scheme to cover Russian literature in the original as well as in translation. The Yudin Collection had in part been classified according to a scheme devised by Alexis V. Babine, which could not be applied to the combined collection, since it took no account of translations and did not follow the notation used in other sections of the Library of Congress classification."

Miss Voegelein developed the present schedule. This schedule lacks both an index and a detailed outline. The lists of Russian names are transliterated in accordance with the Library of Congress system of transliteration. These lists contain full names and dates and many syndetic devices. There are auxiliary tables for one number and Cutter number authors and anonymous works.

CLASS Q

The first edition of Class Q, Science, was published in 1905. James David Thompson was responsible for subclasses Q, Sciences (General); QA, Mathematics; QB, Astronomy; QC, Physics; QD, Chemistry; and, QE, Geology. F. B. Weeks worked with Thompson on subclass QE. Subclass QK, Botany, was developed by S. C. Stuntz. J. Christian Bay prepared the remaining subclasses, QH, Natural history; QL, Zoology; QM, Human anatomy; QP, Physiology; and, QR, Bacteriology. Thompson served as editor for the entire class in the first edition. The second edition appeared in 1913 with Clarence Perley as editor. Perley also served as editor of the third edition which was issued in 1921. The fourth edition was published in 1948 with Miss Voegelein as the editor. She served as editor of the fifth edition published in 1950.

INTERNAL TABLES

There are very few problems in the use of this schedule. There are no auxiliary tables and the application of the internal tables is obvious. An example of this is the geology of individual states of the United States. Each is assigned two numbers with the direction, "The second number assigned to each state is used for special localities (i. e., counties or physiographic divisions) arranged alphabetically. " California is assigned the numbers "QE 89-90". (See Figure 67.) The first of these is to be used for works on geology of the state in general and the second for particular regions. The California Journal of Mines and Geology is classed "QE 89. A2".

California Journal of Mines and Geology.

QE------ The double letters for the subclass, geology.

89 ------ The integral number meaning a general work on the geology of California.

.A2 ----- The Cutter number used to place this journal at the beginning of the subdivision.

John Maxson's Death Valley: Origin and Scenery is classed in the second number for specific regions of California as "QE 90 . D35M3". In this case the first Cutter number is used for the specific region, Death Valley.

Q

SCIENCE

Q	Science (General)	
QA	Mathematics	
	801–935	Analytic mechanics
QB	Astronomy	
	275–341	Geodesy
QC	Physics	
	81–119	Weights and measures
	122–168	Experimental mechanics
	811–849	Terrestrial magnetism
	851–999	Meteorology
		Temperature, rain, wind, weather, etc.
QD	Chemistry	
	901–999	Crystallography
QE	Geology	
	Cf. GB, GC	
	351–499	Mineralogy and petrology
	701–996	Paleontology. Paleozoology. Paleobotany
QH	Natural history	
	201–277	Microscopy
	301–705	Biology (General)
QK	Botany	
QL	Zoology	
	801–950	Anatomy (General)
	951–991	Embryology
QM	Human anatomy	
QP	Physiology	
	351–499	Physiological psychology
	501–801	Physiological chemistry
	903–981	Experimental pharmacology
QR	Bacteriology	
	180–185	Immunity and immunization

Maxson's <u>Death Valley: Origin and Scenery</u>.

QE------ The double letters for the subclass, Geology.

90 ------ The integral number meaning a regional or local
work on the geology of California.

.D35 ---- The first Cutter number for the region, Death
Valley.

M3------ The second Cutter number for the main entry,
Maxson.

BOOK NUMBERS

One unusual classification device used in Class Q is called
"Book numbers." One use of these numbers is shown under "QB
543-544" for Solar eclipses. (See also Figure 68.)

QB   Astronomy.

Solar eclipses.

543   1800-1899.[1]

544   1900-1999.[1]

[1]Book number-last two figures of the year, followed by
author number. e.g. QB 544.47U6 U.S. National
Almanac Office, Total eclipse of the sun, May 20,
1947.

"Book numbers" are decimal extensions of integral numbers indicating a particular decade and year of a predetermined century.
Another example of the use of "book numbers" to subdivide an integral number chronologically by year is the U.S. Nautical Almanac
Office's Total Eclipse of the Sun, June 30, 1954 classed "QB 544.54
U6". ".54" is the "book number" which refers to the year of the
particular eclipse in the century "1900-1999"; or, ".54" means 1954.

<u>Total Eclipse of the Sun, June 30, 1954</u>.

QB------ The double letters for the subclass, Astronomy.

544 ----- The integral number meaning a 20th century solar
eclipse.

.54 ----- The "book number" meaning 1954, the date of the
eclipse.

U6 ------ The first Cutter number for the main entry, U.S.
Nautical...

The use of "book numbers" precludes the use of the first decimal point for the first Cutter number. Astronomical Data for the Solar Eclipse, 15 February 1961 by A. Kranjc published in 1960 is similarly classed "QB 544. 61 K7". The "book number" is taken from the date of the eclipse not the date of publication of the individual book.

Astronomical Data for the Solar Eclipse (15 February 1961) by A. Kranjc.

QB------ The double letters for the subclass, Astronomy.

544 ----- The integral number meaning a 20th century solar eclipse.

.61 ----- The "book number" meaning 1961, the date of the eclipse.

K7 ------ The first Cutter number for the main entry, Kranjc.

Perhaps the only major problem that may occur in using Class Q is the terminology of the schedule. In many cases the latest scientific terminology is not employed. Both the arrangement and the terminology of this schedule reflect scientific thought at the turn of the century. There are, however, many notes and examples which make the schedule easier to use.

It should be noted that Cutter numbers are often used for subject subdivisions in Class Q. For instance, "QD 181, " the number in chemistry for special elements, uses Cutter numbers from the symbols of the Periodic Table for further subdivisions. (See also Figure 26 in Chapter 3.)

.A1 A. Argon.

.A2 Ac. Actinium.

.A3 Ag. Silver (Argentum).

.A4 Al. Aluminum.

.A5 Am. Americium.

       Antimony, see .S3.

.A7 As. Arsenic.

.A8 At. Astatine.

.A9 Au. Gold (Aurum).

CLASS R

Class R, Medicine, was developed by J. Christian Bay in 1904. The first edition of Class R was not published until 1910 at which time Clarence Perley prepared the schedule for the printer. The second edition under Perley's editorship was issued in 1921 and in 1953 the third edition was published.

There are no major auxiliary tables for this class although there are many internal tables which employ both double Cutter numbers and successive Cutter numbers. The problems of arrangement and terminology in Class R are similar to those in Class Q. Class R was developed to classify medical literature within a general library not in a medical library.

There are specialized classifications for medical libraries that are superior to Class R. One of these schemes which is directly related to the Library of Congress classification is that of another federal library, the National Library of Medicine. This library was formerly the U. S. Army Medical Library. In the early 1940's a survey showed the need for a special classification for the Army Library. In 1948 a preliminary edition of this classification was prepared by Mary Louise Marshall. This edition was modified and revised by Dr. Frank B. Rogers in 1950 and issued as the first edition of the Army Medical Library Classification in 1951. The second edition was published in 1956 as the National Library of Medicine Classification. The third edition appeared in 1964. This scheme makes use of the unused letter "W" in Library of Congress classification as well as the unused double letters in Class Q of L. C. classification for preclinical sciences. By this device the remainder of L. C. classification can be used by the National Library of Medicine for its nonmedical books. Class R is not used and Class W is used in its place. Many other libraries with large medical collections also do this. The following is synopsis of Class QS-QZ, Preclinical Sciences, and Class W.

PRECLINICAL SCIENCES

QS	Human Anatomy	QW	Bacteriology and Immunology.
QT	Physiology		
QU	Biochemistry.	QX	Parasitology.
QV	Pharmacology.	QY	Clinical Pathology.
		QZ	Pathology.

R

MEDICINE

R   Medicine (General)

RA   State medicine.   Hygiene

         421– 772   Public hygiene. Social hygiene.   Sanitation. Prevention of disease

         773– 788   Personal hygiene

         791– 955   Medical geography and climatology

         960– 996   Hospitals. Dispensaries.   Ambulance service

         1001–1171   Medical jurisprudence

         1195–1260   Toxicology

RB   Pathology

RC   Practice of medicine

         321–630   Diseases of the nervous system, including insanity

RD   Surgery

RE   Ophthalmology

RF   Otology. Rhinology.   Laryngology

RG   Gynecology and obstetrics

RJ   Pediatrics

RK   Dentistry

RL   Dermatology

RM   Therapeutics

         214–261   Alimentation.   Diet

         300–676   Action of remedies.   Patent medicines

         695–737   Physiological therapeutics: Blood-letting, chiropractic, etc.

         738–800   Serum therapy: Smallpox, rabies, etc.   Animal extracts

         801–822   Hydrotherapy.   Baths (Turkish, medicated, etc.)

         831–859   Phototherapy. Radiotherapy. X rays. Radium

         865–891   Thermotherapy. Fever therapy. Electrotherapy

         893–951   Magnetotherapy, hypnotism, suggestive therapeutics, etc.

RS   Pharmacy and materia medica

RT   Nursing

RV   Botanic, Thomsonian, and eclectic medicine

RX   Homeopathy

RZ   Miscellaneous schools and arts

         301–397   Osteopathy

         400–406   Mental healing.   Psychotherapeutics

MEDICINE AND RELATED SUBJECTS

W	Medical Profession	WJ	Urogenital System
WA	Public Health	WK	Endocrine System
WB	Practice of Medicine	WL	Nervous System
WC	Infectious Diseases	WM	Psychiatry
WD100	Deficiency Diseases	WN	Radiology
WD200	Metabolic Diseases	WO	Surgery
WD300	Diseases of Allergy	WP	Gynecology
WD400	Animal Poisoning	WQ	Obstetrics
WD500	Plant Poisoning	WR	Dermatology
WD600	Diseases Caused by Physical Agents	WS	Pediatrics
WD700	Aviation and Space Medicine	WT	Geriatrics. Chronic Disease
WE	Musculoskeletal System	WU	Dentistry. Oral Surgery
WF	Respiratory System	WV	Otorhinolaryngology
WG	Cardiovascular System	WW	Ophthalmology
WH	Hemic and Lymphatic Systems	WX	Hospitals
		WY	Nursing
WI	Gastrointestinal System	WZ	History of Medicine

Class W employs many original features for a classification
scheme. For instance serials are not classified but rather are
separated by form in one of six broad categories. Books printed
prior to the nineteenth century are arranged alphabetically by author
within the century. Nineteenth century materials (1801-1913) are
divided into 80 broad subject classes. Only twentieth century material is classed in the scheme developed in Class W. Cutter numbers
are not used widely for subject subdivisions but usually only for
authors. There are brief outlines at the beginning of each class.
Bibliography in medicine is prefaced by the letter Z followed by
the class number for the particular subject of the bibliography. For
example, the American Medical Association's bibliographic work
entitled Health Publications is classed "ZWB 120 A512h". "Z"
means the work is bibliographic in nature; "WB 120" is the class

number for "Popular medicine (general)"; and, "A512" is the author number for American Medical Association and "h" is the workmark for the title. About fifty percent of the major medical libraries now use this scheme.

The advantages of using this arrangement are the currency of the arrangement of material and use of terminology, its compatibility with the Medical Subject Headings List, and availability of the call numbers appearing on the printed cards of the National Library of Medicine and in the National Library of Medicine, Current Catalog. Further all shared cataloging of medical literature done by the National Library of Medicine for the Library of Congress will show both Class R and Class W numbers. Class W is well worth the serious study of any student of classification and is truly an example of a current classification scheme.

CLASS S

S. C. Stuntz of the United States Department of Agriculture developed Class S, Agriculture--Plant and Animal Industry, on a plan outlined by Chief Classifier Charles Martel. Stuntz used existing bibliographies and classification schemes to formulate the details of the subclasses. One subclass SD, Forestry, was based "on corresponding sections of the systematic catalog of the K. Sächsische Forstakademie (more recently known as the Forstliche Hochschule) at Tarandt. " The first edition of Class S was published in 1911. George M. Churchill prepared this edition for the printer. The second edition was issued in 1928 under the editorship of Clarence Perley. Miss Voegelein prepared the third edition of this class which was published in 1948.

GEOGRAPHICAL DISTRIBUTION TABLES

There are no major problems in the use of this schedule and there are only two auxiliary tables. These are simple tables of geographical distributions. The following is an excerpt from the beginning of these tables. (See also Figure 69.)

Geographical Distribution Tables

In countries to which two numbers are assigned:

(1) General.

(2) Local, A-Z.

I		
21		America.
22		North America.
23		United States.
24	II	States, A-W.
26-27	1-2	Canada.
28-29	3-4	Mexico.
30-31	5-6	Central America.
32-33	7-8	West Indies.
34	9	South America.
36-37	11-12	Argentine Republic.

S

AGRICULTURE—PLANT AND ANIMAL INDUSTRY

S		Agriculture (General)
	560–575	Farm economics. Farm management
	583–589	Agricultural chemistry and physics
	590–599	Soils
	605–623	Land improvement, reclamation, irrigation, etc.
	631–667	Fertilizers and soil improvement
	671–760	Farm machinery and engineering
SB		Plant culture (General)
	107– 109	Economic botany
	183– 317	Field crops
	320– 466	Horticulture
	469– 479	Landscape gardening
	481– 485	Parks and public reservations
	599–1100	Pests and diseases
SD		Forestry
	411–428	Forest protection and preservation. Forest reserves
	430–668	Exploitation and utilization
SF		Animal culture
	601–1100	Veterinary medicine and surgery
SH		Fish culture and fisheries
	401–691	Angling
SK		Hunting sports
	351–579	Game and bird protection
	601–605	Camping. Outdoor life

An example of the use of one of these two tables is under the history of veterinary medicine and surgery, "SF 621-723".

SF   Veterinary Medicine and Surgery.

                     History.

615   General works.

621-723   By country.   Table I.

                     Add number in Table I to 600.

J. F. Smithcors' The American Veterinary Profession, its Background and Development is classed "SF 623 . S65." The number "23" in Table I for United States is added to "600" to give "SF 623."

  Smithcors' The American Veterinary Profession, its Background and Development.

  SF----- The double letters for the subclass, Animal culture.

          600--the base number for veterinary medicine.

          23--the number in Table I meaning the United
          ___   States.
          623

  623 ---- The integral number meaning the history of veterinary
           medicine in the United States.

  . S65 --- The Cutter number for the main entry, Smithcors.

An individual state in the United States uses number "24" from Table I. This number is then subarranged alphabetically by state, A-W. For instance, the Bulletin of the Montana State Veterinary Surgeon is classed "SF 624 . M93."

  Bulletin of the Montana State Veterinary Surgeon.

  SF----- The double letters for the subclass, Animal culture.

          600--the base number for veterinary medicine.

          24--the number in Table I meaning a state in the
          ___   United States.
          624

624------ The integral number meaning a general historical
work on veterinary medicine in an individual
state in the United States.

. M93 ---- The Cutter number for the individual state, Montana.

HUNTING AND FISHING

The sports of hunting and fishing are included in the schedules
for subclasses SH, Fish Culture and Fisheries; and, SK, Hunting
Sports. This is probably a far more useful location for this material than classing hunting and fishing with other sports in subclass
GV.

CLASS T

The original schedules for Class T, Technology, were first
the responsibility of Clarence Perley; he developed the schedules
for subclasses T through TT in 1903. S. C. Stuntz completed the
schedules with the development of subclass TX, Domestic science.
In 1905 H. H. B. Meyer restructured the schedules into four main
classes: the Engineering and Building group, the Mechanical group,
the Chemical group, and the Composite group. Subclasses TH,
Building construction, and TK, Electrical engineering and industries,
and the part of TA, Engineering (General) and Civil engineering,
relating to structures and materials were developed by A. Lau
Voge in 1907. At this point Perley again became the editor for
the schedule and prepared it for the printer. The first edition of
Class T appeared in 1910; the second edition was issued in 1922.
In 1937 the third edition was published, the fourth edition appeared
in 1948 and in 1965 a separate supplement of additions and changes
to Class T was issued.

The major problem in the use of this schedule results from
the separately published supplement. This causes much double
checking to result from consulting a class number in both the
schedule and supplement. A new edition of this class will, of
course, solve this problem. Also Class T, just as Class Q, is
very dated in its terminology and arrangement of material.

AUXILIARY TABLES

The auxiliary tables create no serious problems in use and
are often used as an introduction to the use of auxiliary tables in
L. C. classification. The following portion of Table I, "History and
Country Divisions, " demonstrates this. (See also Figure 70 for the
first page of this four-page table.)

Table I

History and Country Divisions

History.

15	General.
16	Ancient.
17	Medieval.
18	Modern
19	19th century.

T

TECHNOLOGY

T   Technology (General)
         201–339   Patents

ENGINEERING AND BUILDING GROUP

TA   Engineering (General)   Civil engineering
         Materials of engineering and construction; surveying, etc.

TC   Hydraulic engineering (harbors, rivers, canals)
         Water-supply engineering; irrigation, drainage, etc.

TD   Sanitary and municipal engineering
         Water supply: source, pollution, purification; sewerage, municipal refuse, etc.

TE   Roads and pavements

TF   Railroad engineering and operation
         855–1124   Electric railways

TG   Bridges and roofs

TH   Building construction
         Building laws, plumbing, heating, ventilation, lighting, etc.
         9111–9599.   Fire prevention.   Fire extinction

MECHANICAL GROUP

TJ   Mechanical engineering and machinery
         Steam, hydraulic and pneumatic machinery; machine-shop practice, etc.

TK   Electrical engineering and industries
         Production, distribution, and application of electric power.   Electric
           lighting, telegraphy, telephony, radio, etc.

TL   Motor vehicles.   Cycles.   Aeronautics

CHEMICAL GROUP

TN   Mineral industries.   Mining and Metallurgy

TP   Chemical technology
         Manufacture of chemicals, alcohol, fuel, pottery, etc.

TR   Photography

COMPOSITE GROUP

TS   Manufactures
         Metal, lumber, leather, paper, textile, packing-house, etc.

TT   Trades
         Wood- and metal-working, dressmaking, laundry work, etc.

TX   Domestic science

20	20th century.
	Special countries.
21	America.
22	North America.
23	United States.

. . . .

24	States, A-W.
25	Cities (or other special), A-Z.
26	Canada and Newfoundland.

The study and teaching of home economics uses the table below.

TX	Home Economics.
	Study and teaching.
165	General.
167	Textbooks.
170	Examinations, questions, etc.
171-274	Special countries. Table I.
	(Add 150 to numbers in the table.)

For example the U.S. Office of Education, Division of Vocational Education's Homemaking Education in Secondary Schools of the United States is classed "TX 173 . A5 1947". "23" is the number in Table I for the United States. "23" added to "150" gives the number "TX 173" for study and teaching of home economics in the United States. ".A5" is the use of an official Cutter number.

U. S. Office of Education. Division of Vocational Education. Homemaking Education in Secondary Schools of the United States.

TX------ The double letters for the subclass, Domestic
             science.

        150--the designated base number in the schedule.
         23--the number from Table I for the United States.
        173

173------ The integral number meaning study and teaching
of home economics in the United States.

.A5 ----- The official Cutter number as this is an official
publication.

1947----- The date of publication.

Mary Stewart Lyle's Educational Needs of Three Socio-economic
Groups of Rural Homemakers in Iowa is an example of study and
teaching of home economics in an individual state of the United
States. "24" is the number in Table I for individual states of the
United States. When this number is added to the base number
"150" the result is "TX 174". The complete call number is "TX
174 . I8L9".

Lyle's Educational Needs of Three Socio-economic Groups
of Rural Homemakers in Iowa.

TX------ The double letters for the subclass, Domestic
science.

150--the designated base number in the schedule.
24--the number from Table I for individual states
174   the United States.

174 ----- The integral number meaning study and teaching
of home economics in an individual state of the
United States.

. I8------ The first Cutter number for the individual state,
Iowa.

L9 ------ The second Cutter number for the main entry,
Lyle.

In addition to the auxiliary tables in Class T there are many uses
of both reserved and successive Cutter numbers.

Another problem in classing in this schedule is the distinction
to be made between pure and applied science. Class Q, Science,
is normally used for pure science and applied science is classed
in Class T, Technology. However, the additional science schedules
create further distinctions. For example, Werner Von Bergen's
American Wool Handbook is classed "TS 1631 . V6" in the technology
subclass for manufactures; however, Archer Butler Gilfillan's
Sheep Culture is properly classed "SF 375 . G5", the correct number in the agricultural subclass for animal culture.

CLASSES U AND V

Class U, Military Science, was originally developed by Charles Martel in 1903 and was first issued in 1910. "The extensive additions incident to the military developments of the First World War made it necessary to issue a second edition in 1928." (Preface) The Third edition was published in 1952 under the editorship of Miss Voegelein.

Class V, Naval Science, was first planned in 1904 by S. C. Stuntz under the direction of Charles Martel. In 1905 Clarence Perley took charge of this schedule and served as the editor of the first edition in 1910. The second edition was issued in 1953 under Miss Voegelein's editorship.

The Classification and Index of the Military Information Division of the Adjutant-General's Office of U. S. War Department served as the basis for Class U as well as for most of Class V. Subclass VK, Navigation, was based on the order of the publications of the British Hydrographic Office.

Neither of these two short schedules is difficult to use; however, no introductory outlines are provided. The auxiliary tables are simplified versions of the "Country Subdivisions Table" in Class T. (See Figure 70.) "Divide-like" notes occur frequently in these schedules, for example, numbers for the National Guard of any state are arranged like the numbers for the first listed state, Alabama, "UA 50-59". One very detailed internal table of reserved Cutter numbers is for material concerning West Point. The following is a portion of that development of reserved Cutter numbers. (See also Figure 71.)

U   Military Science (General)

410   U. S. Military Academy, West Point.
              Administration.

. . . .

     . F8   Special days and events. By date.

     . G3   Information for graduates.

     . H2   Rosters of officers, etc. (U. S. Army)

              Registers.

     . H3   Official annual.

     . H4   Other official. By date.

U

MILITARY SCIENCE

U	Military science (General)
UA	Armies. Organization and distribution
UB	Administration
UC	Maintenance and transportation
UD	Infantry
UE	Cavalry
UF	Artillery
UG	Military engineering
UH	Other services
	201–655 Medical and sanitary service

V

NAVAL SCIENCE

V	Naval science (General)
	750–980 War vessels. Construction, armament, etc.
VA	Navies. Organization and distribution
VB	Naval administration
VC	Naval maintenance
VD	Naval seamen
VE	Marines
VF	Naval ordnance
VG	Other services of navies
	100–475 Medical and sanitary service
VK	Navigation
	600– 794 Tide and current registers
	798– 995 Sailing directions. Pilot guides
	1000–1249 Lighthouse service. Lists of lights
	1300–1491 Saving of life and property
	1500–1661 Pilots and pilotage
VM	Shipbuilding and marine engineering

Nonofficial.

. H5   Cullom's register.

. H7-8   Other.

. J1   Student publications. Annuals, etc.

      Graduate publications.

. K1   Reunions of graduates' associations.

. K3   Bulletins of graduates' associations.

. K5-7   Other.

. L1   History and general works on the academy.

         . A1-5   Official works.

. L3   Illustrated works. Views.

. M1   Biography, A-Z.

. N1   Class histories. By date.

. P1   Descriptive works. "Life at West Point."

An official history entitled <u>Building Leaders: the Story of West Point</u> issued in 1949 uses the reserved Cutter number ".L1". The complete call number is "U 410 . L1A4 1949". "A4" is used to indicate that this is an official work.

<u>Building Leaders: the Story of West Point.</u>

U------- The single letter for the subclass, Military
                science (general).

410 ----- The integral number meaning the U.S. Military
                Academy, West Point.

. L1----- The reserved Cutter number meaning a history.

A4------ The official Cutter number meaning this is an
                official work.

1949 ---- The date of publication.

A history of West Point that is not an official work such as Sidney Forman's <u>West Point, A History of the United States Military Academy</u> is classed "U 410 . L1F6".

Forman's <u>West Point, A History of the United States Military Academy</u>.

U------ The single letter for the subclass, Military science (general).

410---- The integral number meaning the U. S. Military Academy, West Point.

. L1---- The reserved Cutter number meaning a history.

F6----- The second Cutter number for the main entry, Forman.

A final example of the use of these reserved Cutter numbers is ". M1" for "Biography, A-Z". An autobiographical work by Marty Maher, <u>Bringing up the Brass; My 55 Years at West Point</u> is classed "U 410 . M1M3".

Maher's <u>Bringing up the Brass; My 55 Years at West Point</u>.

U------ The single letter for the subclass, Military science (general).

410---- The integral number meaning the U. S. Military Academy, West Point.

. M1 --- The reserved Cutter number for biography.

M3 ---- The second Cutter number for the subject and author of the biography, Maher.

The only possible problem in using these schedules is that they are somewhat dated in arrangement and terminology. The location of material on air forces is not as natural as the other locations. It is scattered throughout Class U.

One interesting device used in subclass UF, Artillery, under the number 565 is the possibility of a Cutter number with double workmarks. Under the heading for Ordnance material the following is listed.

565   Other countries, A-Z.

     e. g.   Great Britain gun handbooks.

        . G7   By inches.

        . G72   By pounds.

Further subdivision is made by adding the
following letters as needed:

B. L.	Breech loading.
M. L.	Muzzle loading.
Q. F.	Quick firing.
H.	Hotchkiss.
N.	Nordenfelt.

Guns of different marks have the numbers added
in parentheses; thus for marks II to IV add
(2-4).

Arrange different editions by date.

Obviously these directions could cause unusual original notations
to result depending on the particular foreign gun handbook.

CLASS Z

Class Z, Bibliography and Library Science, was the first schedule of L. C. classification to be prepared. It was completed in 1898 and published in 1902. Charles Martel developed the original schedules for this class. The second edition was issued in 1910 and the third edition in 1926. The fourth and present edition was published in 1959. A discussion of the historical development of this schedule is contained in the first chapter of this guide.

Class Z is designed to contain all bibliographies classed in Library of Congress classification. There are separate ranges of numbers for National Bibliography (Z1201-4941), Subject Bibliography (Z5051-7999), and Personal Bibliography (Z8001-8999). The classifier must apply the subdivisions of the subject bibliography section as these subdivisions do not parallel the overall subject structure of Library of Congress classification. This difference may be cited as a weakness in the classification scheme. Also the fact that all bibliographies are separately classed in Class Z often causes criticism; however, where all bibliographies are shelved in a reference collection, a separate class for them is most useful. It should be noted that Class M: Music does contain numbers for bibliographies of music, and there are numbers projected for law bibliographies in Class K: Law.

NATIONAL BIBLIOGRAPHY

There are six auxiliary tables to be used with Class Z: Table I, II and III for National Bibliography and Table IV, V, and VI to be used with Subject Bibliography. The basic use of all six of these tables as illustrated by Table I is usually direct numerical transfer or matching of final digits. The following is an abridgement of Table I which may be studied in its entirety in Figure 72.

Table I

(1)	General bibliography.
(2)	Bibliography of early works.
(3)	Publishers' catalogs.
(5)	Periodicals.
(6)	Societies.
(7)	Collections.
(9)	Government publications.

Z

BIBLIOGRAPHY and LIBRARY SCIENCE

(10)	Biobibliography.
(11)	Literature (General).
	By period.
(12)	Early to 1800.
(13)	1801-1950.
(13. 3)	1951—
(14)	Special topics, A-Z.
(15)	Philology.
(16)	History and description (General).
	By period.
(17)	To 1500.
(17. 5)	16th century.
(18)	17th-18th centuries.
(19)	19th century.
(20)	Early 20th century.
(20. 3)	1945—
(21)	Special topics not in (17)-(20), A-Z.
	Local.
(23)	General.
(24)	Special, A-Z.
(27)	Special topics not otherwise provided for, A-Z.
(29)	Catalogs.

In the schedules Great Britain is assigned a range of numbers
"Z 2001-2029" for national bibliography. The classifier is instructed in the schedules to use Table I with this range of numbers.
The British National Bibliography Cumulated Subject Catalogue is
classed "Z 2001 . B752". In this case the first number in Table I
for general bibliography is applied to the first number in Great
Britain's range.

British National Bibliography Cumulated Subject Catalogue.

Z------ The single letter for the class, Bibliography and
library science.

2001 --- The integral number meaning a general British
national bibliography.

.B752-- The Cutter number for main entry, British...

Pollard and Redgrave's Short Title Catalogue is classed as a bibliography of early works, the second number in Table I. Great
Britain's second number is "Z2002". The complete call number
is "Z 2002 .P77 1946".

Pollard and Redgrave's Short Title Catalogue, 1946.

Z------ The single letter for the class, Bibliography and
library science.

2002 --- The integral number meaning British national bibliography of early works.

.P77--- The first Cutter number for the main entry, Pollard.

1946 --- The date of publication.

Literature, philology and history are all treated as subdivisions of Table I for national bibliography. This material, if
of a national scope, is then treated by the Library of Congress as
national bibliography and not subject bibliography. The 11th number of Table I is for general national bibliography of literature.
"Z2011" is the eleventh number in Great Britain's range. George
Watson's The Concise Cambridge Bibliography of English Literature,
600-1950 is classed "Z 2011 .W3".

Watson's The Concise Cambridge Bibliography of English
Literature.

Z------ The single letter for the class, Bibliography and
library science.

2011 --- The integral number meaning a general bibliography
of British literature.

.W3 --- The Cutter number for the main entry, Watson.

The Royal Historical Society's Writing on British History, 1940-
1945 is classed as a general national bibliography of history using

the 16th number in Table I. Great Britain's 16th number is "Z 2016".

The Royal Society's Writing on British History, 1940-1945.

Z------ The single letter for the class, Bibliography and
library science.

2016 --- The integral number meaning a general bibliography
of British history.

.R882-- The Cutter number for the main entry, Royal...

Finally William Matthew's British Autobiographies; an Annotated
Bibliography uses the 27th number for "Special topics not otherwise
provided for, A-Z." It is classed "Z 2027 .A9M3". ".A9" in this
case is the Cutter number for the subject of the special topic, autobiography.

Matthew's British Autobiographies; an Annotated Bibliography.

Z------ The single letter for the class, Bibliography and
library science.

2027 --- The integral number for British bibliographies of
special topics not provided for otherwise.

.A9---- The first Cutter number for the special topic,
autobiography.

M3 ---- The second Cutter number for the compiler, Matthew.

In addition to these tables the fourth edition of Class Z has a
special scheme for a special collection of Library of Congress publications. This scheme is designed "to be used exclusively for
complete sets of all Library of Congress publications." Many libraries may prefer to ignore this table as individual Library of
Congress publications are classed separately elsewhere.

Class Z is often the most criticized schedule in the entire
classification, and it has many weaknesses, especially of arrangement. The problems with subject bibliographies can be solved in
various ways. For instance some libraries that do not class their
periodicals use the subject numbers for periodicals in B-Z for
bibliographies. Such a device may easily be adopted if the library
assumes the responsibility for the necessary original classing of
all subject bibliographies.

BIBLIOGRAPHY

Class A

U. S. Library of Congress. Classification Division. Classification. Class A: General Works, Polygraphy. Washington: Govt. Print. Off., 1911.

_____. _____. Adopted 1911. As in force June, 1915. Washington: Govt. Print. Off., 1915.

U. S. Library of Congress. Subject Cataloging Division. Classification. Class A: General Works, Polygraphy. 3d ed. Washington: 1947, reprinted with supplementary pages, 1963.

Class B

U. S. Library of Congress. Classification Division. Classification. Class B, Part I, B-BJ: Philosophy. Printed as Manuscript. Washington: Govt. Print. Off., 1910.

U. S. Library of Congress. Subject Cataloging Division. Classification. Class B, Part I, B-BJ: Philosophy. 2d ed. Washington: 1950, reprinted with supplementary pages, 1960.

U. S. Library of Congress. Classification Division. Classification. Class B, Part II, BL-BX: Religion. Printed as manuscript. Washington: Govt. Print. Off., 1927.

U. S. Library of Congress. Subject Cataloging Division. Classification. Class B, Part II, BL-BX: Religion. 2d ed. Washington: 1962.

Class B: Readings

Butz, Helen S. "Princeton Theological Seminary Library and the Library of Congress Classification for Church History. " Unpublished Master's thesis, Drexel Institute of Technology, 1955.

Davis, N. E. "Modification and Expansions of the Library of Congress Classification Schedule at the University of Chicago, " Proceedings of the Seventh Annual Conference, American Theological Library Association, Evanston, Illinois, June 11-12, 1953. Dayton, Ohio: Bonebrake Theological Seminary, 1953. Pp. 23-4.

Headicar, B. M. "Library of Congress Classification: Classes B, N, R, and Z, " Library Association Record, 12:515-6, 1910.

Mueller, Theodore A. "Workshop on the Library of Congress Classification and its New BL-BX Schedules, " Summary of Proceedings, Fifteenth Annual Conference, American Theological Library Association, Wesley Theological Seminary, Washington, D. C., June 13-15, 1961. Austin, Texas: Episcopal Theological Seminary of the Southwest, 1961. Pp. 68-83.
This is a detailed discussion on the classification of religion with many invaluable statements by the principal developer of the second edition of Subclasses BL-BX.

Satory, M. Max. "Class B--Philosophy and Religion of the Library of Congress Classification Schedules, " Library Journal, 62:450-3, June 1, 1937.

Stouffer, M. I. "Princeton and the Library of Congress Schedule, " Summary of Proceedings, Seventh Annual Conference, American Theological Library Association, Evanston, Illinois, June 11-12, 1953. Dayton, Ohio: Bonebrake Theological Seminary, 1953. Pp. 21-3.

Stouffer, M. I. "Round Table on Library of Congress Classification, " Summary of Proceedings, Ninth Annual Conference, American Theological Library Association (Union Theological Seminary), New York, New York, June 15-17, 1955. Maywood, Ill.: Chicago Lutheran Theological Seminary, 1955. Pp. 46-7.

Turner, D. "Report of Round Table on Library of Congress Classification, " Summary of Proceedings, Third Annual Conference, American Theological Library Association (Chicago Theological Seminary) Chicago, Illinois, June 20-21, 1949. Evanston, Ill.: Garrett Biblical Institute, 1949, Pp. 47.

Uhrich, H. B. "Abridgement of the LC Schedule in Religion, " Summary of Proceedings, Seventh Annual Conference, American Theological Library Association, Evanston, Illinois, June 11-12, 1953, Dayton, Ohio: Bonebrake Theological Seminary, 1953. Pp. 24-27.

Class B: Modifications of BL-BX

Jacobsen, Karl Theodor. Library of Congress Classification Schedules for the Lutheran Church, Modified and Expanded, Together with an Alphabetical List of Lutheran Synodical Organizations. Monograph series, Vol. 2, No. 4. Minneapolis: Board of Christian Education, Evangelical Lutheran Church, 1953.

Lynn, Jeannette Murphy. An Alternate Classification for Catholic
　　Books: Ecclesiastical Literature, Theology, Canon Law, Church
　　History. For Use with the Dewey Decimal, Classification
　　Decimale, Library of Congress Classifications. 2d ed., rev.
　　by Gilbert C. Peterson. Washington: Catholic University of
　　America Press, 1954. (1965 suppl. by Thomas G. Pater.)

Markley, Lucy W. A Methodist Book Classification. 2d ed., rev.
　　by Delbert E. Hollenberg. Evanston, Ill.: The Library,
　　Garrett Theological Seminary, 1964.

Peterson, K. G. "Further Expansion of Library of Congress Classi-
　　fication Schedules for the Lutheran Church Based upon the Mod-
　　ification and Expansion as Compiled by Karl T. Jacobsen. "
　　Pacific Lutheran Theological Seminary, Berkeley, California, n. d.

Class C

U. S. Library of Congress. Classification Division. Classification.
　　Class C: Auxiliary Sciences of History. Printed as manu-
　　script. Washington: Govt. Print. Off., 1915.

U. S. Library of Congress. Subject Cataloging Division. Classifi-
　　cation. Class C: Auxiliary Sciences of History. Subclass
　　CN: Epigraphy. Washington: Govt. Print. Off., 1942.

_____. Classification. Class C: Auxiliary Sciences of
　　History. 2d ed. Washington: 1948, reprinted with supple-
　　mentary pages, 1961.

Class D

U. S. Library of Congress. Classification Division. Classification.
　　Class D: Universal and Old World History. Printed as manu-
　　script. Washington: Govt. Print. Off., 1916.

_____. Classification. Universal and Old World History.
　　European War, D501-659. Printed as manuscript. Washing-
　　ton: Govt. Print. Off., 1921.

U. S. Library of Congress. Subject Cataloging Division. Classifica-
　　tion. Universal and Old World History. European War, D501-
　　725. 2d ed. as in force August 1933. Washington: 1933, re-
　　printed with supplementary pages, 1954.

_____. _____. Classification. Class D, Supplement 2,
　　Second World War. Preliminary edition as of June 1946.
　　Washington: Govt. Print. Off., 1947.

_____. _____. Classification. History: Class D, General
　　and Old World. 2d ed. Washington: 1959, reprinted with sup-
　　plementary pages, 1966.

Class D: Readings

Veryha, Wasyl. "Problems in Classification of Slavic Books with
Library of Congress Classification Schedules and Subject
Headings, " College and Research Libraries, 28: 277-283,
July 1967.

Class E-F

U.S. Library of Congress. Classification Division. America: History
and Geography. Preliminary and Provisional Scheme of Classification, January 1901. Washington: Govt. Print. Off., 1901.

_____. Classification. Class E-F: America. 2d ed. Printed
as manuscript. Washington: Govt. Print. Off., 1913.

U. S. Library of Congress. Subject Cataloging Division. Classification. History: Class E-F, America. 3d ed. Washington:
1958, reprinted with supplementary pages, 1965.

Class G

U. S. Library of Congress. Classification Division. Classification.
Class G: Geography, Anthropology, Sports and Games. Printed
as manuscript. Washington: Govt. Print. Off., 1910.

_____. Classification GR: Folk-lore. GT: Manners and Cus-
toms. Completing Class G: Geography, Anthropology, Sports
and Games. Printed as manuscript. Washington: Govt. Print.
Off., 1915.

_____. Classification. Class G: Geography, Anthropology,
Folklore, Manners and Customs, Sports and Games. 2d ed.
Washington: Govt. Print. Off., 1928.

U. S. Library of Congress. Subject Cataloging Division. Classification. Class G: Maps, G3160-9999. Preliminary draft.
Washington: Govt. Print. Off., 1946.

U. S. Library of Congress. Subject Cataloging Division. Classification. Class G: Geography, Anthropology, Folklore, Manners and Customs, Recreation. 3d ed. Washington: 1954,
reprinted with supplementary pages, 1966.

Class G: Readings

Allen, F.P. "Anthropology: Its Library Classification Problems, "
Special Libraries, 24: 90-93, May 1933.

Class H

U. S. Library of Congress. Classification Division. Classification. Class H: Social Sciences. Printed as manuscript. Washington: Govt. Print. Off., 1910.

U. S. Library of Congress. Catalog Division. Classification HT. Social Groups: Communities, Classes, Races. Completing Class H: Social Sciences. Printed as manuscript. Washington: Govt. Print. Off., 1915.

U. S. Library of Congress. Classification Division. Classification. Class H: Social Sciences. 2d ed. Printed as manuscript. Washington: Govt. Print. Off., 1920.

U. S. Library of Congress. Subject Cataloging Division. Classification. Class H: Social Sciences. 3d ed. Washington: 1950, reprinted with supplementary pages, 1965.

Class H: Readings

Bogardus, Janet. "Classification Schemes for Business and Financial Libraries, " Special Libraries, 43:409-410, December 1952.

Hagedorn, Ralph. "Random Thoughts on L. C. Classification, " Special Libraries, 52:256-257, May 1961.

"Library of Congress: Class H, Social Sciences, " American Journal of Sociology, 17:418, November 1911.

Class J

U. S. Library of Congress. Classification Division. Classification. Class J: Political Science. Printed as manuscript, subject to revision. Washington: Govt. Print. Off., 1910.

U. S. Library of Congress. Subject Cataloging Division. Classification. Class J: Political Science. 2d ed. Washington: 1924, reprinted with supplementary pages, 1966.

Class K

U. S. Library of Congress. Subject Cataloging Division. "Classification. Class KF. Law of the United States. " Final draft (revised as of May 1, 1967). Washington: [Photoduplication Services of the Library of Congress] 1967. Electrostatic copy.

Class K: Variants

Benyon, Elizabeth V. Classification. Class K. Law. Printed as manuscript. Washington: The Library of Congress, 1948.

Canada. Parliament Library. Class K, Law, Based on Law Library of Congress Classification Scheme. Ottawa: Parliamentary Library, 1956.

Los Angeles County Law Library. Classification: Class K: Law. Rev. ed. Los Angeles: Los Angeles County Law Library, 1965.

U. S. Department of Justice. Library. "Tentative Law Classification Scheme with Annotations, " Washington: June, 1940.

Class K: Readings

Benyon, Elizabeth V., "Classification of Law Books, " Law Library Journal, 50: 542-65, 1957.

Charpentier, A. A. and others. "Library of Congress Classification Schedule for Anglo-American Law (panel with discussion), " Law Library Journal, 57: 352-376, November 1964.

Ellinger, Werner B., "Progress of Class K, " Law Library Journal, 50: 542-565, 1957.

Wagman, F. H., "Class K. Law, " Library of Congress Information Bulletin, 8:4-5, May 24-30, 1949.

Class L

U. S. Library of Congress. Classification Division. Classification. Class L: Education. Washington: Govt. Print. Off., 1911.

_____. _____. 2d. ed. Washington: Govt. Print. Off., 1929.

U. S. Library of Congress. Subject Cataloging Division. Classification. Class L: Education. 3d ed. Washington: 1951, reprinted with supplementary pages, 1966.

Class M

U. S. Library of Congress. Division of Music. Classification. Class M, Music; Class ML, Literature of Music; Class MT, Musical Instruction. Adopted December, 1902; as in force April, 1904. Washington: Govt. Print.Off., 1904.

U. S. Library of Congress. Subject Cataloging Division. Classification. Class M: Music and Books on Music. 2d ed. Washington: 1917, reprinted with supplementary pages, 1963.

Class M: Readings

Bryant, Eric Thomas. Music Librarianship: A Practical Guide.
London: J. Clarke; New York: Hafner, 1959.
Pp. 154-161 cover a discussion of the possible uses of Class
M in a music library. A comparison with the Decimal Clas-
sification is made.

Cunningham, Virginia. "The Library of Congress Classed Catalog
for Music, " Library Resources & Technical Services, 8:285-
288, Summer 1964.
This article discusses the classed catalog of the Music Division of the Library of Congress including its use of mnemonic
"imaginary numbers" (decimal extensions to numbers used
in the classed catalog but not used in the classification numbers of books).

U.S. Library of Congress. The Music Division in the Library of
Congress. Washington: 1960.

Class N

U.S. Library of Congress. Classification Division. Classification.
Class N: Fine Arts. Printed as manuscript. Washington:
Govt. Print. Off., 1910.

_____. _____. Adopted 1909. As in force April, 1917.
Washington: Govt. Print. Off., 1917.

U.S. Library of Congress. Subject Cataloging Division. Classification. Class N: Fine Arts. 3d ed. Washington: 1922, reprinted with supplementary pages, 1962.

Class N: Readings

Headicar, B.M. "Library of Congress Classification: Classes B,
N, R, and Z, " Library Association Record, 12: 515-516,
1910.

Class P

U.S. Library of Congress. Subject Cataloging Division. Classification. Class P, P-PA: Philology, Linguistics, Classical
Philology, Classical Literature. Washington: 1928, reprinted
with supplementary pages, 1964.

304

_____. Class P, Subclass PA Supplement: Byzantine and Modern Greek Literature, Medieval and Modern Latin Literature. Washington: 1942, reprinted with supplementary pages, 1964.

_____. Classification. Class P, Subclasses PB-PH: Modern European Languages. Washington: 1933, reprinted with supplementary pages, 1966.

_____. Classification. Class P, Subclass PG, in part: Russian Literature. Washington: 1948, reprinted with supplementary pages, 1965.

_____. Classification. Class P, Subclasses PJ-PM: Languages and Literatures of Asia, Africa, Oceania, America, Mixed Languages, Artificial Languages. Washington: 1935, reprinted with supplementary pages, 1965.

U. S. Library of Congress. Classification Division. Classification. Philology. Index to Languages and Dialects in the Volumes P-PA, PB-PH, PJ-PM. Printed as manuscript. Washington: Govt. Print. Off., 1936.

U. S. Library of Congress. Subject Cataloging Division. Classification. Class P, Subclasses P-PM Supplement: Index to Languages and Dialects. 2d ed. Washington: 1957, reprinted with supplementary pages, 1965.

_____. Classification. Class P, Subclasses PN, PR, PS, PZ: Literature (General), English and American Literatures, Fiction in English, Juvenile Literature. Washington: 1915, reprinted with supplementary pages, 1964.

_____. Classification. Class P, Subclass PQ, part 1: French Literature. Washington: 1936, reprinted with supplementary pages, 1966.

_____. Classification. Class P, Subclass PQ, part 2: Italian, Spanish and Portuguese Literatures. Washington: 1937, reprinted with supplementary pages, 1965.

_____. Classification. Class P, Subclass PT, part 1: German Literature. Washington: 1938, reprinted with supplementary pages, 1966.

_____. Classification. Class P, Subclass PT, part 2: Dutch and Scandinavian Literatures. Washington: 1942, reprinted with supplementary pages, 1965.

Class P: Readings

Immroth, Phillip. "To PZ or not to PZ, " The Colorado Academic
Library, 3:17-19, Winter 1966.

Noe, A. C. von. "The New Classification of Languages and Literatures by the Library of Congress. " Bibliographical Society
of America, Papers, 6:59-65, 1911.

Pincherle, Alberto. "La Literatury y la Historia Italians a Traves
de las Classificaciones Dewey y del Congress, Fenix. Re-
vista de la Biblioteca Nacional, 3:459-84, 1945.

Zirny, L. J. [Review of PQ, part 2] Casopis Ceskoslovenskych
Knihovniku, 17:56, 1938.

Class Q

U. S. Library of Congress. Classification Division. Classification.
Class Q: Science. Preliminary, July 1, 1905. Washington:
Govt. Print. Off., 1905.

_____. _____. Adopted 1905. As in force November,
1912. Washington: Govt. Print. Off., 1913.

_____. _____. 3d ed. Washington: Govt. Print. Off.,
1921.

U. S. Library of Congress. Subject Cataloging Division. Classification. Class Q: Science. 4th ed. Washington: Govt. Print.
Off., 1948.

_____. _____. 5th ed. Washington: [Govt. Print. Off.]
1950, reprinted with supplementary pages, 1966.

Class Q: Readings

Allen, F. P. "Pure Science: L. C. vs. D. C., " Library Journal,
58:124-127, February 1, 1933.

Bartle, Robert G. "One Mathematician Looks at the Classification
of Mathematics, " The Role of Classification in the Modern
American Library. Papers Presented at an Institute Con-
ducted by the University of Illinois Graduate School of Library
Science, November 1-4, 1959. Champaign, Ill.: Illini Union
Bookstore, 1959. Pp. 93-102.

306

Class R

U.S. Library of Congress. Classification Division. Classification. Class R: Medicine. Printed as manuscript. Washington: Govt. Print. Off., 1910.

_____. _____. 2d ed. Washington: Govt. Print. Off., 1921.

U.S. Library of Congress. Subject Cataloging Division. Classification. Class R: Medicine. 3d ed. Washington: 1952, reprinted with supplementary pages, 1966.

Class R: Readings

Hallam, B. B. and Mrs. O. K. Goodman. "Library of Congress Classification with Emphasis on Edition 3, 1952 of Class R: Medicine," Medical Library Association Bulletin, 41:353-356, October 1953.

Haykin, David J. "The Classification of Medical Literature in the Library of Congress," Libri, 3:104-106, 1954.

Class S

U.S. Library of Congress. Classification Division. Classification. Class S: Agriculture--Plant and Animal Industry. Printed as manuscript. Washington: Govt. Print. Off., 1911.

_____. Classification. Class S: Agriculture, Plant and Animal Industry, Fish Culture and Fisheries, Hunting and Sports. 2d ed. Washington: Govt. Print. Off., 1928.

U.S. Library of Congress. Subject Cataloging Division. Classification. Class S: Agriculture, Plant and Animal Industry, Fish Culture and Fisheries, Hunting Sports. 3d ed. Washington: 1948, reprinted with supplementary pages, 1965.

Class T

U.S. Library of Congress. Classification Division. Classification. Class T: Technology. Printed as manuscript. Washington: Govt. Print. Off., 1910.

_____. _____. 2d ed. Washington: Govt. Print. Off., 1922.

_____. _____. 3d ed. Washington: Govt. Print. Off., 1937.

U.S. Library of Congress. Subject Cataloging Division. Classification. Class T: Technology. 4th ed. Washington: 1948, reprinted, 1953.

_____. _____. Supplement to the Fourth Edition. Additions and Changes to October 1964. Washington: 1965.

Class U

U. S. Library of Congress. Classification Division. Classification. Class U: Military Science. Printed as manuscript. Washington: Govt. Print. Off., 1910.

_____. _____. 2d ed. Washington: Govt. Print. Off., 1928.

U. S. Library of Congress. Subject Cataloging Division. Classification. Class U: Military Science. 3d ed. Washington: 1952, reprinted with supplementary pages, 1966.

Class V

U. S. Library of Congress. Classification Division. Classification. Class V: Naval Science. Printed as manuscript. Washington: Govt. Print. Off., 1910.

U. S. Library of Congress. Subject Cataloging Division. Classification. Class V: Naval Science. 2d ed. Washington: 1953, reprinted with supplementary pages, 1966.

Class W

U. S. Army Medical Library. "Classification: Medicine, " Preliminary ed. Washington: [Govt. Print. Off.] 1948. (Mimeographed)

U. S. Army Medical Library. Army Medical Library Classification: Medicine. Preclinical Sciences: QS-QZ, Medicine and Related Subjects: W. 1st ed. Washington: Govt. Print. Off., 1951.

U. S. National Library of Medicine. National Library of Medicine Classification. A scheme for the shelf arrangement of books in the field of medicine and its related sciences. 2d ed. Washington: Govt. Print. Off., 1956.

U. S. National Library of Medicine. National Library of Medicine Classification: A Scheme for the Shelf Arrangement of Books in the Field of Medicine and its Related Sciences. 3d ed. Public Health Service Publication No. 1108. Bethesda, Md.: U. S. Department of Health, Education, and Welfare, Public Health Service, National Library of Medicine, 1964.

Class W: Readings

The National Medical Library: Report of a Survey of the Army Medical Library. Financed by the Rockefeller Foundation and made under the auspices of the American Library Association, by Keyes D. Metcalfe, Janet Doe, Thomas P. Fleming, Mary Louise Marshall, L. Quincy Mumford, and Andrew D. Osborn. Chicago: American Library Association, 1944.

Class Z

U. S. Library of Congress. Classification Division. Classification. Class Z: Bibliography and Library Science. Adopted 1898. As in force January 1, 1902. Washington: Govt. Print. Off., 1902.

_____. _____. Adopted 1898. As in force January, 1910. Washington: Govt. Print. Off., 1910.

_____. _____. 3d ed. January, 1926. Washington: Govt. Print. Off. , 1927.

U. S. Library of Congress. Subject Cataloging Division. Classification. Class Z: Bibliography and Library Science. 4th ed. Washington: 1959, reprinted with supplementary pages, 1965.

The Outline of the Classes

U. S. Library of Congress. Classification Division. Classification. Outline Scheme of Classes. Washington: Govt. Print. Off., 1903.

_____. _____. Washington: Govt. Print. Off., 1904.

_____. _____. Washington: Govt. Print. Off., 1906.

_____. _____. Washington: Govt. Print. Off., 1907.

_____. _____. Preliminary, December, 1909. Washington: Govt. Print. Off., 1910.

_____. _____. Preliminary. Rev. to January, 1914. Washington: Govt. Print. Off., 1914.

_____. _____. Rev. to February, 1917. Washington: Govt. Print. Off., 1917.

_____. _____. Rev. to August, 1920. Washington: Govt. Print. Off., 1920.

U. S. Library of Congress. Subject Cataloging Division. Outline of the Library of Congress Classification. Revised and enlarged edition of "Outline Scheme of Classes. " Washington: 1942, reprinted, 1965.

Figure 49

AZ   HISTORY OF THE SCIENCES IN GENERAL   **AZ**

	History.
	General works.
	Prefer CB, D, P, Q.
200–208	**Early.**
200	Latin.
201	English.
202	French.
203	German.
204	Italian.
208	Other.
211–218	19th century.
	Subdivided like AZ201–208.
221–228	20th century.
	Subdivided like AZ201–208.
	By period.
	Prefer CB, D, P, Q.
301	Antiquity.
311	Ancient Oriental.
	Assyro-Babylonian, Egyptian, etc.
321	Middle ages.
331	Renaissance.
341	Modern.
346	16th–17th centuries.
351	18th century.
356	19th century.
361	20th century.
501–908	**By country.**
	Prefer DA–DU, P, Q.
	Under each:

I	II	III	IV	
10 nos.	5 nos.	3 nos.	1 no.	
(0)	(1)	(1).A1–A3	.A1–A2	Collections.
(1)	(2)		.A5–Z3	.A5–Z3 General works. History.
(2)				Early. Origins.
(3)				Middle ages.
(4)				Modern.
(6)				General special. Relations, aspects, etc.
(7)	(3)	.Z5	.Z5	Addresses, essays, lectures. Pamphlets.
(8)	(4)	(2)	.Z7A–Z	States, provinces, etc. Under each: (1) Collections. (2) History. (3) Other: Minor.
[9]	[5]	[3]	[.Z8A–Z]	Cities, *see* DA–DU, E, F.

Figure 50

TABLES OF SUBDIVISIONS
(CT210–3150)

	I			II	
0	Serials. Yearbooks.		0	Serials. Yearbooks.	
1	Collections.		1	Collections.	
2	Early works to 1800.		3	General and miscellaneous works.	
3	Dictionaries, 1801–				
4	General works, 1801–		4	Minor works.	
5	General special. Special aspects.			By period.	
				Ancient, *see* D.	
6	Miscellaneous and minor.			Medieval, *see* D.	
7	Juvenile.			Modern.	
	By period.		5	To 1800.	
(8)	Ancient, *see* D.		6	1801–	
(9)	Medieval, *see* D.		7	Local divisions, A–Z.	
	Modern.			Cities, *see* D–F.	
10	15th–16th centuries.			Rulers, *see* D–F.	
11	17th–18th centuries.		8	Individual biography, A–Z.	
12	19th–20th centuries.			Including correspondence.	
13	20th century.		.Z9	Persons not known by name.	
14	Colonies (General).				
	Prefer CT278–3090.				
15	Local divisions, A–Z.				
(16)	Cities, *see* D.				
(17)	Rulers, *see* D–F.				
18	Individual biography, A–Z.				
	Including correspondence.				
.Z9	Persons not known by name.				

BIOGRAPHY BY SUBJECT

Based on general Library of Congress classification.
Numbers in parentheses are for added entries in card shelflist only.

Biography of women.
Cf. CT7205, 8240–8273.

3200	Periodicals. Collections.
	General works.
3201	To 1800.
3202	1801–

Figure 51

DC   FRANCE   **DC**

History, 1815–
  By period.
    20th century.
      Fourth Republic, 1947–   —Continued.
        Biography and memoirs.
406   Collective.
407   Individual, A–Z.

>   e. g.   .M4   Mendès-France, Pierre.
>   .P5   Pinay, Antoine.
>   .S3   Schuman, Robert.

408   Auriol, Vincent, 1947–1953.
409   Coty, René, 1954–

LOCAL HISTORY AND DESCRIPTION

600   **Islands of France (General).**
>   Individual islands, *see* DC 611, 801; DT 469, etc.
         Larger geographical divisions.
>   For subarrangement, *see* table under DC 611.
601.1–9   North.   Northeast.
603.1–9   East.
605.1–9   Central.
607.1–9   South.   Gulf of Lyons.
608.1–9   Riviera.
>   Cf. DG 975.R6, Italian Riviera.
609.1–9   West.
611   **Regions, provinces, departments, etc., A–Z.**
>   Local history during the Revolution and Consulate,
>   *see* DC 195.
>   Under each:
>   (1)   Periodicals.   Societies.
>   (2)   Sources and documents.   Collections.
>   (23) Gazetteers.   Directories.   Dictionaries,
>   etc.
>   (25) Biography (Collective).
>   (3)   General works.   Description and travel.
>   Guidebooks.
>   (4)   Antiquities.
>   (5)   History (General).
>   By period (History and description).
>   (6)   Early.
>   (7)   Medieval and early modern.
>   (8)   Modern.
>   (9)   Special topics.

Figure 51a

611   **Regions, provinces, departments, etc., A–Z—Con.**

Notes on table (p. 180):

> The table shows the sequence of topics when nine basic numerals are available. If eleven are indicated (23), (25), (3), etc., become (3), (4), (5), etc. If fewer are available, longer decimal or cutter numbers may be introduced, as for example (23) and (25) above; or a number may cover more than one topic, e. g. (1) may cover (1) and (2), or (5) may cover (5) through (8). When one numeral only is indicated, .A1–9 or .A1A–Z may be used for serials.

> Some variations in the application of the table at the Library of Congress are presented in the following list.

.A16   Agenais.

.A26–27   Ain.

> .A261   Sources and documents.   Collections.

.A298–299   Aisne.

> Including old district, Thiérache.

.A3   Alais.

.A33–35   Albigeois.

.A435–437   Allier.

.A553–557   Alpes (Basses-, Hautes-, Maritimes).

> Cf. DQ 821–829, Swiss Alps.

> .A553   Periodicals.   Societies.
> .A554   Sources and documents.   Collections.
> .A555   Gazetteers.   Dictionaries, etc.
> .A556   Description and history.
> .A557   Other.

Alsace, *see* DD 801.A31–69, Alsace and Lorraine (Germany).

.A601–609   Anjou.

.A645–666   **Aquitaine.**

> .A645   Periodicals.   Societies.
> .A646   Sources and documents.   Collections.
> .A647   Collected works.
> .A648   Biography.
> .A649   Gazetteers.   Directories, etc.
> A65   Description and travel.
> .A652   Antiquities.
> .A654   Ethnography.

Figure 52

611   Regions, provinces, departments, etc., A–Z—Con.
.B394–396   Beauvais.
.B425–428   Belfort.
.B521–523   Bernaville.
.B531–533   Berry.
.B574–576   Béziers.
.B6   Boisbelle (Cher).
.B751–753   Bouches-du-Rhône.
             Bouillon, *see* DH 801.B6.
             Boulogne, *see* DC 801.B75–77.
.B764–768   Bourbonnais.
.B771–79   **Burgundy** (Bourgogne).
             .B771   Periodicals. Societies.
             .B772   Sources and documents. Collections.
             .B7723   Gazetteers. Directories. Place names, etc.
             .B7725   Biography (Collective).
             .B773   General works. Description and travel.
             .B774   Antiquities.
                      History.
             .B775   General works.
                          By period.
             .B776   Early and medieval to 1477.
             .B777   Early to 843.
             .B778   843–1032.
             .B779   1032–1361, Dukes of the Capetian
                              dynasty.
             .B78   1361–1477, Dukes of Burgundy.
             .B781   1467–1477, Charles le Téméraire.
             .B782   1477–1789.
             .B785   1789–
             .B787   Other special.
.B841–915   **Brittany** (Bretagne).
             .B841   Periodicals. Societies.
             .B842   Sources and documents. Collections.
             .B843   Collected works.
             .B844   Minor works. Pamphlets, etc.
             .B845   Biography (Collective).
             .B846   Gazetteers. Directories, etc.
             .B847   General works.
             .B848   Description and travel.
                        Including the picturesque.
             .B85   Antiquities.
             .B851   Social life and customs. Civilization.
             .B852   Ethnography.
                      History.
             .B854   General works.
             .B855   General special.

Figure 53

UNITED STATES LOCAL HISTORY

SUBDIVISIONS UNDER STATES
TABLE I
(Continued)

(13) **Metropolis. Chief city.**

> Thus far subdivision (13) has been used only for Boston, New York, and Philadelphia at the Library of Congress.
>
> For subarrangement, *see* Table IV.

(14) **Cities, towns, etc., A–Z.**

> Class here historical and descriptive matter on a town or city and its subdivisions; local biography; genealogy; vital records; histories of colonial churches reaching back to the settlements; local societies of a historical character; centennial and other local celebrations; old home week; views; historic buildings; etc.
>
> Class here, also, estates and townships not located within the limits of any town or city, e. g. F 234.S865, Stratford Hall, Westmoreland Co., Va.

(15) **Elements in the population.**

> Works on racial and ethnic groups including religious bodies which have significance in the history of a state (Cf. BX, Special churches and sects) are classed here.
>
> In .A1, General works, include material on foreign elements in general, minorities, race conflicts, etc.
>
> For individual elements, consult a representative list of elements (with cutter numbers) under E 184, p. 27–29.

TABLE II [1]

(1) Periodicals. Societies. Collections.
(3) Museums. Exhibitions, exhibits.
(4) Gazetteers. Dictionaries. Geographic names.
(4.3) Guidebooks.
   Directories.
> State directories are no longer classified at the Library of Congress.

(4.5) General.
(4.6) Elite.
(4.7) Business.
(5) Biography (Collective). Genealogy (Collective).
(5.2) Historiography.
   Historians, *see* E 175.5.
(5.5) Study and teaching.
(6) General works. Histories.
(6.3) Juvenile works.
(6.5) Minor works. Pamphlets, addresses, essays, etc.
(6.6) Anecdotes, legends, pageants, etc.
(7) Historic monuments. Illustrative material.

---

[1] For scope and meaning of subdivisions in Table II. *see* Table I

Figure 53a

UNITED STATES LOCAL HISTORY

SUBDIVISIONS UNDER STATES

TABLE II [1]

(Continued)

(8)	Antiquities (Non-Indian).
(9)–(11)	By period.

e. g.   (9)   Early to 1775.
         (10)   1775–1865.
         (11)   1865–1950.
         (11.2)   1951–

(12)	Regions, counties. etc., A–Z.
(13)	Metropolis. Chief city.

Thus far, subdivision (13) has been used only for Chicago at the Library of Congress.

For subarrangement, *see* Table IV.

(14)	Cities, towns, etc., A–Z.
(15)	Elements in the population.

.A1   General works.
.A2–Z   Individual elements.

TABLE III [1]

Identical with Table II except that subdivision (6), General works, also covers the period "Early to 1950"; and subdivisions (9)–(11) are used differently.

e. g.   (9) Early to 1950, *see* Subdivision (6).
         (10) 1951–

SUBDIVISIONS UNDER A METROPOLIS

TABLE IV [1]

.1	Periodicals. Societies. Collections.
.15	Museums. Exhibitions, exhibits.
.18	Guidebooks.
(.2)–(.24)	Directories.

City directories are no longer classified at the Library of Congress.

.25	Biography (Collective). Genealogy (Collective).

Including vital records and epitaphs. Collections from two or more cemeteries are classed here. Those from a single cemetery are classed preferably in subdivision (.61).

.27	Historiography.
.29	Study and teaching.
.3	General works. Histories.
.33	Juvenile works.
.35	Minor works. Pamphlets, addresses, essays, etc.
.36	Anecdotes, legends, pageants, etc.
.37	Historic monuments. Illustrative material.
.39	Antiquities (Non-Indian).

[1] For scope and meaning of subdivisions in Tables II, III, and IV, *see* Table I.

Figure 54

UNITED STATES LOCAL HISTORY

Michigan. Table III.[1]

572   Regions, counties, etc., A–Z—Continued.

    .W4   Wayne Co.
    .W5   Wexford Co.

574   Cities, towns, etc., A–Z.

    e. g. .A2   Ann Arbor.
         .B3   Bay City.
         .D2   Dearborn.
         .D4   Detroit.
         .G7   Grand Rapids.
         .K1   Kalamazoo.
         .L2   Lansing.
         .M9   Muskegon.
         .S15   Saginaw.
         .S3   Sault Ste. Marie.

575   Elements in the population.

    .A1   General works.
    .A2–Z Individual elements.

        For a list of racial, ethnic, and religious elements (with cutter numbers), *see* E 184, p. 27–29.

576–590   **Wisconsin.** Table II.[1]

576   Periodicals. Societies. Collections.
578   Museums. Exhibitions, exhibits.
579   Gazetteers. Dictionaries. Geographic names.
  .3   Guidebooks.
580   Biography (Collective). Genealogy (Collective).
  .2   Historiography.

        Historians, *see* E 175.5.

  .5   Study and teaching.
581   General works. Histories.
  .3   Juvenile works.
  .5   Minor works. Pamphlets, addresses, essays, etc.
  .6   Anecdotes, legends, pageants, etc.
582   Historic monuments (General). Illustrative material.
583   Antiquities (Non-Indian).

    By period.

584   Early to 1848.

        Biography: Thomas Pendleton Burnett, etc.

585   1836–1848. Wisconsin Territory.
586   1848–1950.

        Admission as a state, May 29, 1848.

        Biography: Benjamin Franklin Hopkins, Morgan Lewis Martin, Cadwallader Colden Washburn, etc.

---

[1] For Tables and interpretation of their numbers, *see* p. 133–140.

Figure 54a

UNITED STATES LOCAL HISTORY

Wisconsin. Table II.[1]

By period.

586   1848–1950—Continued.

    Cf. D 570.85.W6–61, World War I, 1914–1918.
    D 769.85.W6–61, World War II, 1939–1945.
    E 537, Civil War, 1861–1865 (General); E 470.4,
      471–478, Military operations and battles.
    E 726.W6, War of 1898 (Spanish-American War).

.2   1951–

587   Regions, counties, etc., A–Z.

  .A2   Adams Co.
        Apostle Islands, *see* F 587.A8.
  .A8   Ashland Co.
          Apostle Islands, Chequamegon Bay, etc.
  .B25   Barron Co.
  .B3   Bayfield Co.
          Chequamegon Bay, *see* F 587.A8.
  .B55   Black River and Valley.
  .B7   Boundaries.
          Cf. F 547.B7, Illinois boundary.
             F 612.B7, Minnesota boundary.
  .B8   Brown Co.
  .B9   Buffalo Co.
  .B95   Burnett Co.
  .C2   Calumet Co.
        Chequamegon Bay, *see* F 587.A8.
  .C48   Chippewa Co.
  .C5   Chippewa River and Valley.
  .C6   Clark Co.
  .C7   Columbia Co.
  .C8   Crawford Co.
        Dalles of the Wisconsin, *see* F 587.W8.
  .D3   Dane Co.
          Cave of the Mounds, Lake Mendota, etc.
        Dells of the Wisconsin, *see* F 587.W8.
  .D6   Dodge Co.
  .D7   Door Co.
  .D8   Douglas Co.
  .D9   Dunn Co.
  .E2   Eau Claire Co.
  .F5   Florence Co.
  .F6   Fond du Lac Co.
  .F65   Forest Co.
  .F7   Fox River and Valley, Wis.
          Cf. F 547.F77, Illinois.
        Lake Geneva, *see* F 587.W18.
  .G5   Grant Co.

---

[1] For Tables and interpretation of their numbers, *see* p. 133–140.

318

F   UNITED STATES LOCAL HISTORY   **F**

Wisconsin. Table II.[1]

587   Regions, counties, etc., A–Z—Continued.

.S2   Sauk Co.

Devil's Lake, Durward's Glen, etc.

.S3   Sawyer Co.
.S45   Shawano Co.
.S5   Sheboygan Co.
.S9   Lake Superior region, Wis.

Cf. F 552, General.

.T3   Taylor Co.
.T79   Trempealeau Co.
.V5   Vernon Co.
.V6   Vilas Co.
W18   Walworth Co.

Lake Geneva, etc.

.W185   Washburn Co.
.W19   Washington Co.
.W2   Waukesha Co.
.W3   Waupaca Co.
.W35   Waushara Co.
.W5   Winnebago Co.
.W8   Wisconsin River and Valley.

Dells (Dalles) of the Wisconsin, etc.

.W9   Wood Co.

589   Cities, towns, etc., A–Z.

e. g.   .G7   Green Bay.
        .K3   Kenosha.
        .L1   La Crosse.
        .M1   Madison.
        .M6   Milwaukee.
        .O8   Oshkosh.
        .P8   Prairie du Chien.
        .R2   Racine.
        .S95 Superior.

590   Elements in the population.

.A1   General works.
.A2–Z   Individual elements.

For a list of racial, ethnic, and religious elements (with cutter numbers), *see* E 184, p. 27–29.

591–596   **The West.** Trans-Mississippi region.

The "Indian country," 1803–1854, *see* F 697.
Louisiana (Province), *see* F 374.
Middle West, *see* F 351–355.
Mississippi River and Valley, *see* F 351–354.
Missouri River and Valley, *see* F 598.
The Northwest (Upper Mississippi Valley), *see* F 597.
Pacific coast, *see* F 851.

---

[1] For Tables and interpretation of their numbers, *see* p. 133–140.

Figure 55

TABLES OF SUBDIVISIONS FOR ATLASES AND MAPS

I

AREA SUBDIVISIONS

Each sequence of two or more numbers assigned to a geographic area is subdivided in accordance with the following plan:

(1) 0 or 5   General.

       e. g.   G 1250   New York State (general atlas number)

              G 3800   New York State (general map number)

(2) 1 or 6   By subject.

         Subarranged by Table II, p. 176–183.

       e. g.   G 1251   New York State (atlas subject-area number)

              .P3   Railroad atlases

              G 3801   New York State (map subject-area number)

              .P3   Railroad maps

(3) 2 or 7   By region, natural feature, etc., when not assigned individual numbers, A–Z.

       e. g.   G 1252   New York State (atlas regional number)

              .A2   Adirondack Mountains atlases

              G 3801   New York State (map regional number)

              .A2   Adirondack Mountains maps

An island without distinctive number is treated as a regional division of the area of which it is a geographical part. This treatment is also preferred if the island is a political unit.

       e. g.   G 3762   Regions, A–Z (Massachusetts)

              .N3   Nantucket Island

                    Not G 3763.N3, Nantucket County

              G 3772   Regions, A–Z (Rhode Island)

              .B5   Block Island

                    Not G 3773.N4, as part of Newport County

              G 3802   Regions, A–Z (New York State)

              .S8   Staten Island

                    Neither G 3803, Richmond County *nor* as a borough of New York City

              G 4982   Regions, A–Z (Bahama Islands)

              .T9   Turks Islands

                    A geographical part of the Bahamas but a political dependency of Jamaica, G 4960–4964

              G 6762   Regions, A–Z (Sicily)

              .P3   Pantelleria

                    Not G 6763.T7, as part of province of Trapani

Figure 55a

SUBDIVISIONS FOR ATLASES AND MAPS

TABLE OF AREA SUBDIVISIONS
(Continued)

(4) 3 or 8   By major political division (Counties, states, provinces, etc.) when not assigned individual numbers, A–Z.

> Arranged alphabetically using one or more successive cutter numbers for each political division, depending upon the number of political subdivisions to be provided for.

> e. g.   G 1253   New York State (atlas county number)
> .W3   Washington County atlases
> .W37   Kingsburg (town[ship] in Washington County) atlases
> G 3803   New York State (map county number)
> .W3   Washington County maps
> .W37   Kingsburg (town[ship]) maps

(5) 4 or 9   By city or town, A–Z.

> Cities and towns of most countries are grouped under the country, not under the political subdivision in which they are located. Exceptions to this rule follow:

> (1) United States cities and towns are classified under each state. New England towns (i. e. townships) and other townships which are urban or suburban in character, are classified with the cities of the state.

> (2) Canadian cities and towns are classified under each province.

> (3) Chinese cities and towns of outlying or former dependencies (Manchuria, Outer Mongolia, Sinkiang, Tibet, and Formosa) are classified under those areas. Cities and towns of China proper are classified in G 2309 (atlases) or G 7824 (maps).

> (4) French West African and French Equatorial African cities and towns are classified under individual colony numbers.

> e. g.   G 1254   New York State (atlas city and town number)
> .R6   Rochester atlases
> G 3804   New York State (map city and town number)
> .R6   Rochester maps
> G 1914   Germany (atlas city and town number)
> .B3   Berlin atlases
> G 6084   Germany (map city and town number)
> .B3   Berlin maps

Call numbers for area atlases consist of three parts; *call numbers* for area maps, three or four parts. For example:

(1) Major area atlas
> G 1251   New York State (area number)
> .A5   American Automobile Association (cutter number for the authority responsible for the atlas)
> 1947   Date of atlas [1]

---

[1] If exact date of atlas or map is unknown, use an approximate date.

Figure 55b

SUBDIVISIONS FOR ATLASES AND MAPS

TABLE OF AREA SUBDIVISIONS
(Continued)

(2) Sub-area atlas
    G 1253   New York State counties (area number)
  .M6M7   Monroe County *and* Monroe County Good Roads Committee (sub-area cutter number plus cutter number for authority responsible for the atlas)
    1943   Date of atlas [1]

(3) Major area map
    G 3800   New York State (area number)
    1947   Date of map [1]
    .C7   Geo. F. Cram Co., Inc. (cutter number for authority responsible for the map)

(4) Sub-area map
    G 3803   New York State counties (area number)
    .M6   Monroe County (sub-area cutter number)
    1943   Date of map [1]
    .M7   Monroe County Good Roads Committee (cutter number for the authority responsible for the map)

Sets of maps, usually cataloged with open entry, are designated by a small "s" after the area number. These set maps are filed ahead of (or separate from) the general or closed entry maps of the same area which are arranged by date. In the call number, the date is replaced by the denominator of the scale "representative fraction," minus the last three digits. For sets of large maps with scales larger than 1:1,000 (e. g. 1:200, 1:950, etc.) use the full scale fraction denominator number with the two final digits enclosed in parentheses. For example:

(1) G 3800s New York State (area number) plus "s" (signifying set)
      25   Scale number (denominator of scale, 1:25,000, minus last three digits)
     .U5   United States Army Map Service (cutter number for authority responsible for the maps)

(2) G 5834s France (major area number) plus "s" (signifying set)
    .P3   Paris (sub-area cutter number)
    5(00)   Scale number (denominator of scale, 1:500, with the two final digits enclosed in parentheses)
    .S5   Seine (Dept.) Préfecture (cutter number for the authority responsible for the maps)

---

[1] If exact date of atlas or map is unknown, use an approximate date.

Figure 55c

SUBDIVISIONS FOR ATLASES AND MAPS

II

SUBJECT SUBDIVISIONS

Subject subdivisions are used in classifying atlases and maps with special subject interest. General atlases and maps and those showing several types of data do not use subject subdivisions. As set up, there are seventeen major subject groups, designated by capital letters followed by numbers representing subtopics. These numbers are not cutter numbers and have no alphabetical significance. If a subject atlas or map of a given area requires closer classification than is provided, insert additional subject numbers in the appropriate subject group; if a broader classification is desired, use subject letter only.

Subject letter-numbers—treated dècimally in call numbers, e. g. .P2, Roads—may be used with any atlas or map subject-area number (e. g. G 1251, 3801) or map sub-area cutter number (e. g. G 3803.M6), but not with an atlas sub-area cutter number.[1]

Call numbers for atlases consist of three parts; *call numbers* for maps, four parts. For example:

(1) Major area subject atlas
    G 1251   New York State (subject-area number)
    .P2A5   Roads *and* American Automobile Association (subject letter-number plus cutter number for the authority responsible for the atlas)
    1947   Date of atlas [2]

(2) Sub-area subject atlas [3]
    G 1253   New York counties (area number)
    .M6M7   Monroe County *and* Monroe County Good Roads Committee (sub-area cutter number plus cutter number for the authority responsible for the atlas
    1943   Date of atlas [2]

(3) Major area subject map
    G 3801   New York State (subject-area number)
    .P2   Roads (subject letter-number)
    1947   Date of map [2]
    .A5   American Automobile Association (cutter number for the authority responsible for the map)

(4) Sub-area subject map
    G 3803   New York counties (area number)
    .M6P2   Monroe County *and* Roads (sub-area cutter number plus subject letter-number)
    1943   Date of map [2]
    .M7   Monroe County Good Roads Committee (cutter number for the authority responsible for the map)

---

[1] Sub-area subject atlases are to be classed with the area atlases.
[2] If exact date of atlas or map is unknown, use an approximate date.
[3] Call number is the same as that of the area atlas.

Figure 55d

SUBDIVISIONS FOR ATLASES AND MAPS

SUMMARY OF SUBJECT SUBDIVISIONS

A Special category atlases and maps.
B Mathematical geography. Cartography and surveying.
C Physical sciences.
D Biogeography.
E Human and cultural geography.
F Political geography.
G Economic geography.
H Mines and mineral resources.
J Agriculture.
K Forests and forestry.
L Fisheries.
M Manufacturing and processing.
N Technology. Engineering. Public works.
P Transportation and communication.
Q Commerce and trade. Finance.
R Military and naval geography.
S Historical geography.

TABLE OF SUBJECT SUBDIVISIONS

A Special category atlases and maps.

   Including atlases and maps which cannot be placed in any of the subject groups, but because of format or special treatment are to be separated from general atlases and maps.

   1   Outline and base maps.
          With cities include atlases and maps of metropolitan area, suburbs, "vicinity."
   2   Index maps.
   3   Aerial views.
   4   Photomaps.
   5   Pictorial maps.
   6   Cartoon maps.
   7   Advertising maps.

B Mathematical geography.

   Atlases and maps illustrating subjects of cartography, surveying, mapping.

   1   Astronomical observatories and observations.
   2   Movements of the earth.
          Including time, time zones, date line.
   3   Geodetic surveys.
          Triangulation and triangulation nets, precise levelling nets, including prime meridians, base lines, meridians.
   5   Surveying.   Extent of areas surveyed.
   7   Cartography.
          Including projections.
   8   Comparative area maps.

Figure 55e

SUBDIVISIONS FOR ATLASES AND MAPS

TABLE OF SUBJECT SUBDIVISIONS
(Continued)

C   **Physical sciences.**

>Atlases and maps constructed to show the distribution of natural phenomena of the earth, including the atmosphere and sub-surface features: "Geological maps," "Weather maps," etc.

1   General.
>"Topographic maps" are classified as general maps.

2   Physiography. Geomorphology.
>Including topography, land forms.

3   Hydrography.
>Including rivers, lakes, ground waters, springs, glaciation, flood control.

5   Geology.
>Including structural geology, paleontology.

55   Earthquakes (Seismology).

7   Oceanography.
>Including tides.

8   Meteorology and climatology.

9   Geophysics.
>Including terrestrial magnetism.

D   **Biogeography.**

>Atlases and maps showing distribution of plant and animal life, exclusive of man and his economic activities.

1   General.
>That is, plant and animal distribution.

2   Plant geography (Phytogeography).

4   Animal geography (Zoogeography).
>*See also* L, Fisheries.

5   Wildlife reservations.

E   **Human and cultural geography.**

>Atlases and maps concerned with man as a physical and social being.

1   Anthropogeography. Ethnography. Genealogy.

2   Population.
>Including density, vital statistics, movements of population.

3   Languages.

4   Religions.

5   Medical geography.

6   Social and cultural geography.
>Including civilizations and customs, intellectual activities (literature, music, fine arts), education, libraries.

7   Material culture.
>Distribution of income, housing, etc.

8   Archeology.

9   Slavery.

Figure 55f

SUBDIVISIONS FOR ATLASES AND MAPS

TABLE OF SUBJECT SUBDIVISIONS
(Continued)

F   **Political geography.**

Atlases and maps constructed to emphasize data on boundaries, administrative and political divisions, sovereignty, spheres of influence, and national .aspirations. Most "general" or "topographic" atlases and maps show political boundaries also.

2   International or external boundaries.

3   Sovereignty.

5   International relations.

      Treaty enforcements, international cooperation (League of Nations, United Nations, Atlantic Pact, Marshall Plan, etc.).

6   Geopolitics.

7   Administrative, judicial, and political divisions.

8   Government.

      Forms of government, administrative districts and centers of government departments and bureaus, laws and law enforcement, legal systems, etc.

9   Political campaigns. Election results.

G   **Economic geography.**

Atlases and maps showing economic information exclusive of the specialized fields of (1) Mines and mineral resources, (2) Agriculture, (3) Forests and forestry, (4) Fisheries, (5) Manufactures and processing, (6) Technology, engineering, public works, (7) Transportation and communication, and (8) Commerce and trade, finance. These fields receive detailed treatment in subject subdivisions H to Q.

1   General.

2   Economic regions.

3   Natural resources.

4   Land utilization. Land ownership.

5   Reservations.

      See also D5, Wildlife reservations.

51   Public lands.

52   Parks.

55   Reservations (Ethnic).

6   Economic conditions.

7   Business organizations.

8   Labor.

H   **Mines and mineral resources.**

Including atlases and maps showing the location of mines and mineral deposits.

1   General.

2   Metallic group.

5   Nonmetallic group.

8   Petroleum and natural gas.

9   Coal. Lignite. Peat.

Figure 55g

SUBDIVISIONS FOR ATLASES AND MAPS

TABLE OF SUBJECT SUBDIVISIONS
(Continued)

J   **Agriculture.**

1	General. Agricultural regions.
2	Systems of agriculture.
3	Soils.
4	Reclamation. Soil conservation.
	Including irrigation, erosion.
5	Animal resources.
6	Crops.

K   **Forests and forestry.**

Atlases and maps indicating the distribution of forest areas, forest types, agents of forest destruction, silviculture, and forest exploitation.

1	General.
2	Distribution of forest area and forest types.
3	Conservation and reforestation.
	Including national and state forests.
5	Forest fires.
6	Exploitation.

L   **Fish and fisheries.**

Atlases and maps on fish and fisheries, including all types of aquatic life: fish, marine vegetation, and pelagic mammals.

1	General.
2	Distribution of fisheries.
3	Exploitation of fisheries.
5	Pelagic mammals.
	Including sealing, whaling.

M   **Manufacturing and processing.**

Industrial processes shown in atlases and on maps.

1	General.
2	Mineral processing and manufacture.
3	Chemical processing and manufacture.
4	Wood processing and manufacture.
5	Paper processing and manufacture.
6	Fiber and textile processing and manufacture.
7	Hides and skins.
8	Food and beverage processing and manufacture.

N   **Technology.   Engineering.   Public works.**

1	Engineering (General).
2	Hydraulic engineering.
	See also G4, Land utilization; J4, Irrigation; P5, Canals.
3	Power.
	Including steam, electric, and hydroelectric power.
4	Power lines.
6	Water supply.
8	Sanitation. Sanitary engineering.

Figure 55h

SUBDIVISIONS FOR ATLASES AND MAPS

TABLE OF SUBJECT SUBDIVISIONS
(Continued)

P   **Transportation and communication.**

    Atlases and maps showing location, type, and importance of transportation and communication routes, or of the location of centers important for their positions in these fields.

1   General.

    Including comparative maps, maps of distances, legal regulation of transportation.

2   Roads, etc.

    Bridges, tunnels, river ferries, bus lines, motor transport (freight and express). Individual items A–Z, where possible, e. g. where subject-area numbers are used.

3   Railroads.

    Electric railways, subways, elevated railways, aerial cableways, conveyor belts, etc., freight, express. Individual companies A–Z, where possible, e. g. where subject-area numbers are used.

4   Pipe lines.

5   Water transportation.

    Inland waterways, canals, marine transportation, aids to navigation (marine). Individual canals, etc., A–Z, where possible, e. g. where subject-area numbers are used.

55   Port facilities.

6   Air transportation.

    Including air lines, aids to aerial navigation.

8   Communication.

    Postal service, telegraph, submarine cables, telephone, radio (wireless telegraph and telephone), television.

Q   **Commerce and trade. Finance.**

    Atlases and maps on commercial activities other than the processing or transportation of products. Flow of goods, independent of specific transportation means, is included.

1   General. Trade routes.

3   Movement of commodities.

4   Fairs, markets, trade centers, trading areas, etc.

5   Tariffs and other trade barriers.

8   Finance.

    Including coins and currencies, foreign exchange. credit.

Figure 55i

SUBDIVISIONS FOR ATLASES AND MAPS

TABLE OF SUBJECT SUBDIVISIONS
(Continued)

R   **Military and naval geography.**

Atlases and maps concerned with the administration and general operation of military and naval forces. Atlases and maps portraying historical events go in subject subdivision S, History.

2   Military and naval districts and establishments.
3   Strategic and tactical plans.
4   Defenses.
       Including fortifications, etc.
5   Logistics.
7   Military operations.
       Including maneuvers, war games, etc.
9   Property in war.

S   **Historical geography.**

Atlases and maps portraying specific historical events, including disposition of troops, battle lines, or a series of events, are classified here. An atlas or map, either contemporary or reconstructed, giving only general geographical information of an area at the time of a given event or series of events is excluded. A chronological subdivision for each area, based on its own series of historical events, is to be preferred to any universal, arbitrary arrangement. Atlases and maps of individual areas involved in a war are to be kept together, e. g. Sherman's "March to the Sea" is classified as U. S. Civil War, G 3701.S.524 not G 3921.S, Georgia history. As an example of an area's chronological subdivisions, the following is presented.

UNITED STATES HISTORY

G 3701.S1	History (General).
.S2	Colonial period.
.S21	Discovery and exploration.
.S22	King Philip's War, 1675–1676.
.S23	King William's War, 1689–1697.
.S24	Queen Anne's War, 1702–1713.
.S25	King George's War, 1744–1748.
.S26	French and Indian War, 1755–1763.
.S3	Revolution, 1775–1783.
.S31	New England. Quebec.
.S311	Maine.
.S312	New Hampshire.
.S313	Vermont.
.S314	Massachusetts.
.S315	Rhode Island.
.S316	Connecticut.

Figure 55j

SUBDIVISIONS FOR ATLASES AND MAPS

TABLE OF SUBJECT SUBDIVISIONS

S   Historical geography.

UNITED STATES HISTORY

	Revolution, 1775–1783—Continued.
G 3701.S32	Middle Atlantic States.
.S321	New York.
.S322	New Jersey.
.S323	Pennsylvania.
.S324	Delaware.
.S325	Maryland.
.S33	South.
.S331	Virginia.
.S332	North Carolina.
.S333	South Carolina.
.S334	Georgia.
.S35	Northwest.
.S4	1783–1861.
.S42	War of 1812.
.S43	Black Hawk War, 1832.
.S44	Mexican War, 1846–1848.
.S46	John Brown's Raid, 1859.
.S5	Civil War, 1861–1865.
.S511	Pennsylvania.
.S512	Maryland.
.S521	Virginia.
.S522	North Carolina.
.S523	South Carolina.
.S524	Georgia.
.S531	Kentucky.
.S532	Tennessee.
.S533	Alabama.
.S534	Mississippi.
.S535	Louisiana.
.S537	Arkansas.
.S538	Oklahoma.
.S539	Texas.
.S6	1865–1898.
.S7	1898–

Figure 56

TABLES OF GEOGRAPHICAL SUBDIVISIONS

I   II

COUNTRY SUBDIVISIONS

.01	America	11–27
.15	Canada	29–30
.16	Mexico	31–32
.17	Central America	33
.18	British Honduras	35–36
.19	Costa Rica	37–38
.2	Guatemala	39–40
.21	Nicaragua	41–41.5
.215	Panama	42–42.5
.22	Salvador	43–43.5
.23	West Indies	45
.24	Bahamas	47–48
.25	Cuba	49–50
.26	Haiti	51–52
.27	Jamaica	53–54
.28	Puerto Rico	55–56
.29	Other islands, A–Z	57
.3	South America	58
.31	Argentina	59–60
.32	Bolivia	61–62
.33	Brazil	63–64
.34	Chile	65–66
.35	Colombia	67–68
.36	Ecuador	69–70
.37	Guiana	71–72
.38	Paraguay	73–74
.39	Peru	75–76
.4	Uruguay	77–78
.41	Venezuela	79–80
.42	Europe	81
.43	Great Britain	83–84
.44	England	85–86
.45	Scotland	87–88
.46	Ireland	89–89.5
.465	Wales	90–90.5
.47	Austria	91–92

Figure 57

Communism—Continued.
651–780   Theories. Communities. By country. Table V.[1]
     Cf. HQ 967, Free love communities.
     Under each:
       4 nos. 1 no.
       (1) .A3   History.
       (2)   General works.
         Works by and about Owen, in HX 696.O9.
         Works by and about Fourier, in HX 704.F7–9.
       (4) .A4–Z Particular communities, A–Z.
         Works on the New Lanark establishment, in HX 696.O9.
785   Communism and health.
791   Communism and education.
     Communism and religion, in HX 536.
795   Communism and war.
    Utopias. The ideal state.
806   General works. History.
     Particular works.
810   Collections.
811   Individual works. By date of first edition.
    Anarchism.
     Cf. HD 6477, Syndicalism.
       HV 6278, Assassination of rulers.
       HV 8037, Provision against anarchists.
821   Periodicals.
     History.
826   General.
828   19th–20th centuries.
833   Treatises.
     Controversial works in HX 841–970.
     Law.
836   General.
837   By country, A–Z.
841–970   By country. Table V.[1]
     Under each:
       4 nos. 1 no.
       (1) .A–Z6 History.
       (2)   General works.
       (4) .Z7   Local, A–Z.
999   Illustrative materials: Stories, fiction, etc.
     Prefer PQ–PT.

[1] For Table V, *see* p. 527–532. Add country number in Table to 650 or 840, as the case requires.

Figure 58

TABLES OF SUBDIVISIONS UNDER STATES AND CITIES IN JS.

Tables.				
1.	2.	3.	4.	Note.—Cities are arranged alphabetically under each country. Others not expressly provided for in the scheme are to be assigned one of the unused numbers, or Cutter numbers.
99 nos.	20 nos.	9 nos.	1 no.	
1	1	1	. A1	Periodicals, societies, etc. (City and local. General periodicals and societies, see JS 39–42.) Manuals, registers, etc., by date, (Police manuals, HV 7525–7625.)
12	2. A1–2	. A3	. A12	Administrative, judicial, etc., districts.
13	. A3	. A5	. A13	Registers, etc.
15	3	. A8	. A15	Separate documents, charters, etc., by date. (Serial documents, see JS 1–37.)
18	4	. A9	. A3	Laws, ordinances, codes, digests, etc.
				History and description.
19	5. A2±	2. A15±	. 2. A19±	Collections: statistics, etc.
20	. A5–Z	. A2	. A2	General.
23	6	. A3	. A3	Early history (Medieval, etc.).
24	. Z7	. A4	. A4	Special topics, A–Z.
25	7	. A5	. A5	19th century to 1880.
27	8	. A8	. A8	Recent history.
33	10	3. A2	. 3. A2	Reform literature, etc., by (imprint) date. (Reprints under original date in brackets.)
				Special.
35	11	3. A3	. 3. A3	Local government and the state. Home rule, etc. Budget. Income and expenditure, see HJ.
37	12	. A6	. A6	Other special, A–Z. e. g. .C7 Commission government. .I3 Incorporation, charters, etc, (Charter texts in (15). (3), (.A8), (.A15). .L2 Lands, public property, etc. .L7 Limits (territorial). Local administrative divisions.

Figure 58a

TABLES OF SUBDIVISIONS UNDER STATES AND CITIES IN JS—Continued.

Tables.				
1.	2.	3.	4.	
99 nos.	20 nos.	9 nos.	1 no.	
38	13	3. A8	. 3. A8	Local government other than municipal. Documents. .A1–2　　Collections.　(Nonserial.) .A3　　　Separate documents. .A6–Z　Other works. Compends.　Textbooks, see subdivisions (20), (25), (27), Table 1; (5), (7), (8). Table 2, etc.
				Executive: Mayor, etc. Administration.
40	14. A1	4. A1	. 4. A1	General　(including　administrative manuals).
41	. A13	. A13	. A13	Special offices, departments, commissions, etc., A–Z.
43	. A15	. A15	. A15	Special subjects, A–Z. Civil service. 　　(Reform　associations,　United States, in JK.)
47	. A2	. A2	. A2	Report.
48	. A3	. A3	. A3	Rules.
49	. A4	. A4	. A4	Other, by date. 　　e. g. Salaries, pensions, etc.
50	15	5	. 5	Legislative: Aldermen, Council, etc.
51	. A1	. A1	. A1	Yearbooks (Nonofficial).
52	. A2	. A2	. A2	Documents (Nonserial).
53	. A3	. A3	. A3	History.
55	. A5	. A5	. A5	Organization. Procedure.
57	. A7	. A7	. A7	Manuals, rules, etc.
59	. A9	. A9	. A9	Other.

Figure 58b

TABLES OF SUBDIVISIONS UNDER STATES AND CITIES IN JS—Continued.

Tables.				
1.	2.	3.	4.	
99 nos.	20 nos.	9 nos.	1 no.	
60	16	6	.6	Judiciary: Municipal courts. (Cf. K; HV.)
61	.AJ	.A1	.A1	Yearbooks (Nonofficial).
62	.A2	.A2	.A2	Documents (Nonserial).
63	.A3	.A3	.A3	History.
65	.A5	.A5	.A5	Organization.
				Procedure.
67	.A7	.A7	.A7	Manuals, rules, etc.
68	.A8	.A8	.A8	Other.
69	.A9	.A9	.A9	Government property, buildings, etc.
69.1	.A91+	.A91+	.A91+	Special.
70	17	7	.7	Citizenship.
				Suffrage.
72	.A3	.A2	.A2	General.
74	.A4	.A4	.A4	Board of election commissioners. Annual report, etc.
75	.A5	.A5	.A5	Lists of voters, etc., by date.
				Election practice and systems.
	18			Election law.
83	.A2	.A7	.A7	Codes, manuals, by date.
85	.A5	.A8	.A8	Separate, by date. .
87	.A7–Z	.A9	.A9	Other, A–Z.
	19	8	.8	Political corruption.
90	.A–Z5	.A–Z5	.A–Z5	General, by author.
95	.Z7	.Z7	.Z7	Special, by date (including Investigations).
99	20	9	.9	Local, by city, borough, parish, district, ward, etc., A–Z. Under each: (1) General. (2) Special, by date. Wards=.Z5 1st, 2d, etc.

Figure 58c

TABLES OF SUBDIVISIONS UNDER STATES AND CITIES IN JS—Continued.

Table 5. Cities to which Cutter numbers are assigned.

To be divided as follows, using successive Cutter numbers in place of (1), (2), (3), as, for example, .B5, 52, 53; .C65, 66, 67:

(1).A1	Periodicals.
.A2	Registers.
.A3	Collections of (charters and) ordinances.
.A4	Charters.
.A5	Ordinances. Codes (Official) by date.
.A6–Z	Nonofficial.
(2)	History. By author, A–Z.
(3).A2	Reform literature. By date.
.A21–29	Special.
.A3	The Executive.
.A4	Civil service.
.A5	The Legislative.
.A6	The Judiciary.
.A7	Citizenship.
.A8	Elections.
.A9	Corruption, etc.

336

Figure 59

United States*—Continued.

5220–5239	Syracuse University, Syracuse, N. Y. (Table II).
5270.T37–46	Tabor College, Hillsboro, Kans.
5271.T17–26	Tabor College, Tabor, Iowa.
	Tacoma, Wash. College of Puget Sound, *see* Puget Sound, College of, LD 4651.P837–846.
.T27–36	Tarkio College, Tarkio, Mo.
.T37–46	Taylor University, Upland, Ind.
.T487–496	Taylorsville Collegiate Institute, Taylorsville, N. C.
5275.T47–56	Temple University, Philadelphia, Pa.
5280–5299	Tennessee. University. Knoxville, Tenn. (Table II).
5305.T47–56	Tennessee Wesleyan College, Athens, Tenn.
	Texas Agricultural and Mechanical College, College Station, Tex., *see* S 537.T6–849.
5311.T377–386	Texas Christian University, Fort Worth, Tex.
.T3937–3946	Texas College of Arts and Industries, Kingsville, Tex.
.T397–406	Texas Holiness University, Greenville, Tex.
.T57–66	Texas Luther College, Sequin, Tex.
5320–5339	Texas. University. Austin, Tex. (Table II).
5351.T217–226	Thiel College, Greenville, Pa.
.T247–256	Tobin College, Fort Dodge, Iowa.
.T257–266	Toledo University, Toledo, Ohio.
.T57–66	Transylvania College, Lexington, Ky.
.T67–76	Transylvania University, Lexington, Ky.
5356.T67–76	Trevecca Nazarene College, Nashville, Tenn.
5361.T27–36	Tri-state College, Angola, Ind.
.T3647–3656	Tri-state Normal University, Scottsboro, Ala.
	Trinity College, Durham, N. C., *see* Duke University, LD 7732.D77–86.
.T37–46	Trinity College, Hartford, Conn.

*For subarrangement under each institution, *see* Tables, p. 173–175.

Figure 60

TABLES OF SUBDIVISIONS

INSTITUTIONS IN AMERICA

(LD–LE)

Use Tables II–V as indicated in the schedules; Table I for all other institutions, substituting for x1, x2 of Table I the initial and first digit or digits of the Cutter numbers assigned to them in the schedules (*see* examples, p. 175).

I	II	III	IV	
x17	0	0	0	Charter (and founding).
x175	.5	.5	.5	College statutes, by-laws, etc.
				Administration.
				General works. Official reports.
x18	1	1	1	Board of regents, trustees, etc.
x19	2	2	2	President (or head of the institution).
	.5	.5	.5	Treasurer.
	.7	.7	.7	Registrar.
x192	.9	.9	.9	Other administrative reports.
				Special.
x193	3	3	3	Finance.
x194	3.5	3.5	3.5	Endowment.
x195	4	4	4	Appropriations and grants. By date.
x197	5	5	5	Bequests, donations, etc.
x198	5.5	6	6	Scholarships.
x199	5.8	6.5	6.5	Policy and organization.
				Catalogs, registers, bulletins, etc.
x2	6	7	7	Annual, semiannual, quarterly.
				Triennial, quinquennial, *see* Biography.
x2a	7	8	9	Announcements, circulars, etc.
x2b	8	9	10	Directories.
x2d	9	10	11	Requirements for admission.
x2e	10	11	12	Entrance examinations, and accredited schools.
x2g	11	12	13	Curriculum.
x2ga	11.2	12.5	14	Syllabi (Collected).
x2gb	11.25	12.7	14.5	Honors courses.
x2h	11.3	13	15	Graduate work and courses.
x2j	11.7	14	17	Degrees and honors.
x2k	11.8	14.5	17.5	Miscellaneous publications.
				Biography.
x21	12	15	18	Collective.
	12.1	15.1	19	Presidents.
	12.2	15.2	20	Faculty or faculties.

Figure 60a

TABLES OF SUBDIVISIONS

INSTITUTIONS IN AMERICA

I	II	III	IV	
				Biography.
				Collective—Continued.
				Alumni.
x21a	12.3	15.3	21	Directories.
x21b	.4	.4	22	General histories.
x21c	.43	.43		Obituary record.
x21d	.45	.45		General special.
x21f	.49	.49	23	General catalogs. Triennial, etc.
x21g	.5	.5	.5	Other catalogs.
x21k	.6	.6	24	By classes.
				Individual.
x213	12.65	15.8	24.5	Founders, benefactors, etc., A–Z.*
x217	12.7	16	25	Presidents, chronologically, by date of inauguration.
x218	12.8	17	26	Other faculty members, A–Z.
x219	12.9	17.5	27	Reminiscences.
				History and description.
				History (including early descriptions).
x22	13	18	28	General.
				By period.
		.3	29	Early.
		.8	30	Recent.
				Description.
x23	14	19	31	General (including guidebooks).
		.2	.2	Y. M. C. A. handbooks.
x233	14.5	19.7	33	Views.
x234	14.6	19.8	34	Dormitories, residence halls, etc.
				Cf. NA 6600–6605, Architecture.
				Laboratories, *see* Q, T, etc.
				Libraries, *see* Z.
				Museums, *see* AM, or special subject.
x238	15	20	35	Individual buildings and places, A–Z.
				Student life and customs.
x24	16	21	36	General works.
				Special.
x241	16.2	21.4	36.5	Student societies and clubs.
				Fraternities, *see* LJ.
				Class days or events.
x242	16.4		(37)	Freshman.
x243	.5		(38)	Sophomore.
x244	.6		(39)	Junior.
x245	.7	22	40	Senior.
				Commencement.
x246	17	23	41	General works.
x247	.2	24	42	Addresses. Orations. Sermons. By date.
x248	.5	25	45	Presidential inaugurations. By date.
x249	.7	26	46	Other special days and events. By date.

*If founder is first president, prefer the latter classification.

Figure 60b

TABLES OF SUBDIVISIONS

INSTITUTIONS IN AMERICA

I	II	III	IV	
				Undergraduate publications.
				Periodicals, *see* LH.
x25	18	27	47	Annuals.
	.3		.3	Handbooks.
	.5		.5	Calendars.
			.7	Almanacs.
				Alumni activities.
				Alumni magazines, *see* LH.
x257	18.7	28	48	Graduate class publications (and exercises).
x26	19	29	49	Alumni associations and graduate clubs.
				.A1–4 Resident.
				.A5–Z Nonresident, by name of place.

TABLE V

(Institutions to which *one number* is assigned)

.A1–7   Official publications.
.A8–Z   Other works, by author.

Examples illustrating application of Table I:

LD 91.A557–566	Albany College.	
.*A557*	Charter. (*x17*)	
.*A5575*	By-laws, statutes. (*x175*)	
.*A558*	Annual report. (*x18*)	
.*A56*	Catalogue. (*x2*)	
.*A56*a	Announcements. (*x2a*)	
.*A562*	History. (*x22*)	
.*A5633*	Views. (*x233*)	
.*A566*	Alumni associations. (*x26*)	
LD 371.B67–76	Beloit College.	
.*B675*	Laws [1850]. (*x175*)	
.*B68*	Annual report of the trustees. (*x18*)	
.*B7*	Annual catalogue. (*x2*)	
.*B749*	Special days and events.	
	.B749 1857 10th anniversary, 1857.	
.*B75*	Student annuals. (*x25*)	
	.B75C6. The Codex.	

Figure 61

TABLE IV

01	America.
02	Spanish America.
03	North America.
05	United States.
07	Colonial period; 18th (and early 19th) century.
10	19th century.
12	20th century.
15	New England.
20	South.
25	West.
28	Pacific states.
30	States, A–Z.
35	Cities, A–Z.
36	Collective biography.
37	Special artists, A–Z.
	Canada.
40	General.
43	Before 1800 (New France).
44	19th century.
45	20th century.
46	Special divisions, A–Z.
47	Special cities, A–Z.
48	Collective biography.
49	Special artists, A–Z.
50–59	Mexico (like 40–49).
60	Central America.
	British Honduras.
70	General.
71	Local.
72	Special artists, A–Z.
73–75	Costa Rica (like 70–72).
76–78	Guatemala (like 70–72).
79–81	Honduras (Republic) (like 70–72).
82–84	Nicaragua (like 70–72).
85–87	Panama (like 70–72).
88–90	Salvador (like 70–72).
91	West Indies.
100–2	Bahamas (like 70–72).
103–5	Cuba (like 70–72).
106–8	Haiti (like 70–72).
109–11	Jamaica (like 70–72).
112–4	Porto Rico (like 70–72).
115	Other, A–Z.

Figure 62

ADDITIONS AND CHANGES TO APRIL 1960

TABLES OF SUBDIVISIONS

Tables I to III–A

I		II	III	III–A
	(Align with "America.") p. 133			
	Spanish America_____	02	02	02
	(Align with "Japan.") p. 134			
84.5	Korea_____	168.5	253.5	273.5
	(Align with "Northern Asia.") p. 134			
86	Other countries, A–Z_____	172	259	279

Table IV

(Align with "Special artists, A–Z.") p. 135

38	Special races and ethnic groups, A–Z.
	e.g. .N5 Negro.
369	*(In second line above, change* "360" *to* "361" *and* "340" *to* "341.") p. 139
519	*(In line above, change* "500" *to* "501.") p. 140
675	*(In line above, change* "Constantinople" *to* "Istanbul.") p. 141
755	*(In line above, insert* "Yugoslavia" *after* "Serbia." *Below, add note and example.)* p. 141

Under each (using three successive cutter numbers):
(1) General works.
(2) Local, A–Z.
(3) Special artists, A–Z.
e.g.   Lithuania.
.L5   General.
.L52   Local, A–Z.
.L53   Special artists, A–Z.

(Indent under "Philippine Islands.") p. 142

828	Local, A–Z.
829	Special artists, A–Z.
842	*(Align with* "General.") p. 142

(Revise "882.") p. 143

881	Egypt.
882	Coptic art.
	Cf. N 7988.

Art cities

Istanbul	7170	p. 144
Saragosso (Zaragoza)	7111.S3	

Figure 63

	Europe.
	Special countries—Continued.
411–423	Italy (like 391–403, except 420, Rome).
425	Dutch, Flemish, and German, collectively.
431–438	Netherlands (like 391–398).
441–453	Holland (like 391–403; 450, Amsterdam).
461–473	Belgium. Flanders.
	(Divided like 391–403; 470, Brussels).
	Slavic art.
476	General works.
	Russia.
481–488	Like 391–398.
	Special division of European Russia.
	Poland. Polish art.
491	General works.
	Finland. Finnish art.
493	General works.
495	Others, A–Z.
	Special cities.
496	St. Petersburg. Petrograd.
497	Others, A–Z.
498	Collective biography.
499	Special artists, A–Z.
	Scandinavia.
501	General works.
502	Ancient.
503	Medieval. Gothic. Romanesque.
504	Modern.
505	14th–16th centuries. Renaissance
506	17th–18th centuries.
507	19th century.
508	20th century.
509	Collective biography.
	Denmark.
511–518	Like 500–508.
519	Special divisions, A–Z.
520	Copenhagen.
521	Other special cities, A–Z.
522	Collective biography.
523	Special artists, A–Z.
541–553	Iceland (like 511–523; 550 omitted).
561–573	Norway (like 511–523; 570, Christiania).
581–593	Sweden (like 511–523; 590, Stockholm).
	Spain and Portugal. Spain.
601–613	Like 511–523; 610, Madrid.
621–633	Portugal (like 511–523; 630, Lisbon).

ARCHITECTURE

SPECIAL CLASSES OF BUILDINGS

Classed by material.
Cf. Domestic architecture, NA 7150–7170.

4100	General works.
4110	Wood.
4115	Half-timbered.
4120	Brick and tile.
4125	Concrete.
4130	Stone.
4135	Iron and steel.
	Cf. NA 6230.
4140	Other.

Classed by form.

4150	Basilicas.
4160	Other special forms.
	e. g. " Zweischiffige zentralbauten."

Classed by use.

4170	**Public buildings.**
4180	International.
	Peace tribunals.
4185	Hague. Palace of peace.
	Other.
4193	Bureau of American republics.
4195	National, state, municipal, etc.
	Including documents of architectural departments.
4201–4384	Special countries. Table II.
	Under each :
	(1) General.
	(2) Local.
4410–4510	**Government buildings.**
	Historical monuments preferably in NA 701–1613.
	Under each :
	0. General.
	1. United States.
	2. States.
	3. Cities.
	5. Foreign countries, A–Z.
	(1) General.
	(2) Local, A–Z.
	e. g. .G3, Germany—General.
	.G4, Germany—Local.
	Contracts and specifications.
	6. United States. By place only, A–Z.
	7. Foreign. By place only, A–Z.

Figure 64a

Government buildings—Continued.

4410–4417	Capitols.
4420–4427	Government offices and bureaus. Prefectures, etc.
4423	United States government offices in special cities, A–Z.
4430–4437	City halls. Town halls.
4440–4447	Official residences.

       e. g. 4443.W3, White House.
       Cf. NA 7710–86, Palaces.

4450–4457	Post offices.
4460–4467	Custom houses.
4470–4477	Court houses.
	[Prisons, in HV.]
4480–4487	Armories, barracks, etc.

       Cf. UC 400–405.

4490–4497	Police stations.
4500–4507	Engine houses.
4510	Other buildings, A–Z.

       e. g. .C7 Community centers.
         .M5 Mints (General).
         .M6N5 Mint, New Orleans.

RELIGIOUS ARCHITECTURE

4600	General works.
4601	Folios.
4610	Non-Christian.

   Temples—General.

       Cf. Greek temples, NA 275.
         Roman temples, NA 323.
         Egyptian temples, NA 215–216.
         Temple of Jerusalem, NA 243.

4620	General works.
4621	Folios.

   Rock temples, Cave temples.

       Cf. DS 401–20, India.

4640	General.
4641	Folios.
4670	Mosques—General.

       Mosques of special countries, see 5801–11, Spain; 5861–
         71, Turkey; 5960–6030, Asia; 6080–90, North Africa.

4690	Synagogues—General.
4710	Bahai temples.

  Christian architecture.

4800	General works.

       Including history, architectural symbolism, etc.
       For symbolism of church art in general, see N 7831–7832.

4801	Folios.

Figure 65

19th century, 1770/1800–1890/1900.
Individual authors—Continued.

4349.B3	Burns, Robert, of Hamilton.
.B5	Burrell, Lady Sophia.
.B53	Burtt, John.
.B6	Butler, Edward.
.B7	Butler, Samuel, 1835-1902.
4350–4398	**Byron, George Gordon, Lord (II).**

Separate works.

4355	Bride of Abydos.
4356	Cain.
4357	Childe Harold's pilgrimage.
4358	Corsair.
4359	Don Juan.
4360	English bards and Scotch reviewers.
4361	Giaour.
4362	Hebrew melodies.
4363	Hours of idleness.
4364	Lara.
4365	Manfred.
4366	Marino Faliero.
4367	Prisoner of Chillon.
4368	Sardanapalus.
4369	Two Foscari.
4370	Vision of Judgment.
4371	Werner.
4372	Other, A–Z.

4399.B3	Byron, Henry James.
4400–4408	Caine, Hall (IV^a).
4405	Plays, A–Z.
4409.C2	Calverley, Charles Stuart.
	Cambridge, Ada, see Cross, Ada (Cambridge).
4410–4414	Campbell, Thomas (VII).
4415.C2	Canton, William.
4416–4417	Carleton, William (XII).
4419.C5	Carlyle, Jane Welsh.
4420–4438	**Carlyle, Thomas (III^a).**

Separate works.

Chartism, see DA.
Choice of books, see Z 1003.
Cromwell's letters and speeches, see DA.
Early kings of Norway (etc.), see DL 460.

4425	Essays.
.A2,	Collected. By date.
.A3,	Minor collections. By date.
.A5–Z,	Separate essays and minor collections. By title.

Frederick the Great, see DD.
French revolution, see DC.

4426	Heroes and hero worship.

Inaugural address, University of Edinburgh, 1866:
Choice of books, see Z 1003.

Figure 65a

ENGLISH LITERATURE

19th century, 1770/1800–1890/1900.
Individual authors.
Carlyle, Thomas (III^a).

	Separate works—Continued.
4427	Latter day pamphlets.
4428	Past and present.
4429	Sartor resartus.
	Schiller, Friedrich, see PT.
	Sterling, John, Life of, see PR 5473.S8.
	Translations from the German, see PT.
4430	Other works, A–Z.
4439	Carl–Carm.
4441–4442	Carman, Bliss (XII).
4443.C6	Carnavon, Henry, 3d earl of.
4451	Carpenter, Edward.
4452.C5	Carr, Joseph William Comyns.
.C7	Casey, John K.
.C8	Cayley, George John.
4453.C17	Chadwick, Sheldon.
.C18	Chambers, James.
.C2	Chambers, Robert.
.C21	Chambers, William.
.C3	Chesson, Nora (Hopper).
.C4	Chesterton, Gilbert Keith (IX^a).
.C5	Cholmondeley-Pennell, Henry.
.C53	Chorley, Henry Fothergill. Cf. ML.
C6	Clare, John.
.C7	Clarke, Charles Cowden.
.C75	Clarke, Marcus.
.C8	Clarke, Mary Victoria (Novello).
	(Mrs. Mary Cowden Clarke).
.C85	Clarke, Stephen.
4454.C2	Clifford, Mrs. Lucy (Lane).
.C3	Clifford, William Kingdon.
	Cf. B and Q.
4455–4459	Clough, Arthur Hugh (VII).
4461.C3	Cobbe, Frances Power.
.C35	Cobbold, Richard.
.C5	Cochrane, James.
4464	Col–Coleridge.
4467–4468	Coleridge, Hartley (XII).
4470–4488	**Coleridge, Samuel Taylor (III^a).**
	Separate works.
4476	Biographia literaria.
4477	Biographia epistolaria.
4478	Poems.
4479	Rime of the ancient mariner.
4480	Other, A–Z.
4489.C2	Coleridge, Mrs. Sara (Coleridge).
.C3	Collins, John Churton.
.C5	Collins, Mortimer.
4490–4498	Collins, Wilkie (IV^a).
4501.C3	Colman, George, jr. (IX^a).

Figure 66

LANGUAGE

	I (900)	II (500)	III (200)	IV (100)	V (50)
Study and teaching:					
General	65	35	19	11	**7**
General special	66	36			
e. g. Educational value.					
By period, *see* I 53–58, 75–87, etc.					
By country, A–Z	68	38			
By school, A–Z	69	39	21	12	
General works:					
Early to 1800	70	40	22		
Treatises (Philology, General)	71	41	23	13	8
General special	73	43			
Relation to other languages	74	44	24	14	
History of the language.					
General works	75	45	25	15	9
Earliest, *see* I 53, etc	(76)				
Middle ages	77	47			
(15th–) 16th century	79				
(16th–) 17th century	81	49			
(17th–) 18th century	83				
19th century	85	51			
20th century	87				
By region, *see* Dialects, I 700–840, etc.					
Compends	91	53			
Outlines	93	55	26	16	
Popular. Minor	95	57	27	17	10
Script	97	58	28		
Grammar—					
Comparative (two or more languages)	99	59	29	18	
Historical	101	61	31	19	
Treatises			33	21	11
To 1800	103	63			
Later	105	64			
General special (Terminology, etc.)	107	65	34	22	12
Text-books			35	23	13
Early to 1870	109	66			
Later, 1871–	111	67			
Readers—					
Series	113	68	36	24	
Primers. Primary grade readers	115	69	37	25	
Intermediate and advanced	117	71			
Outlines, Syllabi, Tables, etc	118				
Examination questions, etc	119				
Manuals for special classes of students, A–Z	120	72	38	26	
e. g., Commercial, Cf. HF.					

Figure 67

GEOLOGY

51	Museums.
	Catalogs, guides, descriptions, etc.
	Cf. QE 386, 716.
55	Dealers' catalogs of specimens.
61	Surveys.
	History, organization, etc.
	Geographical divisions.
	Official publications stand at the head of each division.
65	Miscellaneous groups.
	e. g. British empire.
70	Arctic regions. Greenland.
.5	America.
71	North America.
	United States.
72	Surveys (General).
73	Surveys, before 1861.
74	Surveys, 1865–1879.
	United States Geological Survey.
75	General publications of the Survey, A–Z.
76	Works about the Survey.
77	General works. Miscellaneous.
	Special regions.
78	Lake region and St. Lawrence.
.3	North. Northeast. East.
.5	South and Southeast.
.7	Central. Mississippi Valley.
79	Western states. Rocky Mountains.
.5	Southwest.
80	States (Collectively).
	By state.
	The second number assigned to each state is used for special localities (i. e., counties or physiographic divisions) arranged alphabetically.
81– 82	Alabama.
83– 84	Alaska.
85– 86	Arizona.
87– 88	Arkansas.
89– 90	California.
91– 92	Colorado.
93– 94	Connecticut.
95– 96	Delaware.
97– 98	District of Columbia.
99–100	Florida.
101–102	Georgia.
103–104	Idaho.

Figure 68

Solar eclipses.
541   General works.
542   Before 1800.
              Cf. CE, Chronology.
543   1800–1899.[1]
544   1900–1999.[1]
551   Spectroscopy of sun and eclipses.
579   Lunar eclipses.
Moon.
581   General works.
583   Distance, parallax.
585   Rotation, libration, and shape.
588   Temperature, radiation, brightness, phases.
591   Surface, physical condition, meteorology.
595   Photographs, maps, drawings.
Planets.
              Cf. QB 54, Plurality of worlds.
                 QB 401–407, Satellites.
                 QB 501, Solar system.
601   General works.
603   Miscellaneous topics.
                 e. g.   Age, brightness, density, rotation.
604   Tables.
606   Inferior planets.
607   Intramercurial planets.
611   Mercury.
                 Cf. QB 515, Transit of Mercury.
621   Venus.
                 Cf. QB 509–513, Transit of Venus.
631   Earth (as a planet).   Astronomical geography.
633   Rotation.
638   Curiosa and miscellany.
639   Superior planets.
641   Mars.
651   Minor planets.
661   Jupiter.
671   Saturn.
681   Uranus.
691   Neptune.
                 Cf. QB ::8, Transit of Neptune.
701   Pluto.

---

[1] Book number=last two figures of the year, followed by author number.
   e. g.   QB 544.47U6   U. S. National Almanac Office, Total eclipse of the
sun, May 20, 1947.

Figure 69

GEOGRAPHICAL DISTRIBUTION TABLES

In countries to which two numbers are assigned:
(1) General.
(2) Local, A–Z.

I	II	
21		America.
22		North America.
23		United States.
24		States, A–W.
26–27	1–2	Canada.
28–29	3–4	Mexico.
30–31	5–6	Central America.
32–33	7–8	West Indies.
34	9	South America.
36–37	11–12	Argentine Republic.
38–39	13–14	Bolivia.
41–42	15–16	Brazil.
43–44	17–18	Chile.
45–46	19–20	Colombia.
47–48	21–22	Ecuador.
49–50	23–24	Guiana.
51	25–26	Paraguay.
52	27–28	Peru.
53	29–30	Uruguay.
54	31–32	Venezuela.
55	33	Europe.
57–58	35–36	Great Britain. England.
59–60	37–38	Wales.
61–62	39–40	Scotland.
63–64	41–42	Ireland.
65–66	43–44	Austria.
67–68	45–46	Belgium.
69–70	47–48	Denmark.
71–72	49–50	France.
73–74	51–52	Germany.
75–76	53–54	Greece.
77–78	55–56	Holland.
79–80	57–58	Italy.
81–82	59–60	Norway.
83–84	61–62	Portugal.
85–86	63–64	Russia.
87–88	65–66	Spain.
89–90	67–68	Sweden.
91–92	69–70	Switzerland.
93–94	71–72	Turkey.
95	73	Other countries of Europe, A–Z.

Figure 70

TABLE I

HISTORY AND COUNTRY DIVISIONS

History.
15	General.
16	Ancient.
17	Medieval.
18	Modern.
19	19th century.
20	20th century.

Special countries.
21	America.
22	North America.
23	United States.
.1	Atlantic coast.
.15	New England.
.2	Appalachian region.
.3	Lake region.
.4	Mississippi Valley.
.5	South. Gulf states.
.6	West.
.7	Northwest.
.8	Pacific coast.
.9	Southwest.
24	States, A–W.
25	Cities (or other special), A–Z.
26	Canada and Newfoundland.
27	Provinces (or other special), A–Z.
27.5	Latin America.
28–29	Mexico.
30	Central America.
31	Special states, B–S.
32	West Indies.
33	Special islands, A–Z.
34	South America.
36–37	Argentine Republic.
38–39	Bolivia.

Figure 71

Military education and training.
By country.
America.
United States.
410   U. S. Military Academy, West Point—Continued.
Administration.
.C3   Regulations.
.C4   General orders.
.C5   Conduct grades.
.C7   Circulars.
.C8   Memoranda.
.E1   Annual report of Superintendent.
.E3   Annual report of Inspectors.
.E4   Annual report of Board of Visitors.
.E45   Special reports, hearings, etc., of Board of
Visitors.
.E5   General congressional documents.
By date.
.E9   Documents relating to hazing. By date.
.F3   Commencement orations.
.F5   Miscellaneous addresses and speeches.
.F7   Other documents, reports, etc.
Including semiofficial material.
.F8   Special days and events. By date.
.G3   Information for graduates.
.H2   Rosters of officers, etc. (U. S. Army).
Registers.
.H3   Official annual.
.H4   Other official. By date.
Nonofficial.
.H5   Cullom's register.
.H7–8   Other.
.J1   Student publications. Annuals, etc.
Graduate publications.
.K1   Reunions of graduates' associations.
.K3   Bulletins of graduates' associations.
.K5–7   Other.
.L1   History and general works on the academy.
.A1–5 Official works.
.L3   Illustrated works. Views.
.M1   Biography, A–Z.
Cf. U 410.H3–8, Registers.

.N1   Class histories. By date.
.P1   Descriptive works. "Life at West Point."

Figure 72

TABLES OF SUBDIVISIONS

I—III: NATIONAL BIBLIOGRAPHY

TABLE I

(1)	General bibliography.[1]
.A1	Bibliography of bibliography.
.A2	Theory, method, etc.
(2)	Bibliography of early works.
	To ca. 1600 or 1800, etc. (Varies with different countries).
(2.5)	History of bibliography.
(3)	Publishers' catalogs.
(5)	Periodicals.
(6)	Societies.
(7)	Collections.
(9)	Government publications.
(10)	Biobibliography.
(11)	Literature (General).
	By period.
(12)	Early to 1800.
(13)	1801–1950.
(13.3)	1951–
(14)	Special topics, A–Z.
	e.g. .D7 Drama.
	.P7 Poetry.
(15)	Philology.
(16)	History and description (General).
	By period.
(17)	To 1500.
(17.5)	16th century.
(18)	17th–18th centuries.
(19)	19th century.
(20)	Early 20th century.
(20.3)	1945–
(21)	Special topics not in (17)–(20), A–Z.
	e.g. .C7 Colonies.
	Local.
(23)	General.
(24)	Special, A–Z.
(27)	Special topics not otherwise provided for, A–Z.
	e.g. .A8 Archaeology. Antiquities.
	.P3 Pamphlets. Broadsides. Proclamations, etc.
	.R4 Relations with other countries.
(29)	Catalogs.

[1] The numbers (1), (2), etc., are not part of the notation. They indicate sequence and are printed to facilitate reference.

INDEX